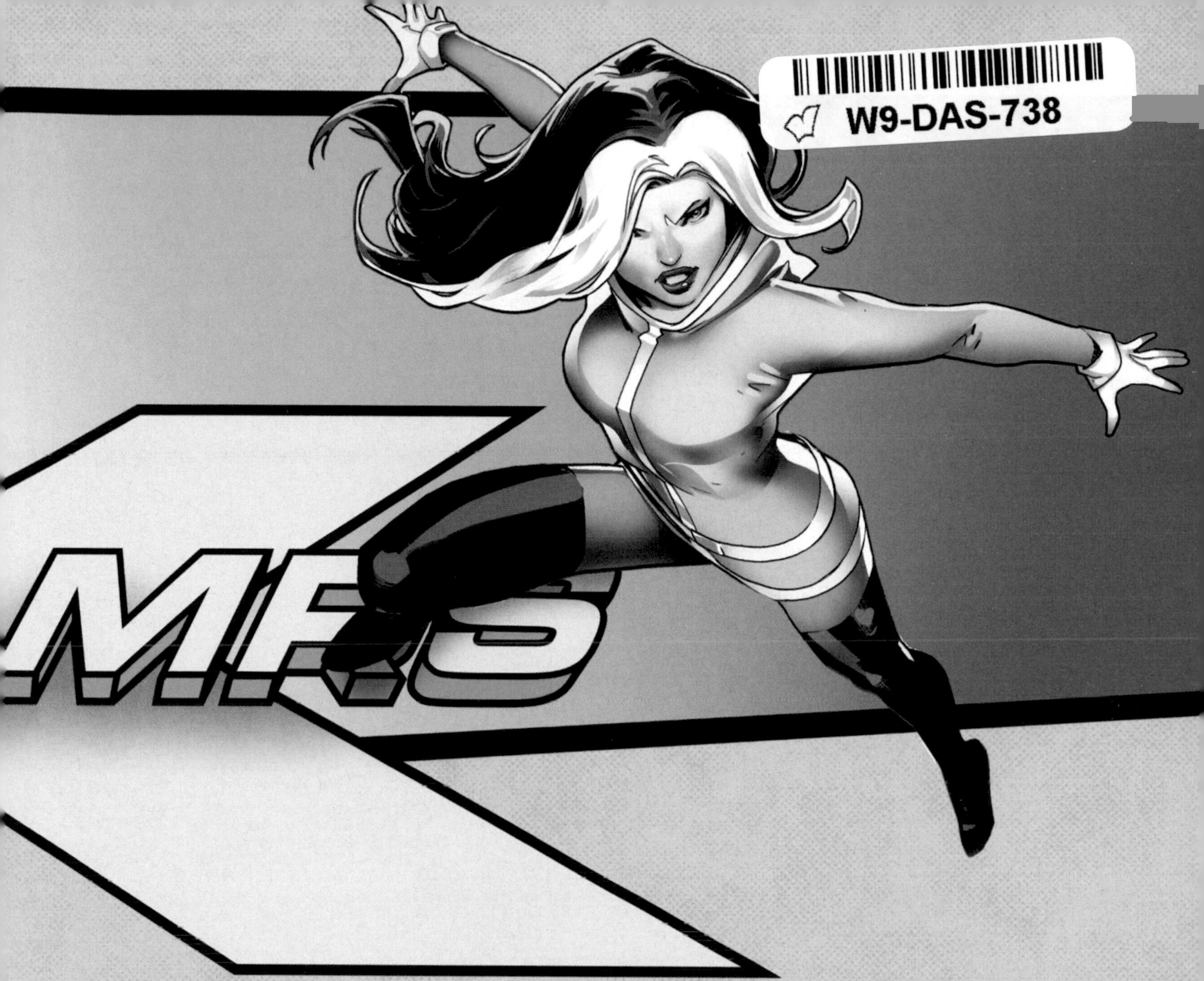

KELLY THOMPSON

WRITER

OSCAR BAZALDUA (#7-11) & **JAVIER PINA** (#12)

ARTISTS

FRANK D'ARMATA

COLOR ARTIST

VC's JOE SABINO

LETTERER

TERRY DODSON & RACHEL DODSON

COVER ART

7

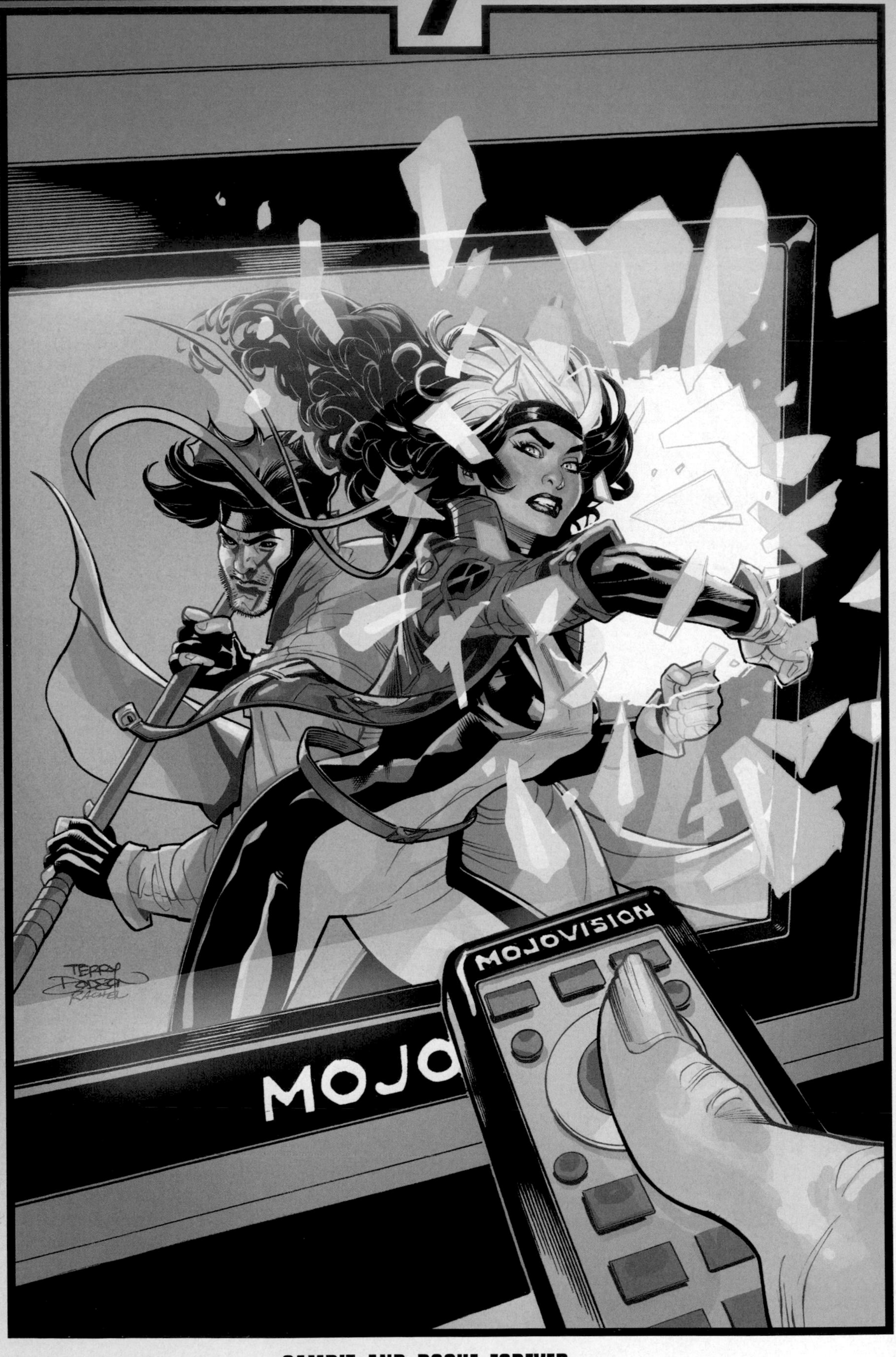
MOJOVISION
MOJOVISION
MOJO
TERRY DODSON RACHEL

GAMBIT AND ROGUE FOREVER PART 1

MR & MRS X

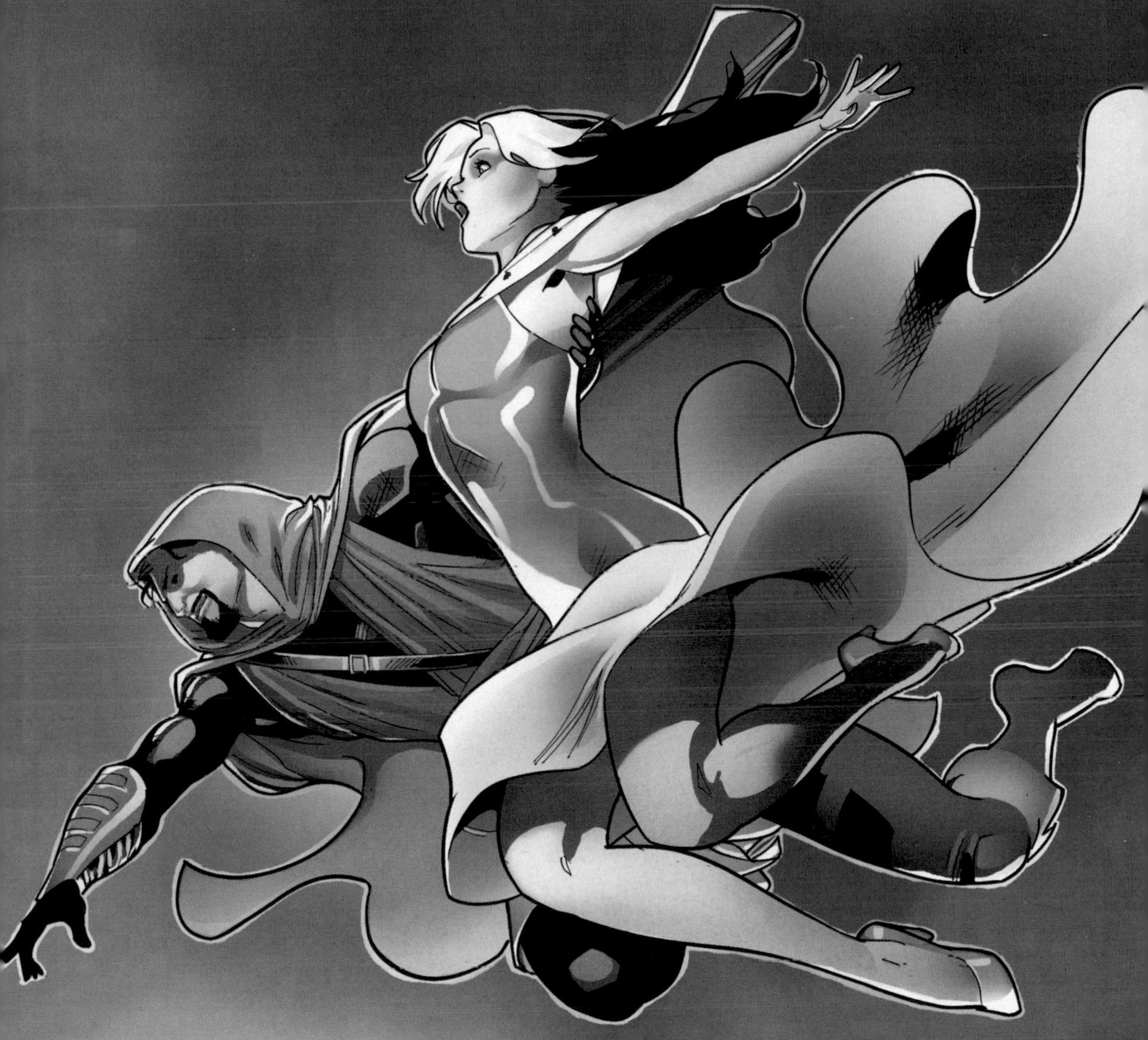

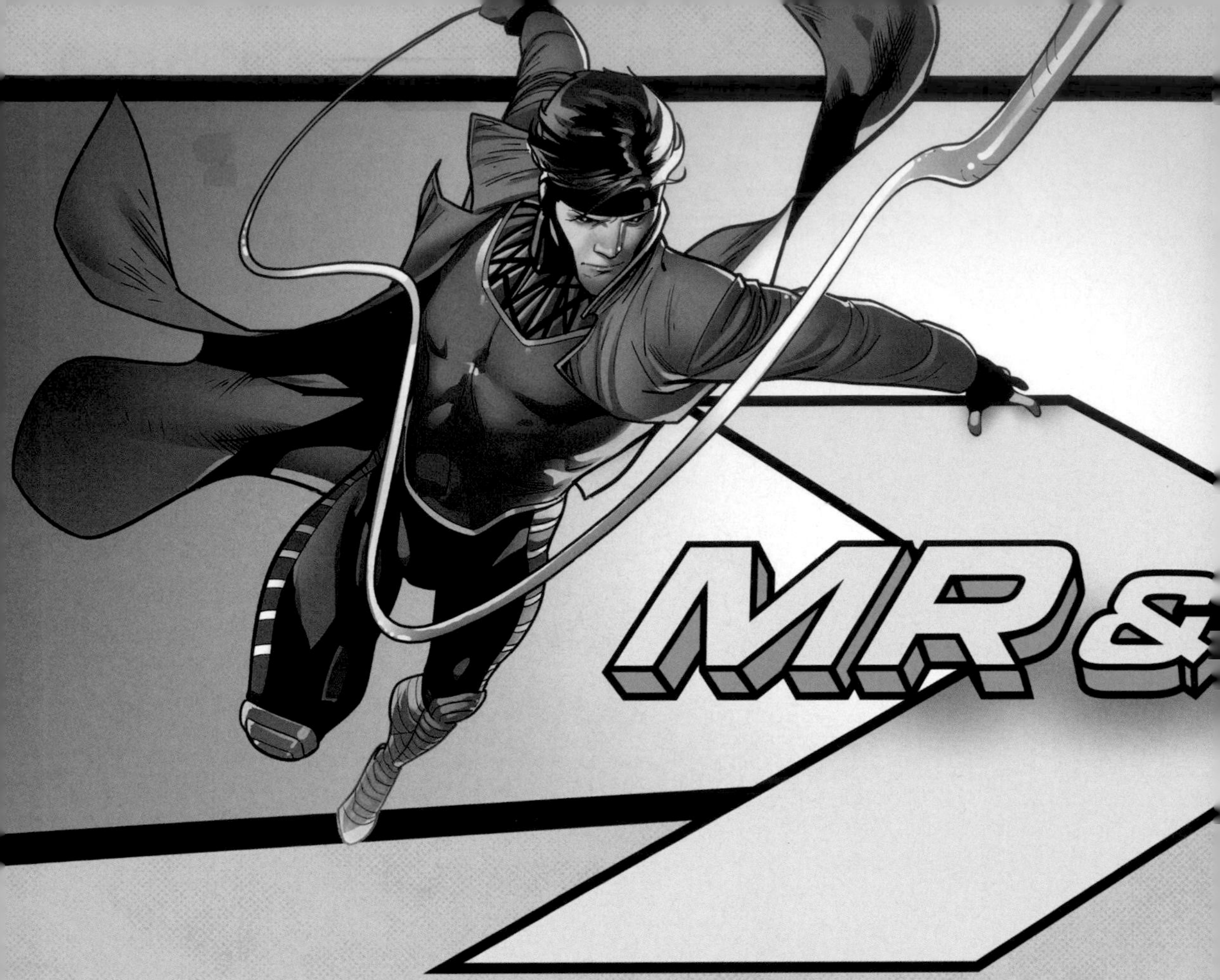
MR &

DANNY KHAZEM & LAUREN AMARO
ASSISTANT EDITORS

DARREN SHAN EDITOR
JORDAN D. WHITE X-MEN GROUP EDITOR

COLLECTION EDITOR **JENNIFER GRÜNWALD** ■ ASSISTANT EDITOR **CAITLIN O'CONNELL** ■ ASSOCIATE MANAGING EDITOR **KATERI WOODY**
EDITOR, SPECIAL PROJECTS **MARK D. BEAZLEY** ■ VP PRODUCTION & SPECIAL PROJECTS **JEFF YOUNGQUIST** ■ BOOK DESIGNER **JAY BOWEN**

SVP PRINT, SALES & MARKETING **DAVID GABRIEL** ■ DIRECTOR, LICENSED PUBLISHING **SVEN LARSEN**
EDITOR IN CHIEF **C.B. CEBULSKI** ■ CHIEF CREATIVE OFFICER **JOE QUESADA** ■ PRESIDENT **DAN BUCKLEY** ■ EXECUTIVE PRODUCER **ALAN FINE**

MR. AND MRS. X VOL. 2: GAMBIT AND ROGUE FOREVER. Contains material originally published in magazine form as MR. AND MRS. X #7-12. First printing 2019. ISBN 978-1-302-91352-6. Published by MARVEL WORLDWIDE, INC., a subsidiary of MARVEL ENTERTAINMENT, LLC. OFFICE OF PUBLICATION: 135 West 50th Street, New York, NY 10020. **Printed in Canada.** DAN BUCKLEY, President, Marvel Entertainment; JOHN NEE, Publisher; JOE QUESADA, Chief Creative Officer; TOM BREVOORT, SVP of Publishing; DAVID BOGART, Associate Publisher & SVP of Talent Affairs; DAVID GABRIEL, SVP of Sales & Marketing, Publishing; JEFF YOUNGQUIST, VP of Production & Special Projects; DAN CARR, Executive Director of Publishing Technology; ALEX MORALES, Director of Publishing Operations; DAN EDINGTON, Managing Editor; SUSAN CRESPI, Production Manager; STAN LEE, Chairman Emeritus. For information regarding advertising in Marvel Comics or on Marvel.com, please contact Vit DeBellis, Custom Solutions & Integrated Advertising Manager, at vdebellis@marvel.com. For Marvel subscription inquiries, please call 888-511-5480. **Manufactured between 6/21/2019 and 7/23/2019 by SOLISCO PRINTERS, SCOTT, QC, CANADA.**

10 9 8 7 6 5 4 3 2 1

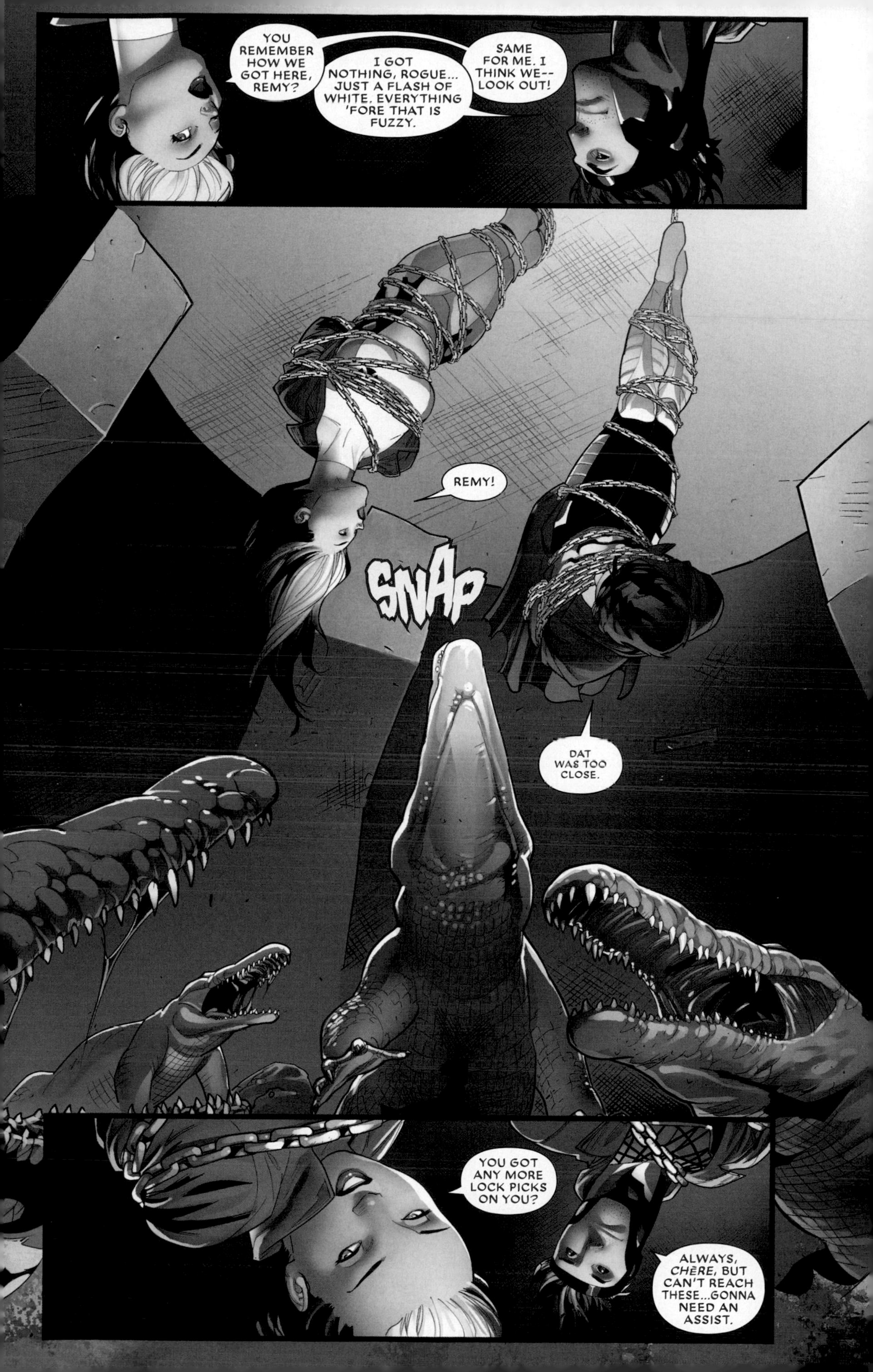
YOU REMEMBER HOW WE GOT HERE, REMY?
I GOT NOTHING, ROGUE... JUST A FLASH OF WHITE. EVERYTHING 'FORE THAT IS FUZZY.
SAME FOR ME. I THINK WE-- LOOK OUT!
REMY!
SNAP
DAT WAS TOO CLOSE.
YOU GOT ANY MORE LOCK PICKS ON YOU?
ALWAYS, CHÈRE, BUT CAN'T REACH THESE...GONNA NEED AN ASSIST.

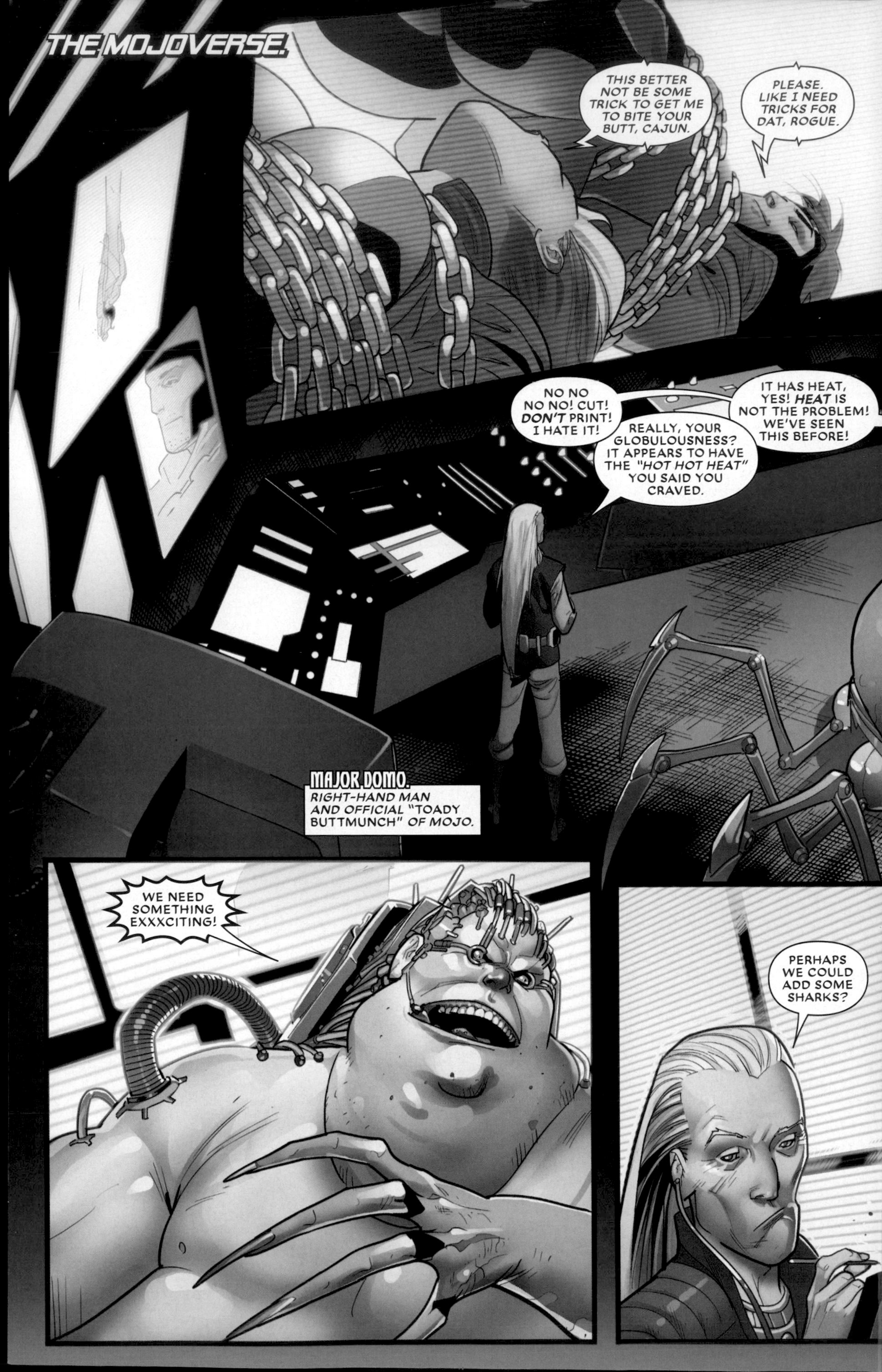
THE MOJOVERSE.
THIS BETTER NOT BE SOME TRICK TO GET ME TO BITE YOUR BUTT, CAJUN.
PLEASE. LIKE I NEED TRICKS FOR DAT, ROGUE.
NO NO NO NO! CUT! DON'T PRINT! I HATE IT!
REALLY, YOUR GLOBULOUSNESS? IT APPEARS TO HAVE THE "HOT HOT HEAT" YOU SAID YOU CRAVED.
IT HAS HEAT, YES! HEAT IS NOT THE PROBLEM! WE'VE SEEN THIS BEFORE!
MAJOR DOMO.
RIGHT-HAND MAN AND OFFICIAL "TOADY BUTTMUNCH" OF MOJO.
WE NEED SOMETHING EXXXCITING!
PERHAPS WE COULD ADD SOME SHARKS?

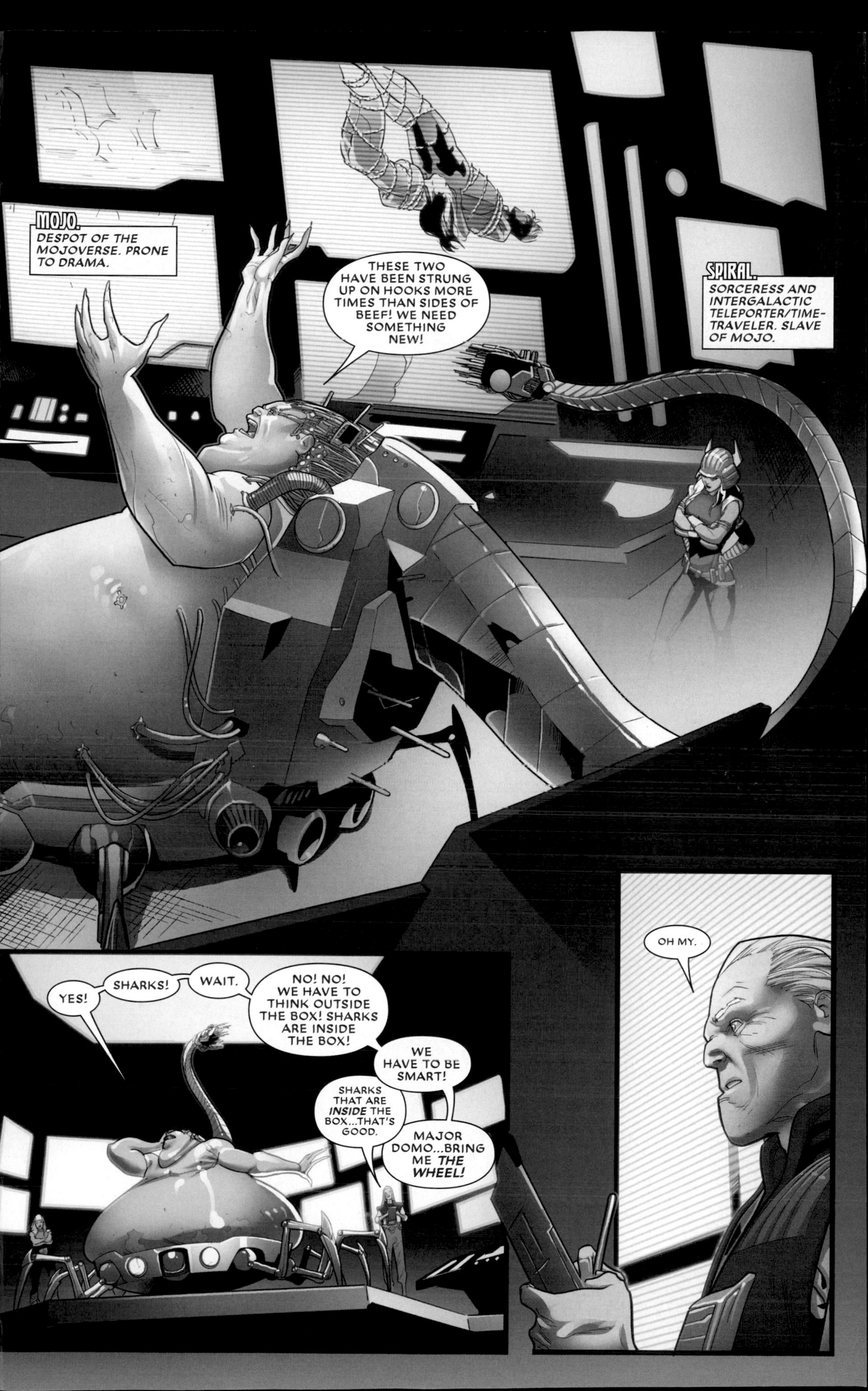
MOJO.
DESPOT OF THE MOJOVERSE. PRONE TO DRAMA.
THESE TWO HAVE BEEN STRUNG UP ON HOOKS MORE TIMES THAN SIDES OF BEEF! WE NEED SOMETHING NEW!
SPIRAL.
SORCERESS AND INTERGALACTIC TELEPORTER/TIME-TRAVELER. SLAVE OF MOJO.
YES!
SHARKS!
WAIT.
NO! NO! WE HAVE TO THINK OUTSIDE THE BOX! SHARKS ARE INSIDE THE BOX!
WE HAVE TO BE SMART!
SHARKS THAT ARE *INSIDE* THE BOX...THAT'S GOOD.
MAJOR DOMO...BRING ME *THE WHEEL!*
OH MY.

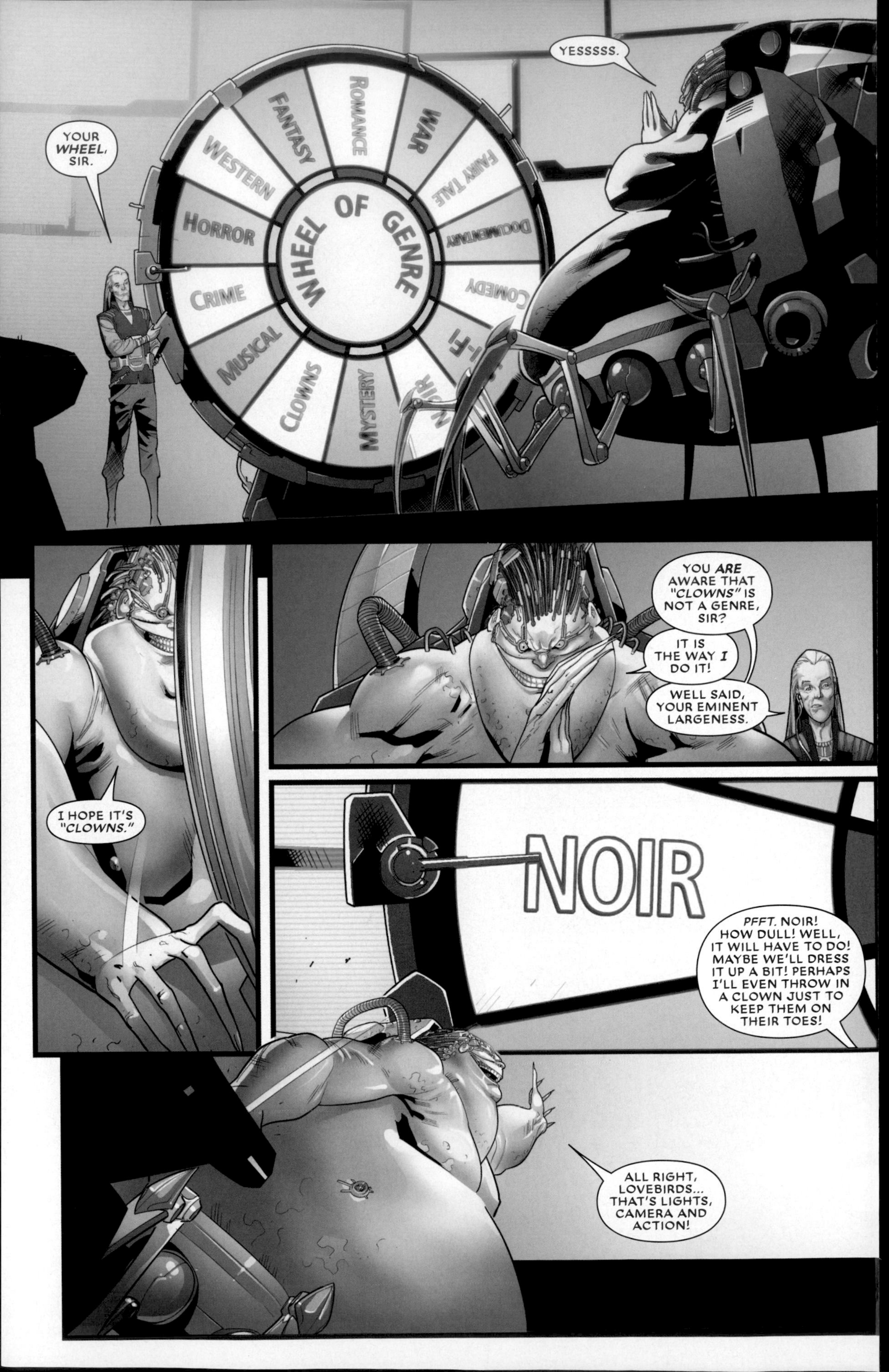
YOUR *WHEEL*, SIR.
YESSSSS.
WHEEL OF GENRE
ROMANCE
WAR
FAIRY TALE
DOCUMENTARY
COMEDY
MYSTERY
CLOWNS
MUSICAL
CRIME
HORROR
WESTERN
FANTASY
I HOPE IT'S "*CLOWNS.*"
YOU *ARE* AWARE THAT "*CLOWNS*" IS NOT A GENRE, SIR?
IT IS THE WAY *I* DO IT!
WELL SAID, YOUR EMINENT LARGENESS.
NOIR
PFFT. NOIR! HOW DULL! WELL, IT WILL HAVE TO DO! MAYBE WE'LL DRESS IT UP A BIT! PERHAPS I'LL EVEN THROW IN A CLOWN JUST TO KEEP THEM ON THEIR TOES!
ALL RIGHT, LOVEBIRDS... THAT'S LIGHTS, CAMERA AND ACTION!

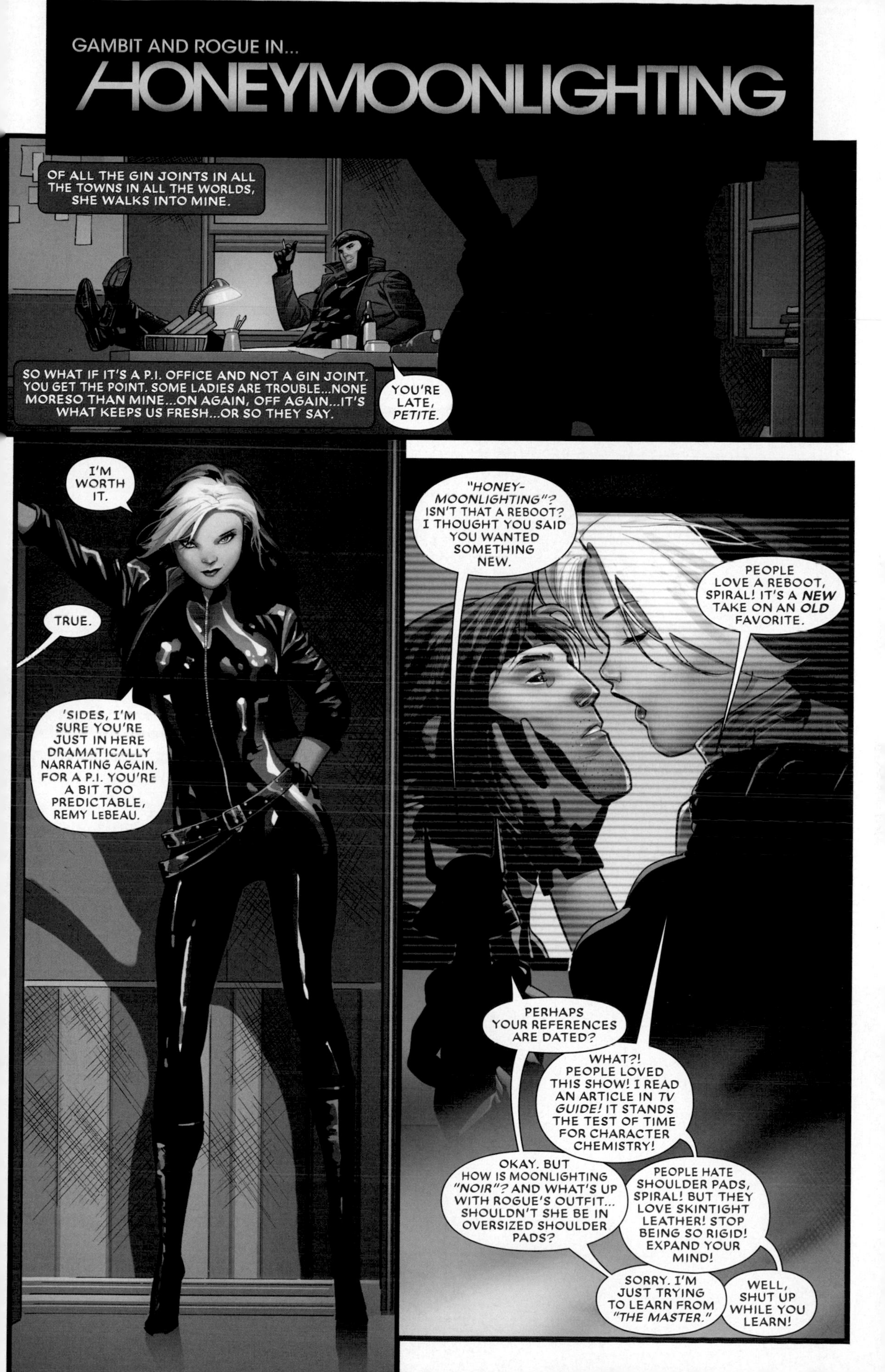
GAMBIT AND ROGUE IN...
HONEYMOONLIGHTING
OF ALL THE GIN JOINTS IN ALL THE TOWNS IN ALL THE WORLDS, SHE WALKS INTO MINE.
SO WHAT IF IT'S A P.I. OFFICE AND NOT A GIN JOINT. YOU GET THE POINT. SOME LADIES ARE TROUBLE...NONE MORESO THAN MINE...ON AGAIN, OFF AGAIN...IT'S WHAT KEEPS US FRESH...OR SO THEY SAY.
YOU'RE LATE, *PETITE.*
I'M WORTH IT.
TRUE.
'SIDES, I'M SURE YOU'RE JUST IN HERE DRAMATICALLY NARRATING AGAIN. FOR A P.I. YOU'RE A BIT TOO PREDICTABLE, REMY LeBEAU.
"HONEY-MOONLIGHTING"? ISN'T THAT A REBOOT? I THOUGHT YOU SAID YOU WANTED SOMETHING NEW.
PEOPLE LOVE A REBOOT, SPIRAL! IT'S A ***NEW*** TAKE ON AN ***OLD*** FAVORITE.
PERHAPS YOUR REFERENCES ARE DATED?
WHAT?! PEOPLE LOVED THIS SHOW! I READ AN ARTICLE IN *TV GUIDE!* IT STANDS THE TEST OF TIME FOR CHARACTER CHEMISTRY!
OKAY. BUT HOW IS MOONLIGHTING *"NOIR"*? AND WHAT'S UP WITH ROGUE'S OUTFIT... SHOULDN'T SHE BE IN OVERSIZED SHOULDER PADS?
PEOPLE HATE SHOULDER PADS, SPIRAL! BUT THEY LOVE SKINTIGHT LEATHER! STOP BEING SO RIGID! EXPAND YOUR MIND!
SORRY. I'M JUST TRYING TO LEARN FROM *"THE MASTER."*
WELL, SHUT UP WHILE YOU LEARN!

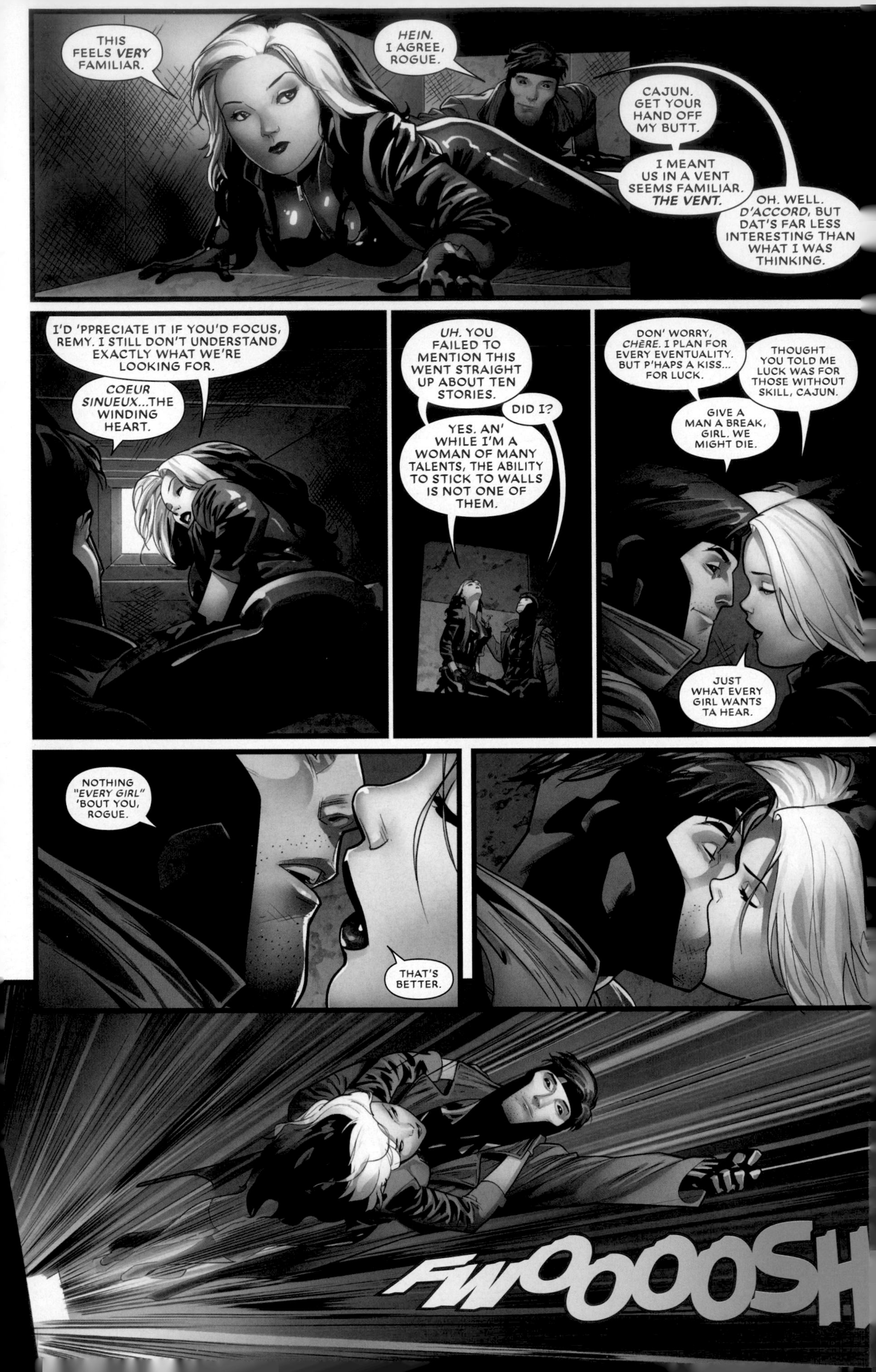
THIS FEELS *VERY* FAMILIAR.
HEIN. I AGREE, ROGUE.
CAJUN. GET YOUR HAND OFF MY BUTT.
I MEANT US IN A VENT SEEMS FAMILIAR. *THE VENT.*
OH. WELL. *D'ACCORD*, BUT DAT'S FAR LESS INTERESTING THAN WHAT I WAS THINKING.
I'D 'PPRECIATE IT IF YOU'D FOCUS, REMY. I STILL DON'T UNDERSTAND EXACTLY WHAT WE'RE LOOKING FOR.
COEUR SINUEUX...THE WINDING HEART.
UH. YOU FAILED TO MENTION THIS WENT STRAIGHT UP ABOUT TEN STORIES.
DID I?
YES. AN' WHILE I'M A WOMAN OF MANY TALENTS, THE ABILITY TO STICK TO WALLS IS NOT ONE OF THEM.
DON' WORRY, *CHÈRE*. I PLAN FOR EVERY EVENTUALITY. BUT P'HAPS A KISS... FOR LUCK.
THOUGHT YOU TOLD ME LUCK WAS FOR THOSE WITHOUT SKILL, CAJUN.
GIVE A MAN A BREAK, GIRL. WE MIGHT DIE.
JUST WHAT EVERY GIRL WANTS TA HEAR.
NOTHING *"EVERY GIRL"* 'BOUT YOU, ROGUE.
THAT'S BETTER.
FWOOOOOSH

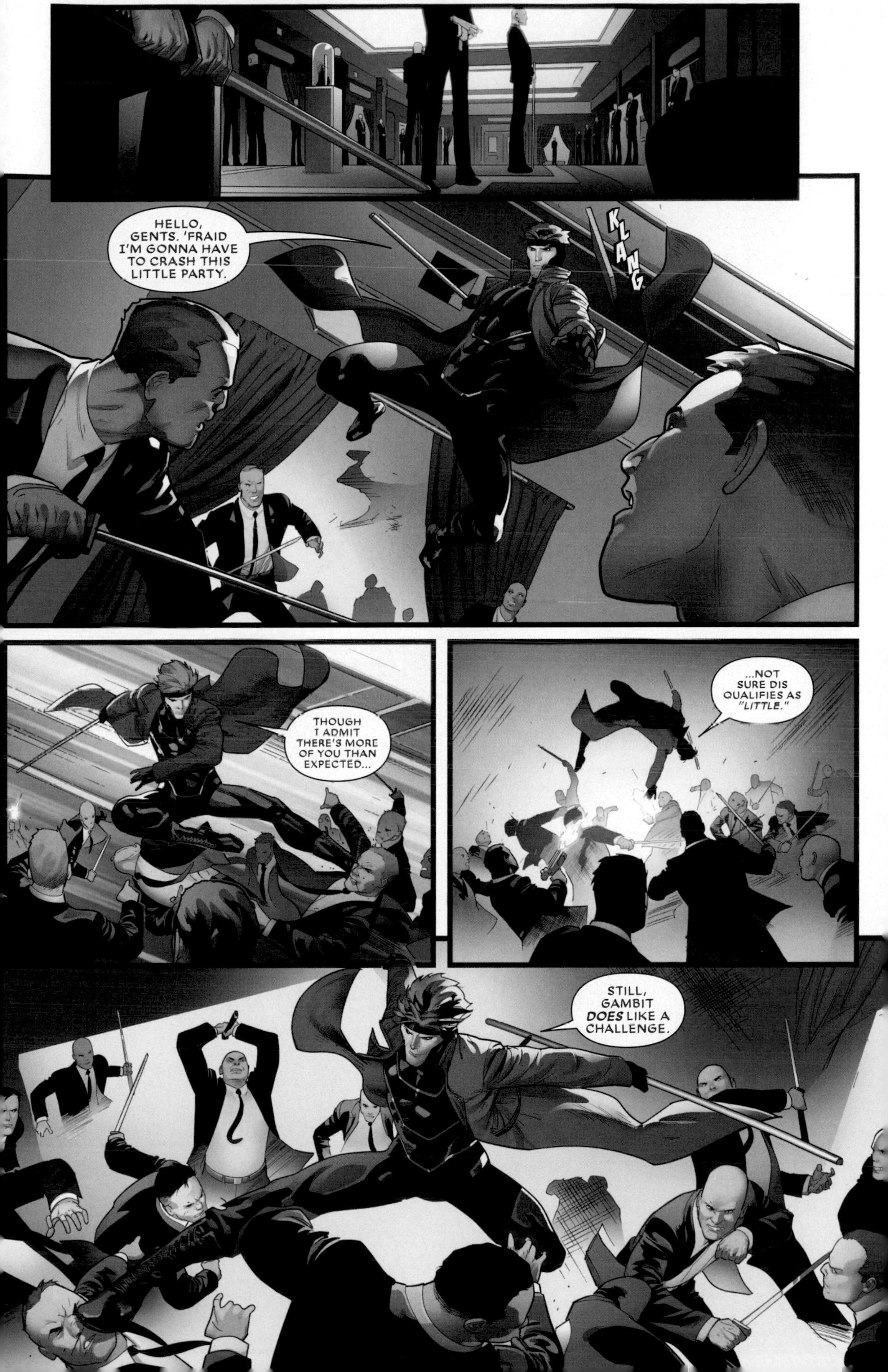
HELLO, GENTS. 'FRAID I'M GONNA HAVE TO CRASH THIS LITTLE PARTY.
KLANG
THOUGH I ADMIT THERE'S MORE OF YOU THAN EXPECTED...
...NOT SURE DIS QUALIFIES AS "LITTLE."
STILL, GAMBIT *DOES* LIKE A CHALLENGE.

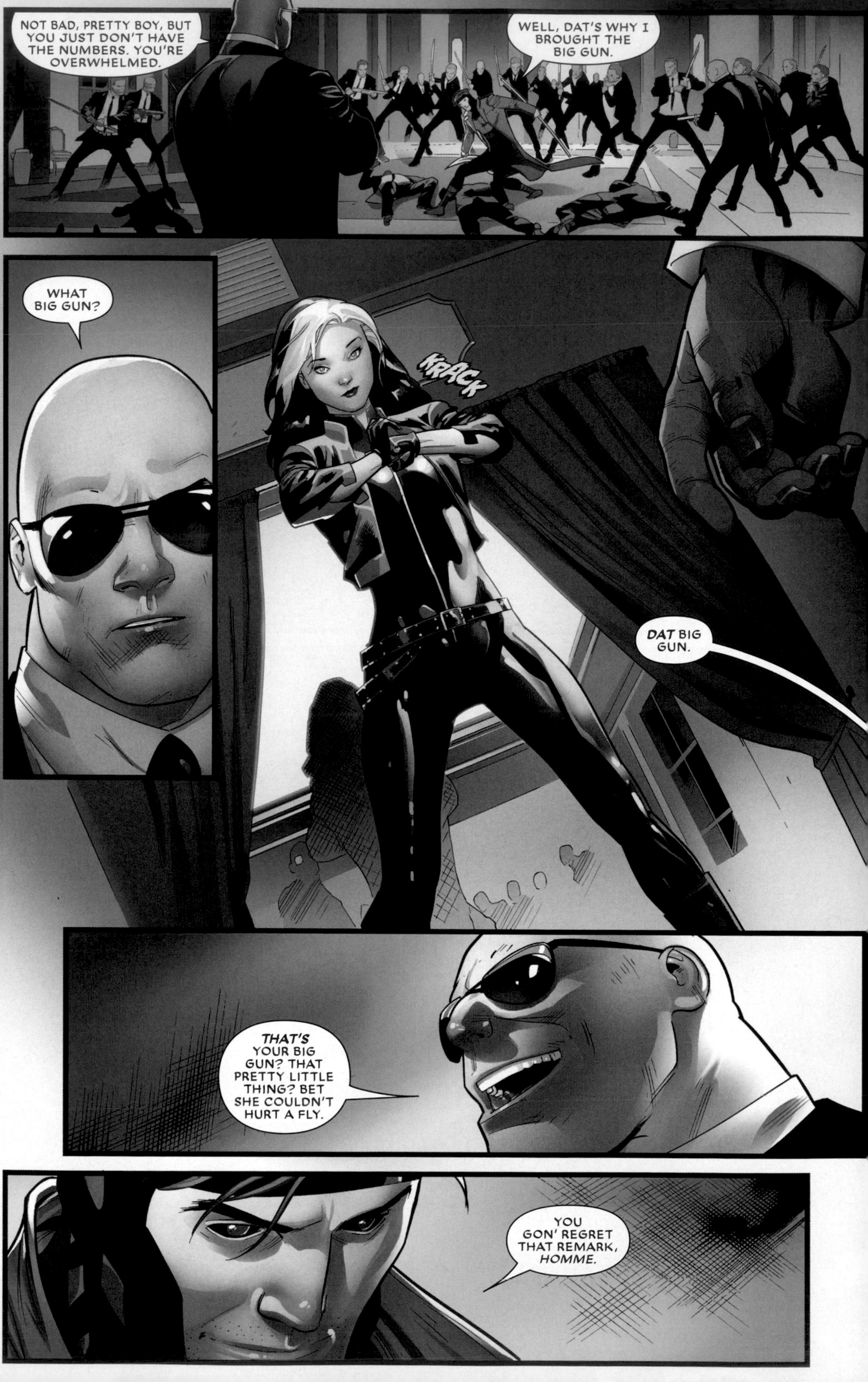
NOT BAD, PRETTY BOY, BUT YOU JUST DON'T HAVE THE NUMBERS. YOU'RE OVERWHELMED.
WELL, DAT'S WHY I BROUGHT THE BIG GUN.
WHAT BIG GUN?
KRACK
DAT BIG GUN.
THAT'S YOUR BIG GUN? THAT PRETTY LITTLE THING? BET SHE COULDN'T HURT A FLY.
YOU GON' REGRET THAT REMARK, HOMME.

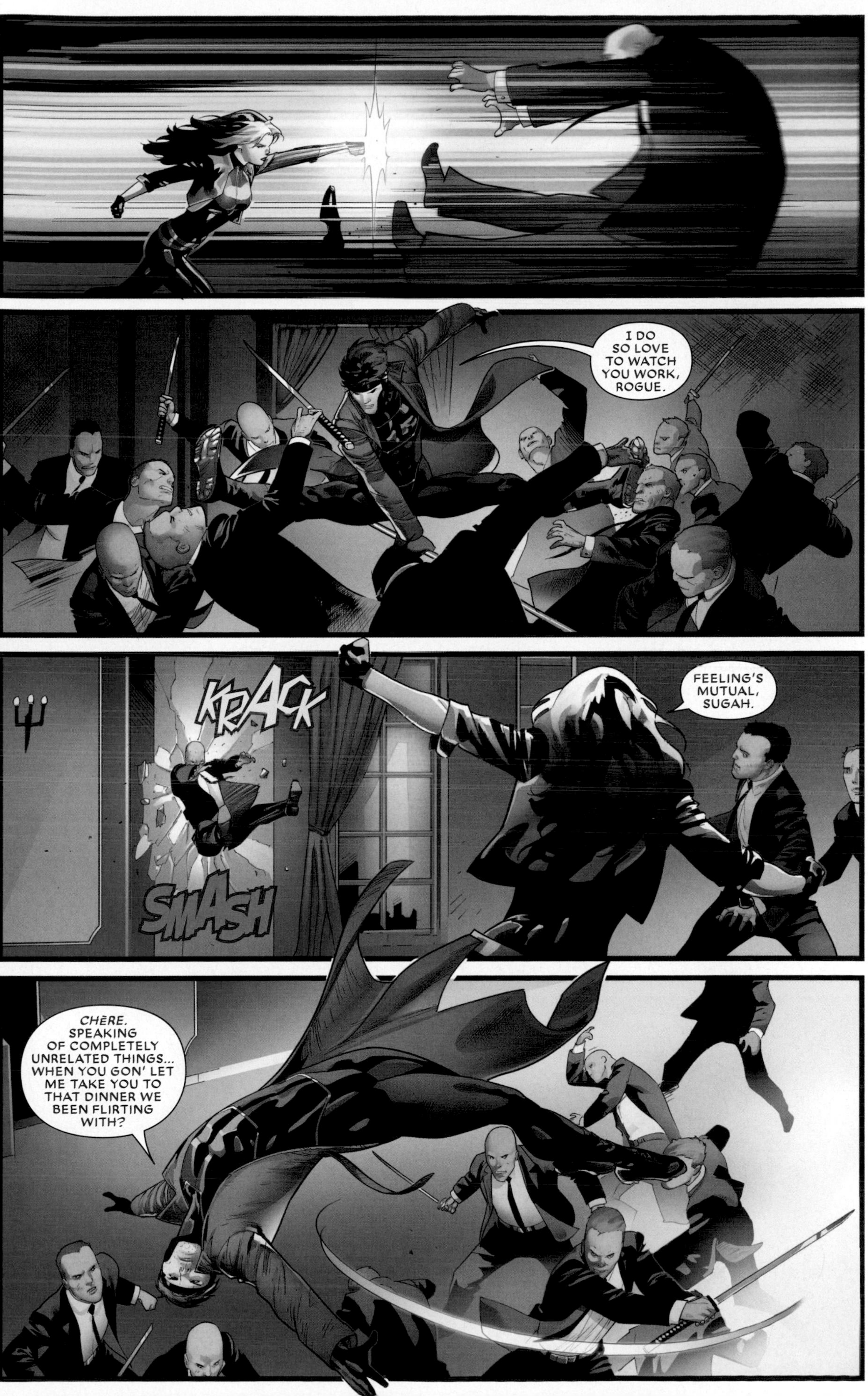
I DO SO LOVE TO WATCH YOU WORK, ROGUE.
KRACK
FEELING'S MUTUAL, SUGAH.
SMASH
CHÈRE. SPEAKING OF COMPLETELY UNRELATED THINGS... WHEN YOU GON' LET ME TAKE YOU TO THAT DINNER WE BEEN FLIRTING WITH?

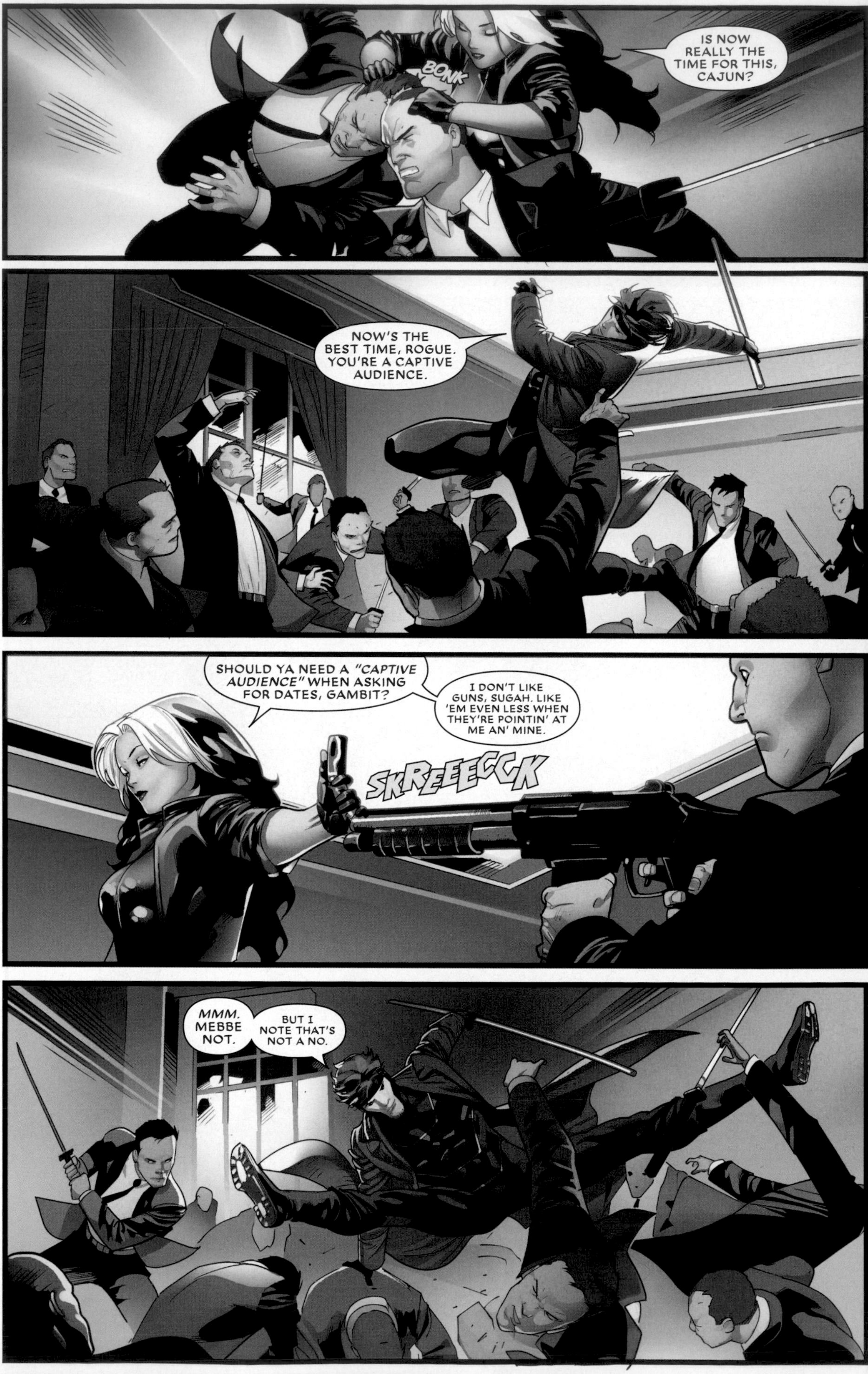
BONK
IS NOW REALLY THE TIME FOR THIS, CAJUN?
NOW'S THE BEST TIME, ROGUE. YOU'RE A CAPTIVE AUDIENCE.
SHOULD YA NEED A "CAPTIVE AUDIENCE" WHEN ASKING FOR DATES, GAMBIT?
I DON'T LIKE GUNS, SUGAH. LIKE 'EM EVEN LESS WHEN THEY'RE POINTIN' AT ME AN' MINE.
SKREEECCK
MMM. MEBBE NOT.
BUT I NOTE THAT'S NOT A NO.

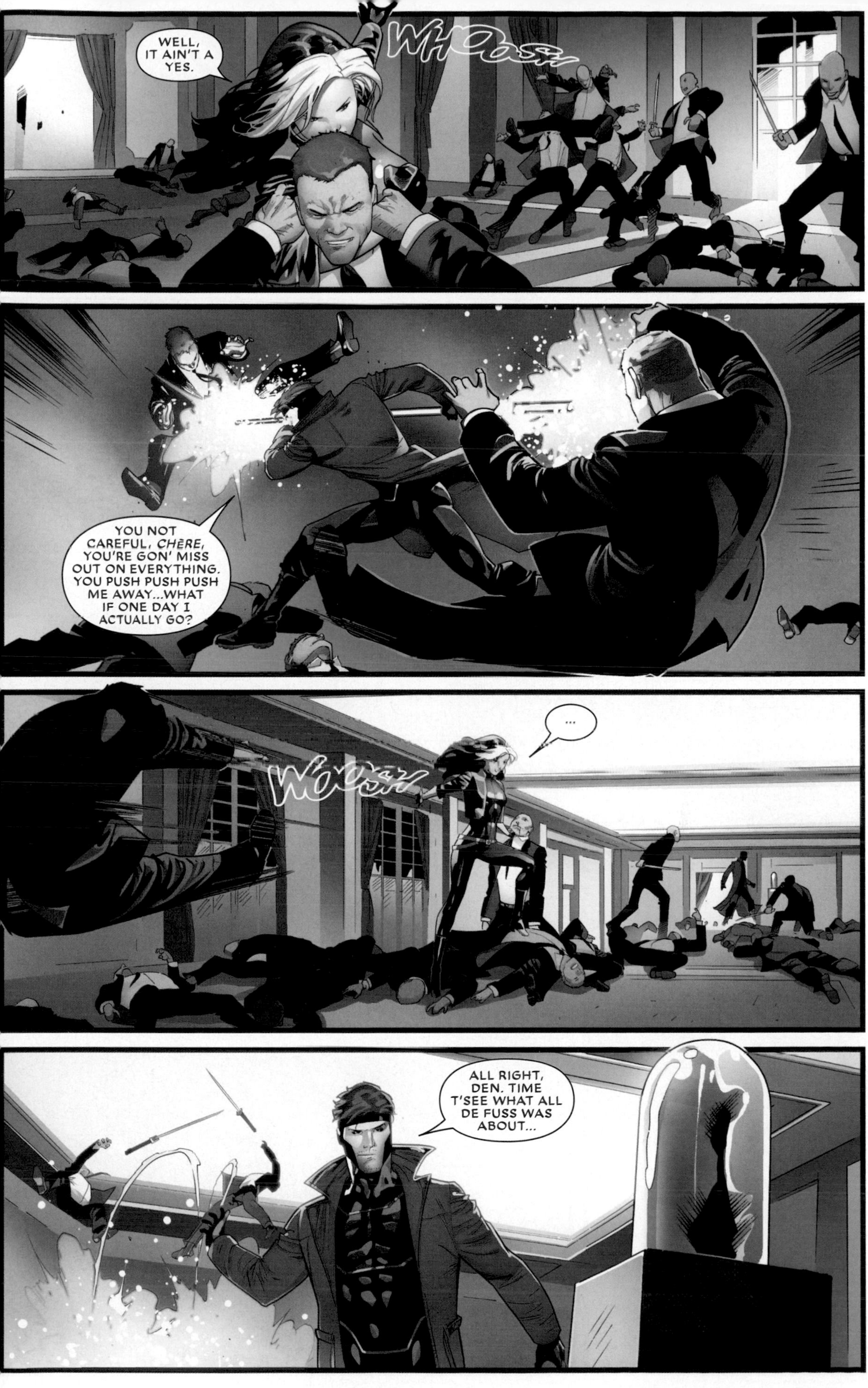
WELL, IT AIN'T A YES.
WHOOSH
YOU NOT CAREFUL, *CHÈRE*, YOU'RE GON' MISS OUT ON EVERYTHING. YOU PUSH PUSH PUSH ME AWAY...WHAT IF ONE DAY I ACTUALLY GO?
...
WOOSH
ALL RIGHT, DEN. TIME T'SEE WHAT ALL DE FUSS WAS ABOUT...

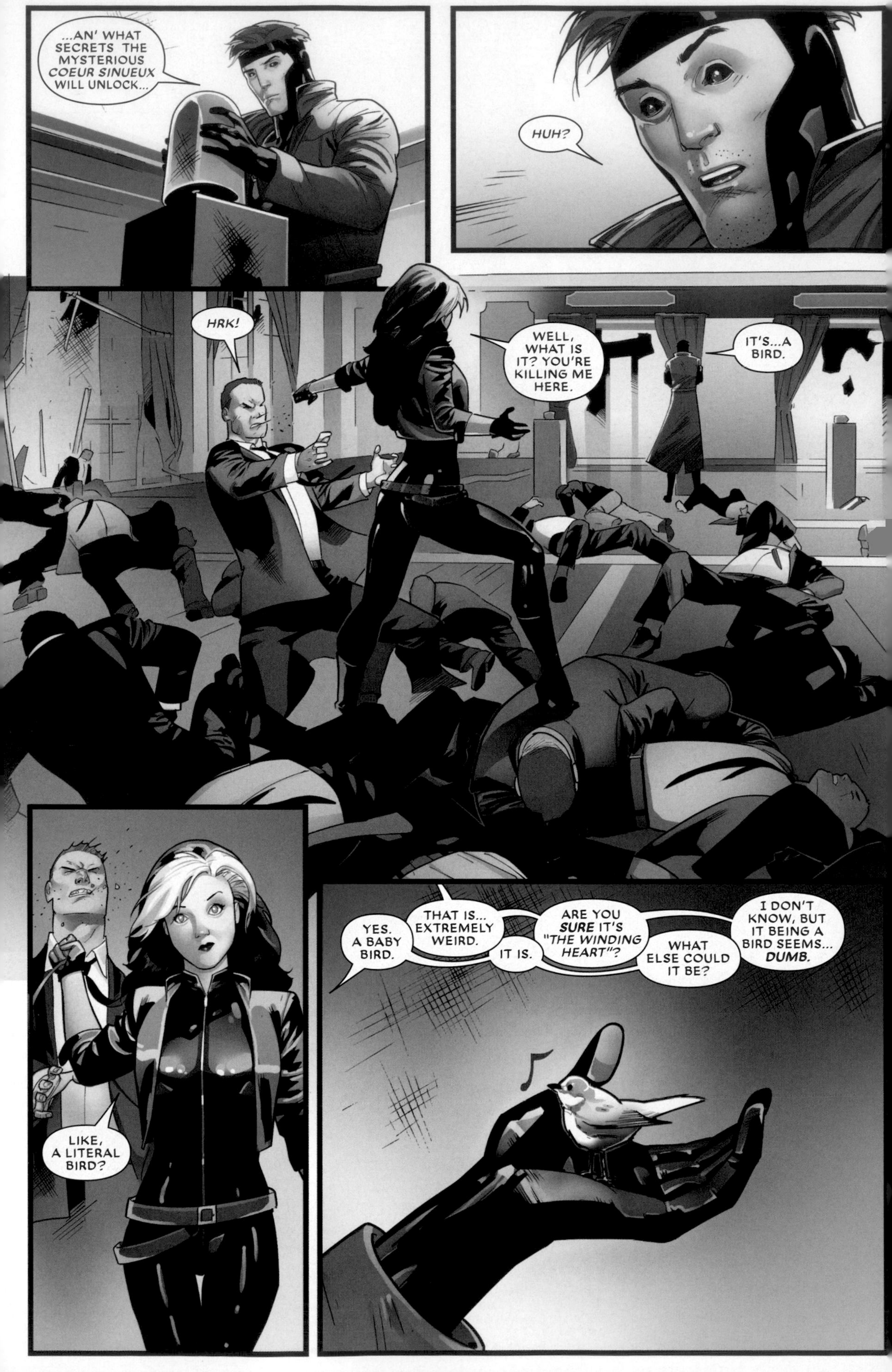
...AN' WHAT SECRETS THE MYSTERIOUS *COEUR SINUEUX* WILL UNLOCK...
HUH?
HRK!
WELL, WHAT IS IT? YOU'RE KILLING ME HERE.
IT'S...A BIRD.
LIKE, A LITERAL BIRD?
YES. A BABY BIRD.
THAT IS... EXTREMELY WEIRD.
IT IS.
ARE YOU ***SURE*** IT'S *"THE WINDING HEART"*?
WHAT ELSE COULD IT BE?
I DON'T KNOW, BUT IT BEING A BIRD SEEMS... ***DUMB.***

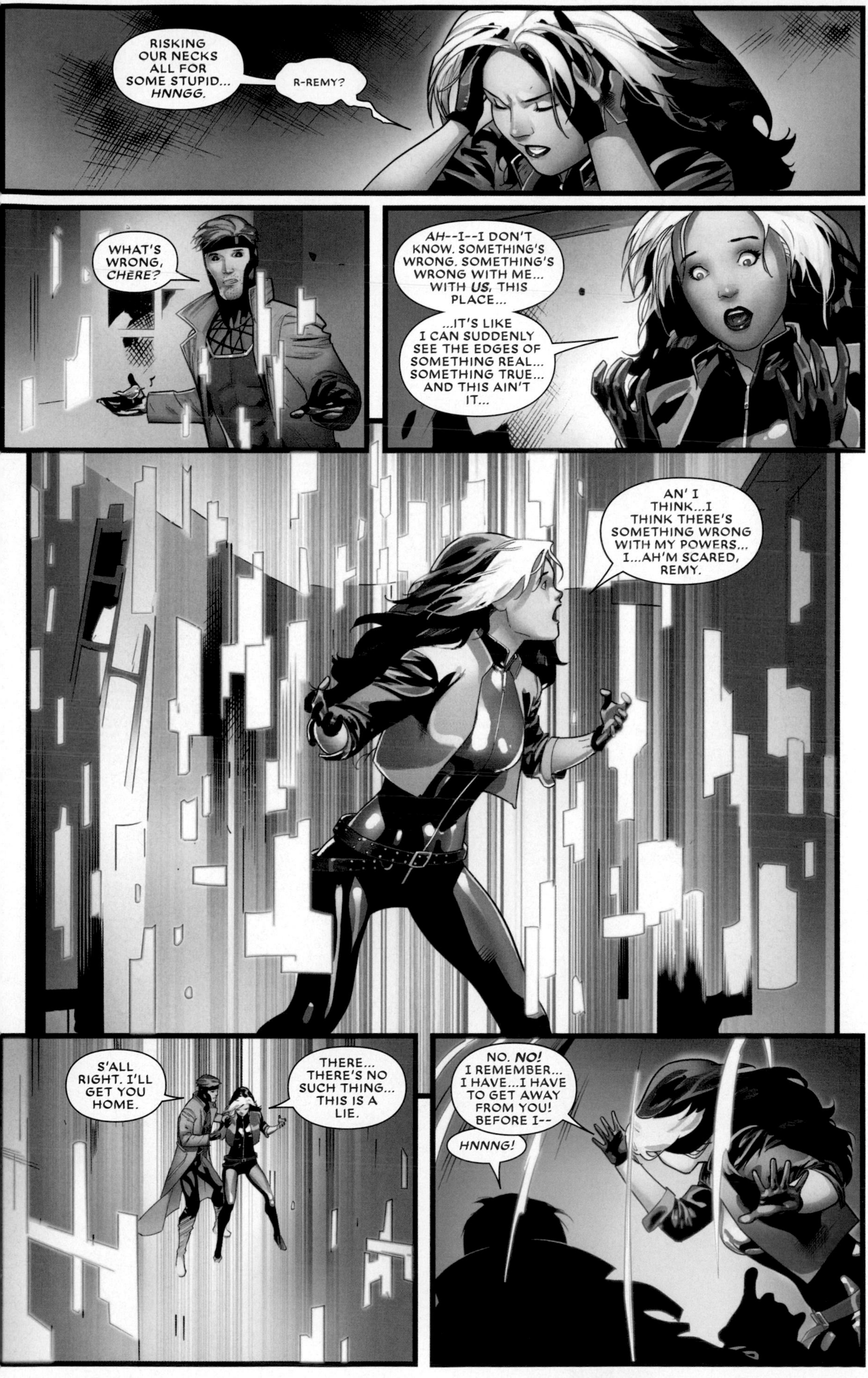
RISKING OUR NECKS ALL FOR SOME STUPID... *HNNGG.*
R-REMY?
WHAT'S WRONG, *CHERE?*
AH--I--I DON'T KNOW. SOMETHING'S WRONG. SOMETHING'S WRONG WITH ME... WITH ***US***, THIS PLACE...
...IT'S LIKE I CAN SUDDENLY SEE THE EDGES OF SOMETHING REAL... SOMETHING TRUE... AND THIS AIN'T IT...
AN' I THINK...I THINK THERE'S SOMETHING WRONG WITH MY POWERS... I...AH'M SCARED, REMY.
S'ALL RIGHT. I'LL GET YOU HOME.
THERE... THERE'S NO SUCH THING... THIS IS A LIE.
NO. ***NO!*** I REMEMBER... I HAVE...I HAVE TO GET AWAY FROM YOU! BEFORE I--
HNNNG!

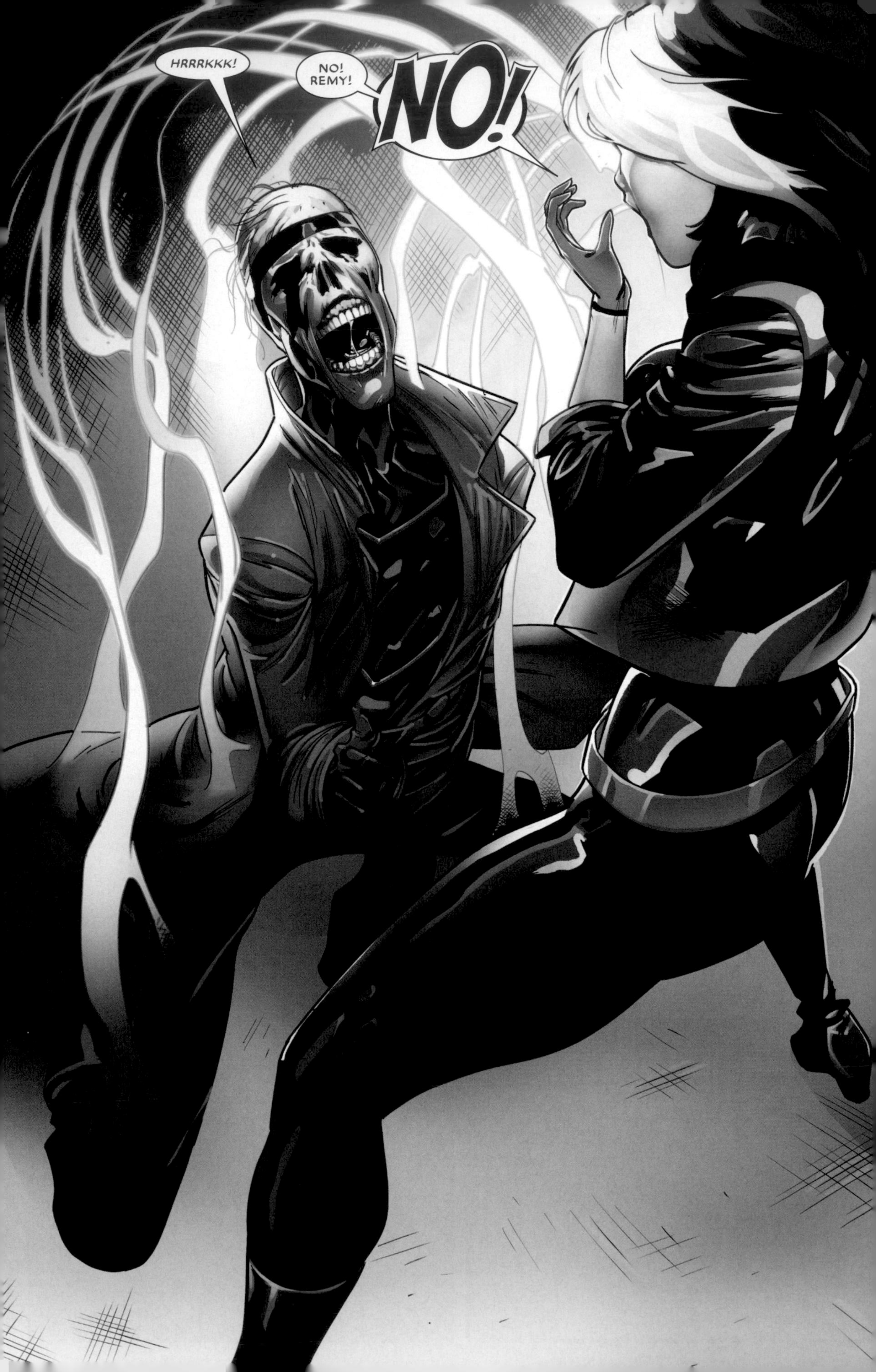
HRRRKKK!
NO! REMY!
NO!

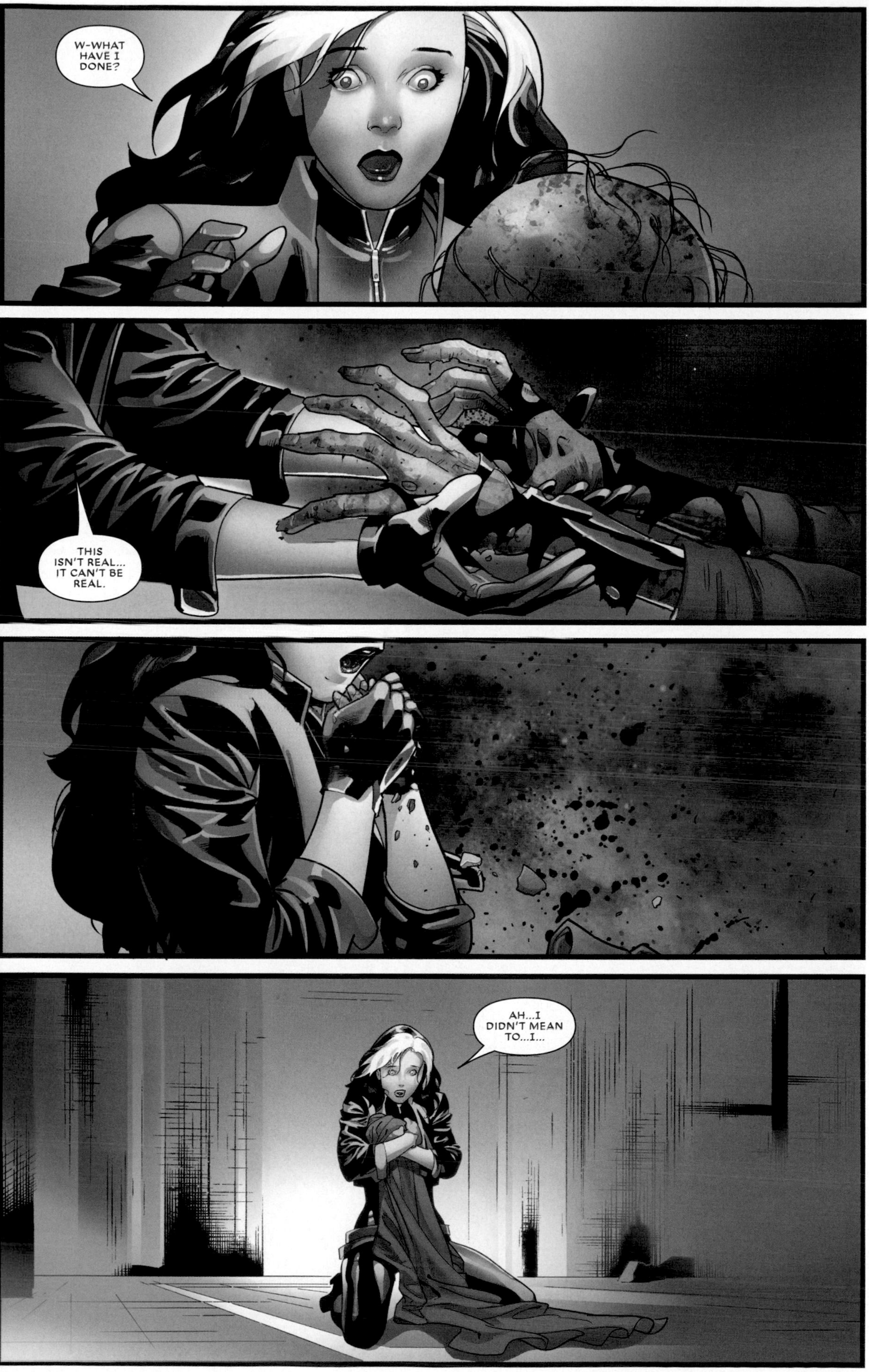
W-WHAT HAVE I DONE?
THIS ISN'T REAL... IT CAN'T BE REAL.
AH...I DIDN'T MEAN TO...I...

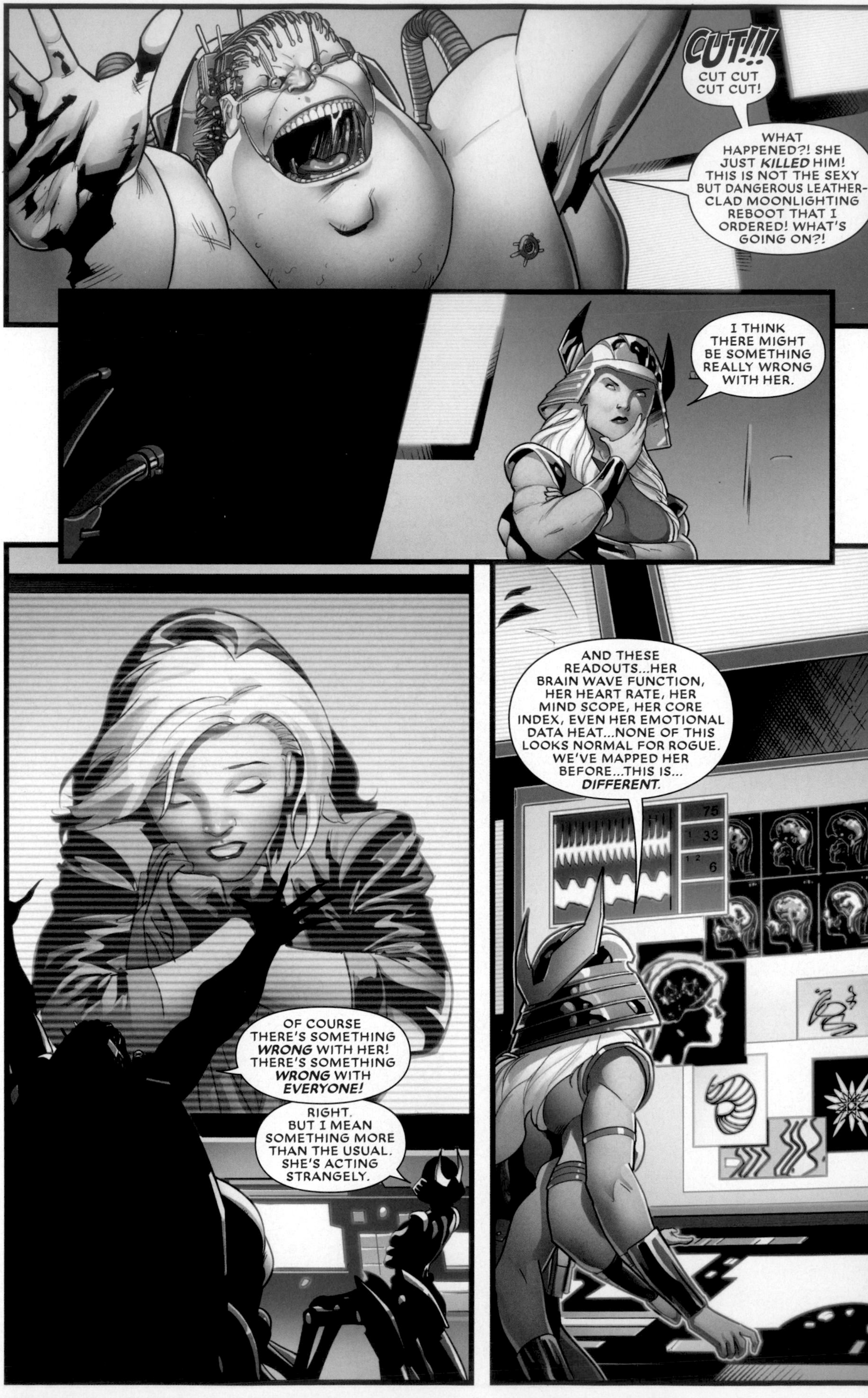
CUT!!!
CUT CUT CUT CUT!
WHAT HAPPENED?! SHE JUST KILLED HIM! THIS IS NOT THE SEXY BUT DANGEROUS LEATHER-CLAD MOONLIGHTING REBOOT THAT I ORDERED! WHAT'S GOING ON?!
I THINK THERE MIGHT BE SOMETHING REALLY WRONG WITH HER.
OF COURSE THERE'S SOMETHING WRONG WITH HER! THERE'S SOMETHING WRONG WITH EVERYONE!
RIGHT. BUT I MEAN SOMETHING MORE THAN THE USUAL. SHE'S ACTING STRANGELY.
AND THESE READOUTS...HER BRAIN WAVE FUNCTION, HER HEART RATE, HER MIND SCOPE, HER CORE INDEX, EVEN HER EMOTIONAL DATA HEAT...NONE OF THIS LOOKS NORMAL FOR ROGUE. WE'VE MAPPED HER BEFORE...THIS IS... DIFFERENT.
75
33
6

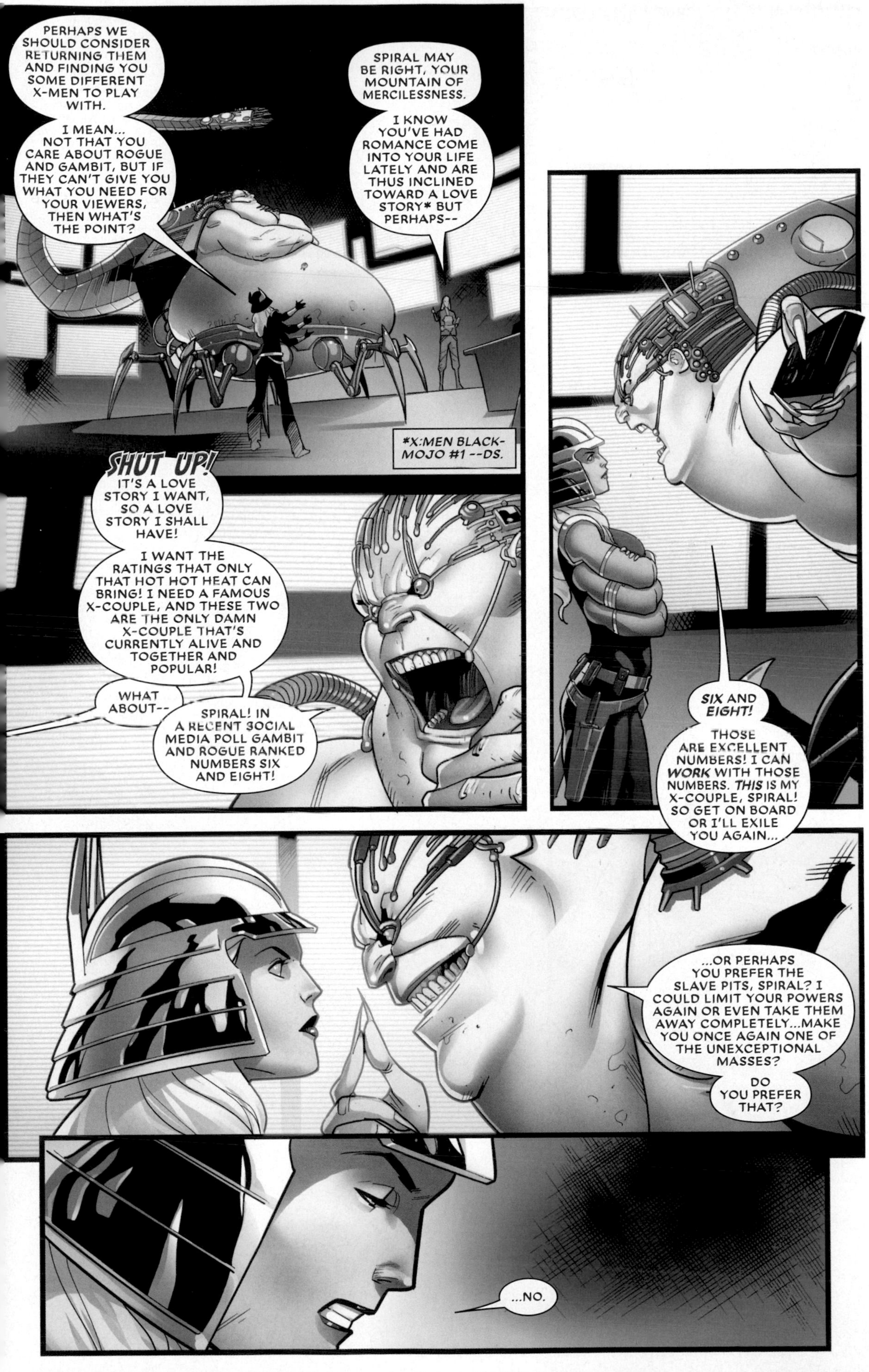
PERHAPS WE SHOULD CONSIDER RETURNING THEM AND FINDING YOU SOME DIFFERENT X-MEN TO PLAY WITH.
I MEAN... NOT THAT YOU CARE ABOUT ROGUE AND GAMBIT, BUT IF THEY CAN'T GIVE YOU WHAT YOU NEED FOR YOUR VIEWERS, THEN WHAT'S THE POINT?
SPIRAL MAY BE RIGHT, YOUR MOUNTAIN OF MERCILESSNESS.
I KNOW YOU'VE HAD ROMANCE COME INTO YOUR LIFE LATELY AND ARE THUS INCLINED TOWARD A LOVE STORY* BUT PERHAPS--
*X-MEN BLACK-MOJO #1 --DS.
SHUT UP!
IT'S A LOVE STORY I WANT, SO A LOVE STORY I SHALL HAVE!
I WANT THE RATINGS THAT ONLY THAT HOT HOT HEAT CAN BRING! I NEED A FAMOUS X-COUPLE, AND THESE TWO ARE THE ONLY DAMN X-COUPLE THAT'S CURRENTLY ALIVE AND TOGETHER AND POPULAR!
WHAT ABOUT--
SPIRAL! IN A RECENT SOCIAL MEDIA POLL GAMBIT AND ROGUE RANKED NUMBERS SIX AND EIGHT!
SIX AND EIGHT!
THOSE ARE EXCELLENT NUMBERS! I CAN WORK WITH THOSE NUMBERS. THIS IS MY X-COUPLE, SPIRAL! SO GET ON BOARD OR I'LL EXILE YOU AGAIN...
...OR PERHAPS YOU PREFER THE SLAVE PITS, SPIRAL? I COULD LIMIT YOUR POWERS AGAIN OR EVEN TAKE THEM AWAY COMPLETELY...MAKE YOU ONCE AGAIN ONE OF THE UNEXCEPTIONAL MASSES?
DO YOU PREFER THAT?
...NO.

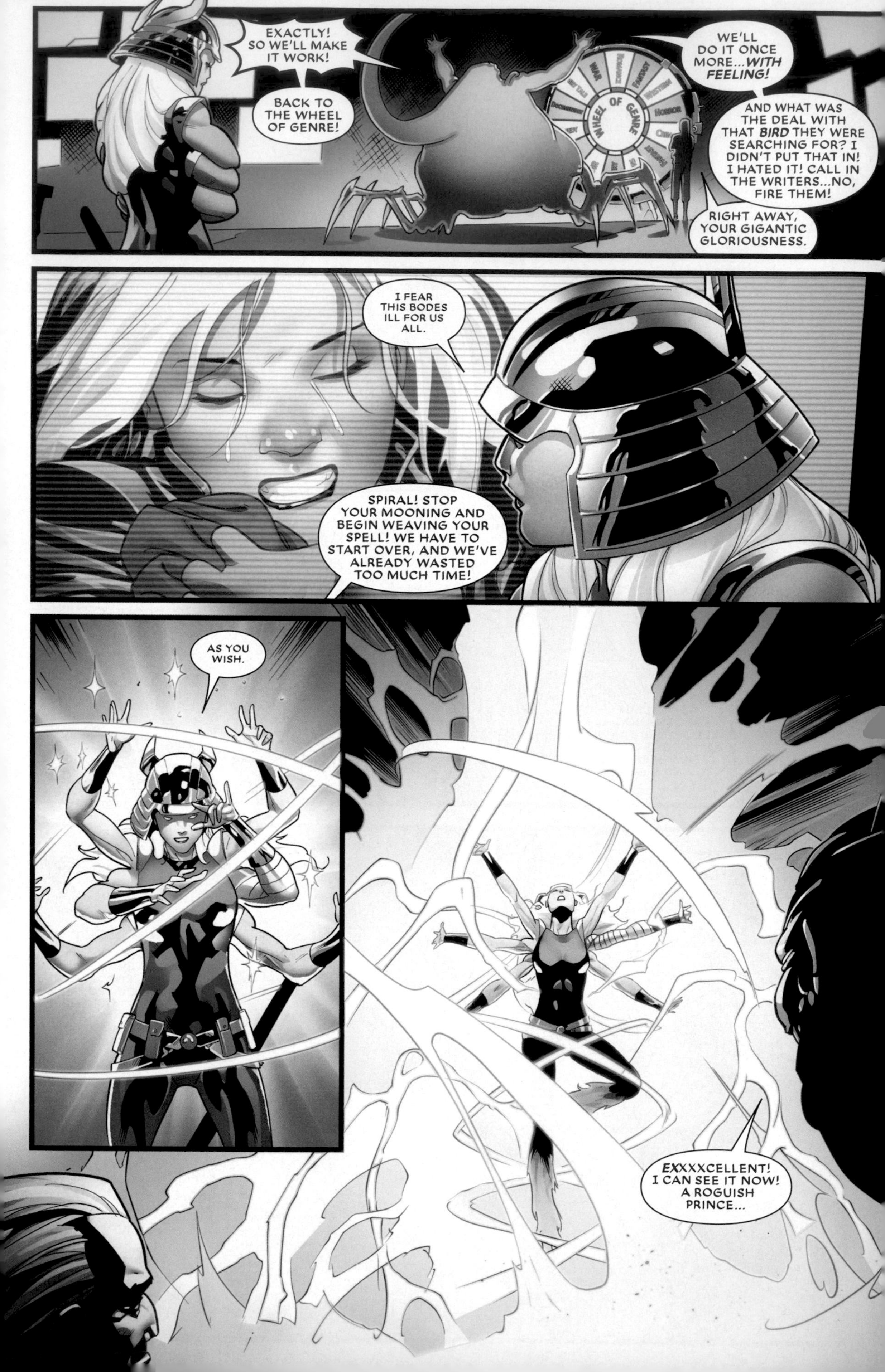

EXACTLY! SO WE'LL MAKE IT WORK!
BACK TO THE WHEEL OF GENRE!
WE'LL DO IT ONCE MORE...WITH FEELING!
AND WHAT WAS THE DEAL WITH THAT BIRD THEY WERE SEARCHING FOR? I DIDN'T PUT THAT IN! I HATED IT! CALL IN THE WRITERS...NO, FIRE THEM!
RIGHT AWAY, YOUR GIGANTIC GLORIOUSNESS.
WHEEL OF GENRE
WAR
ROMANCE
FANTASY
WESTERN
HORROR
DOCUMENTARY
I FEAR THIS BODES ILL FOR US ALL.
SPIRAL! STOP YOUR MOONING AND BEGIN WEAVING YOUR SPELL! WE HAVE TO START OVER, AND WE'VE ALREADY WASTED TOO MUCH TIME!
AS YOU WISH.
EXXXXCELLENT! I CAN SEE IT NOW! A ROGUISH PRINCE...

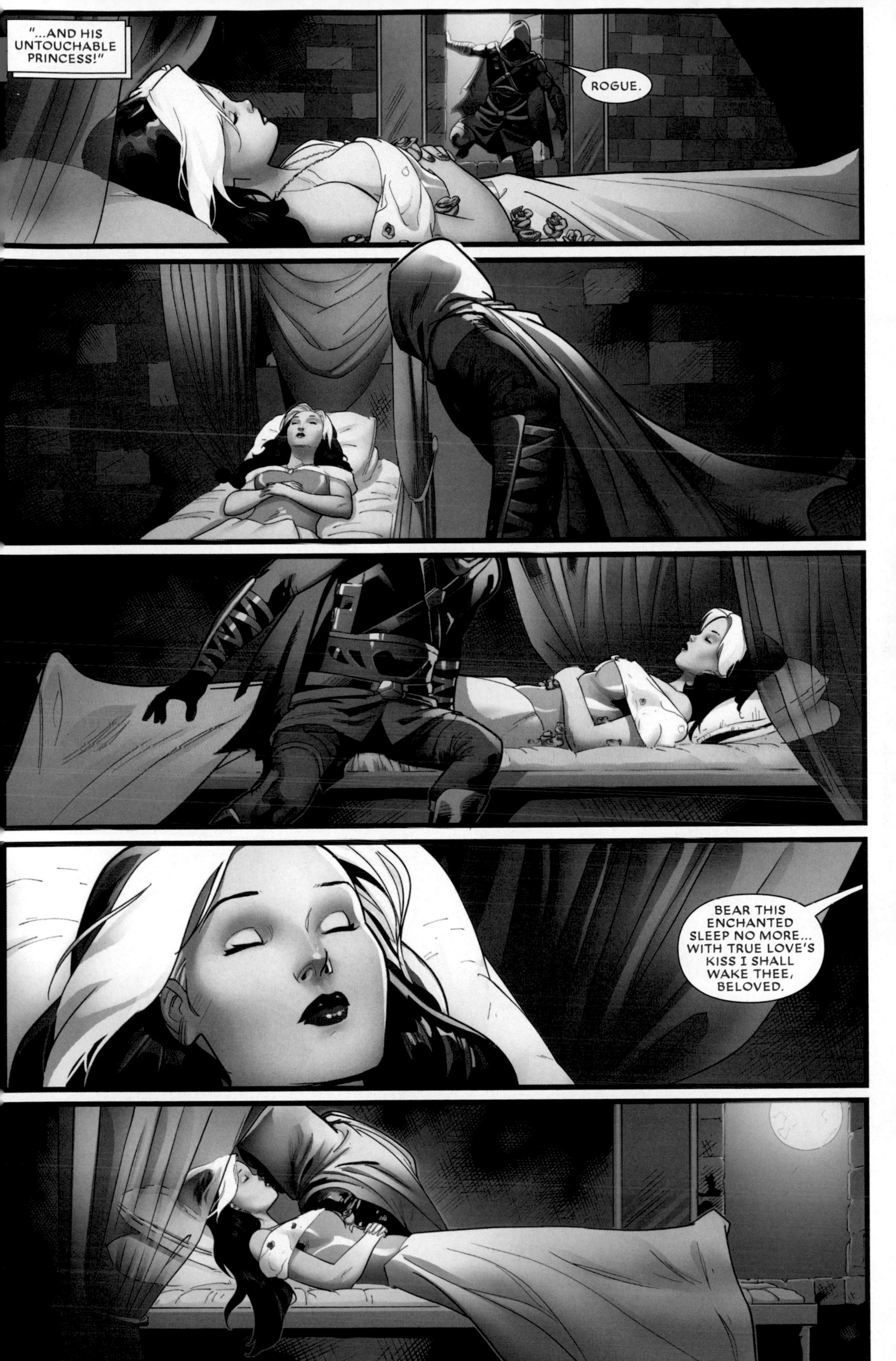
"...AND HIS UNTOUCHABLE PRINCESS!"
ROGUE.
BEAR THIS ENCHANTED SLEEP NO MORE... WITH TRUE LOVE'S KISS I SHALL WAKE THEE, BELOVED.

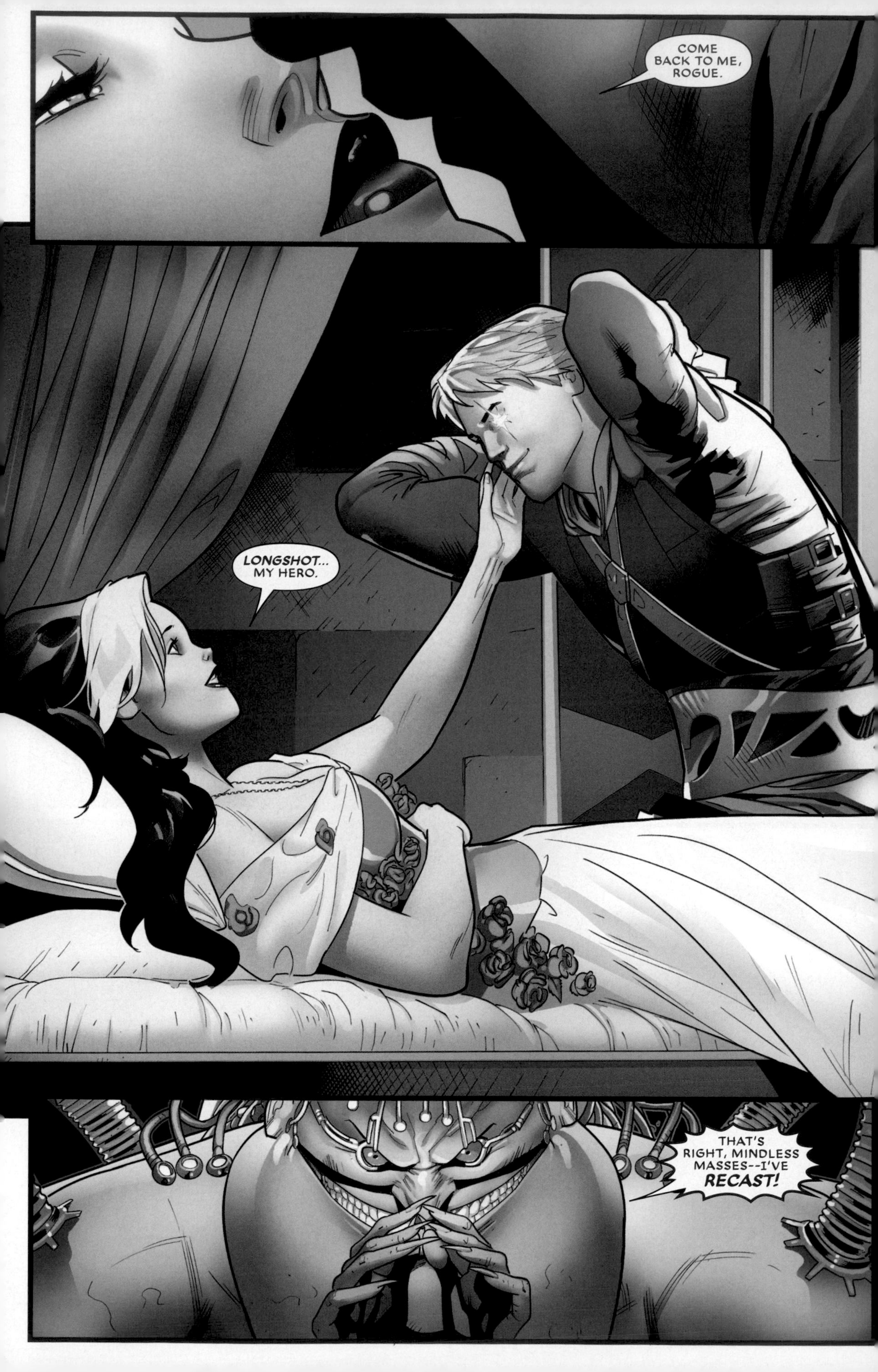
COME BACK TO ME, ROGUE.
LONGSHOT... MY HERO.
THAT'S RIGHT, MINDLESS MASSES--I'VE ***RECAST!***

8

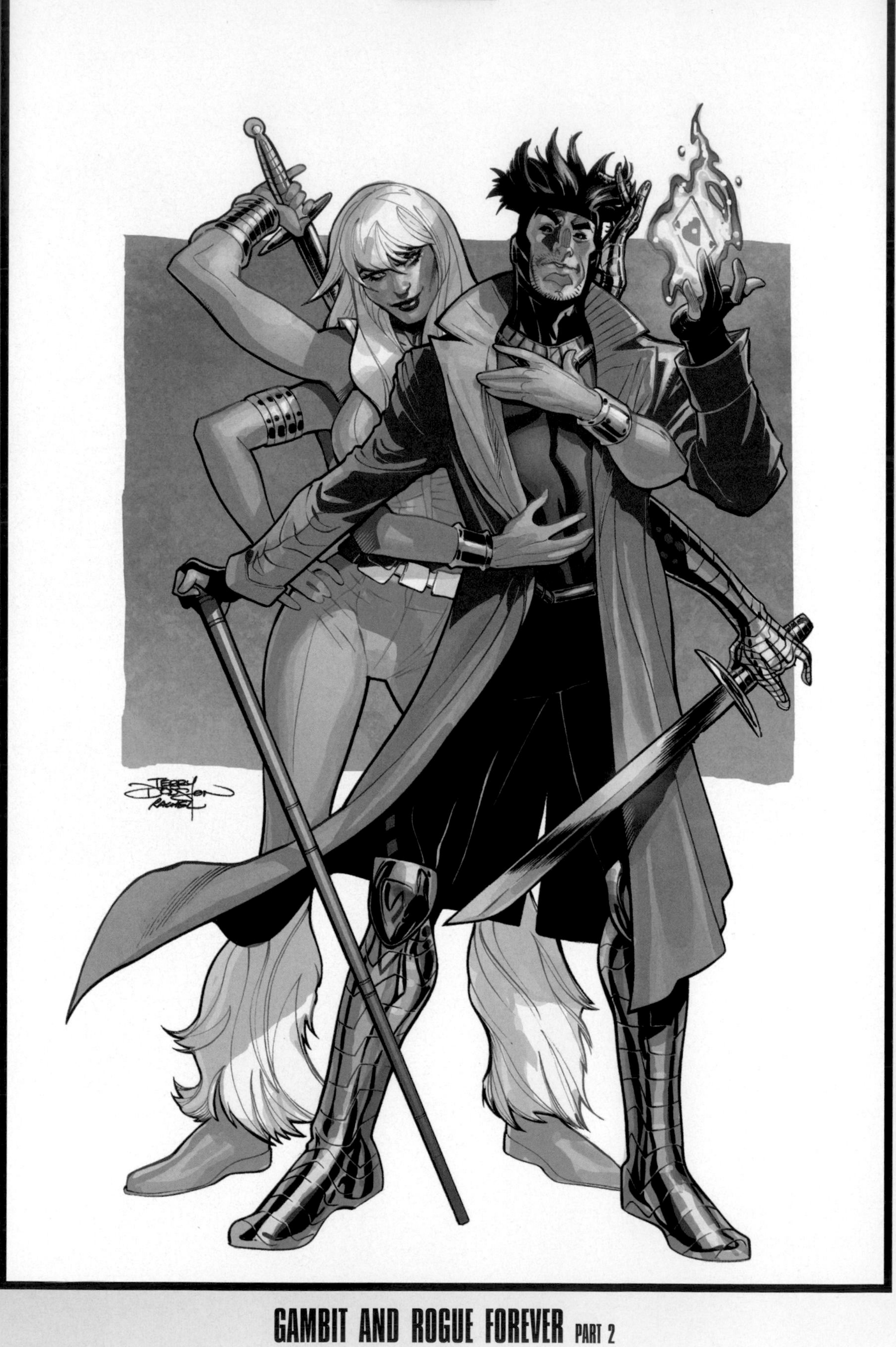

GAMBIT AND ROGUE FOREVER PART 2

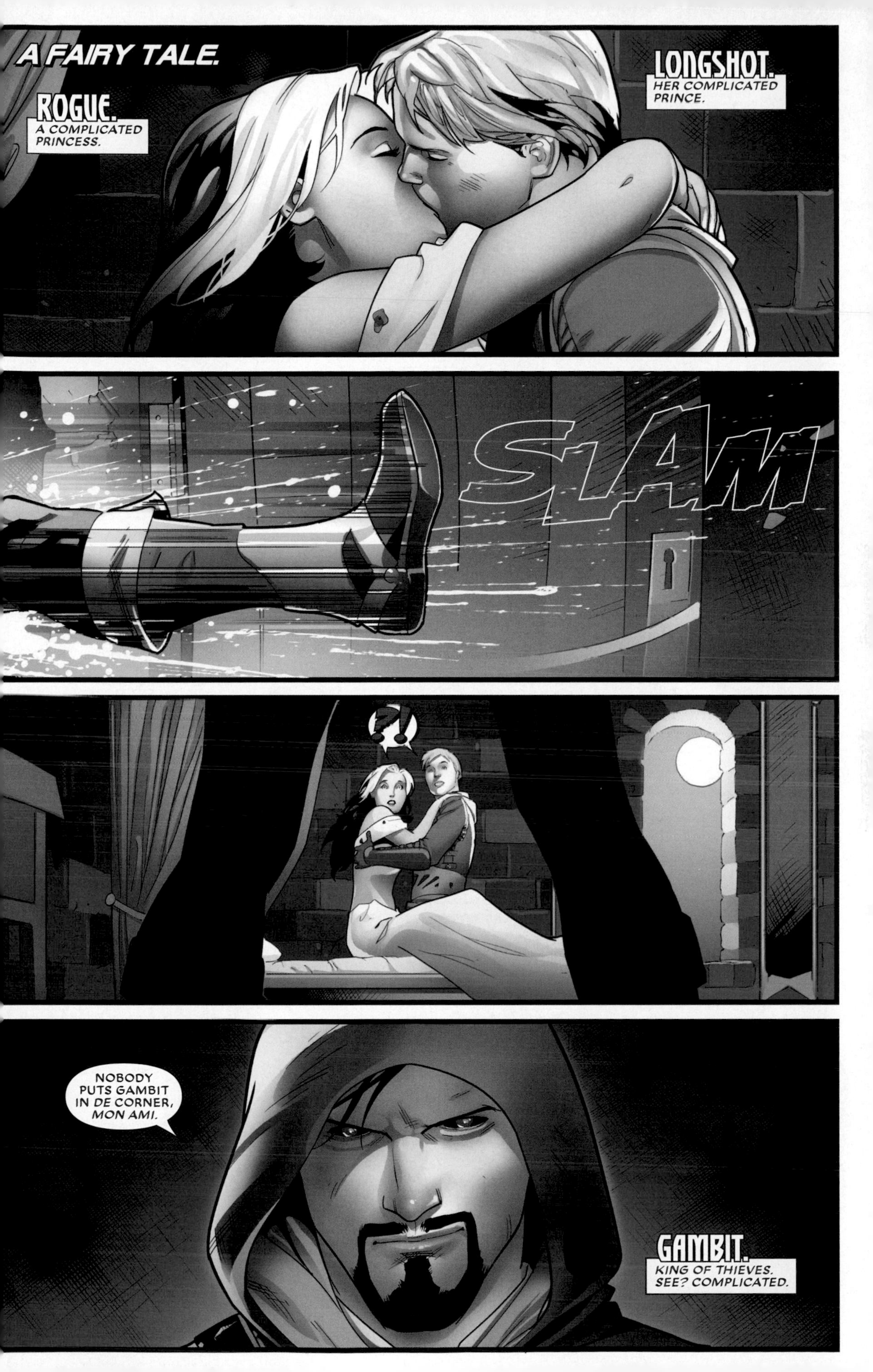
A FAIRY TALE.
ROGUE.
A COMPLICATED PRINCESS.
LONGSHOT.
HER COMPLICATED PRINCE.
SLAM
?!
NOBODY PUTS GAMBIT IN DE CORNER, MON AMI.
GAMBIT.
KING OF THIEVES. SEE? COMPLICATED.

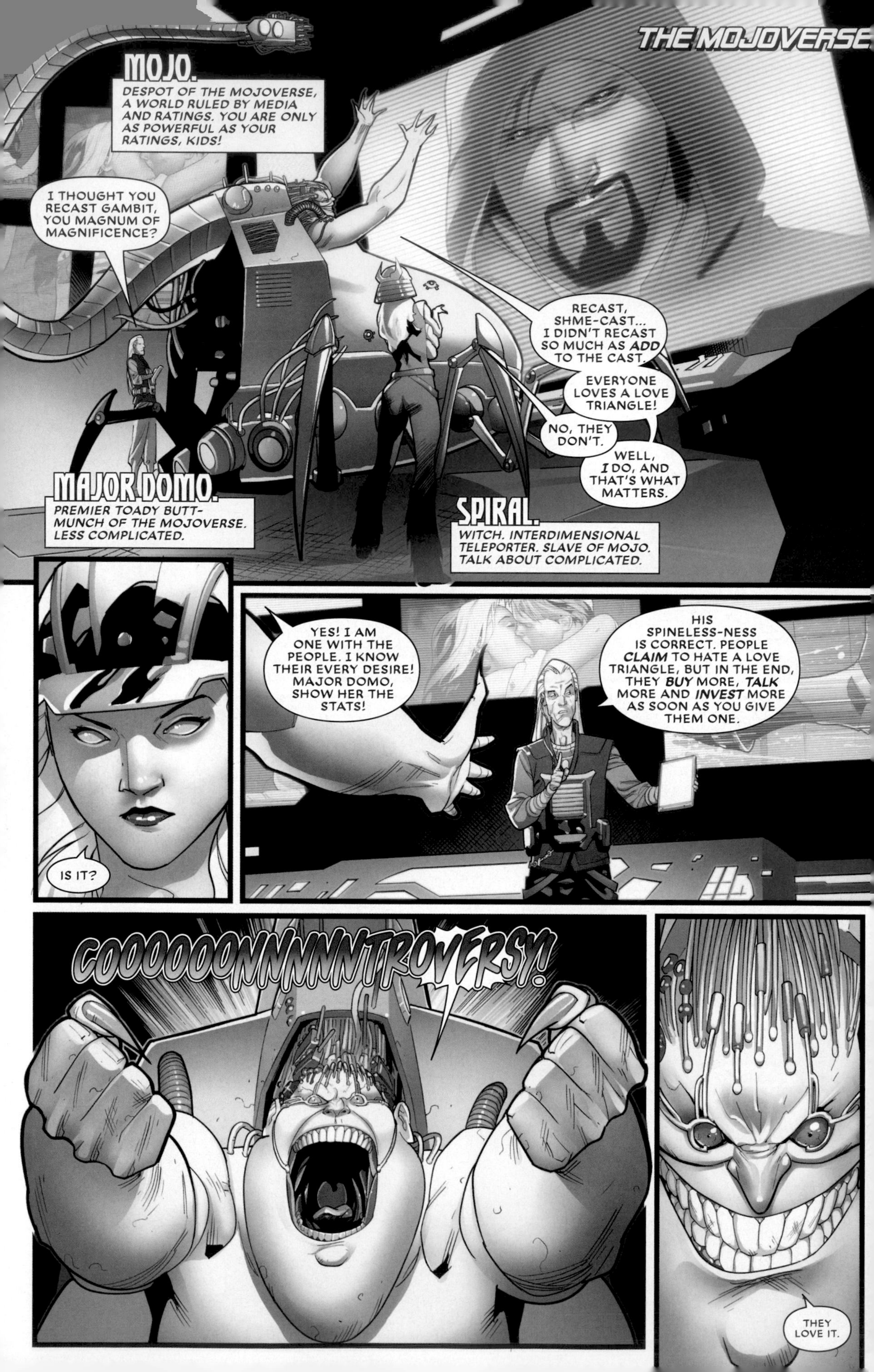
THE MOJOVERSE.
MOJO.
DESPOT OF THE MOJOVERSE, A WORLD RULED BY MEDIA AND RATINGS. YOU ARE ONLY AS POWERFUL AS YOUR RATINGS, KIDS!
I THOUGHT YOU RECAST GAMBIT, YOU MAGNUM OF MAGNIFICENCE?
RECAST, SHME-CAST... I DIDN'T RECAST SO MUCH AS ADD TO THE CAST.
EVERYONE LOVES A LOVE TRIANGLE!
NO, THEY DON'T.
WELL, I DO, AND THAT'S WHAT MATTERS.
MAJOR DOMO.
PREMIER TOADY BUTT-MUNCH OF THE MOJOVERSE. LESS COMPLICATED.
SPIRAL.
WITCH. INTERDIMENSIONAL TELEPORTER. SLAVE OF MOJO. TALK ABOUT COMPLICATED.
IS IT?
YES! I AM ONE WITH THE PEOPLE. I KNOW THEIR EVERY DESIRE! MAJOR DOMO, SHOW HER THE STATS!
HIS SPINELESS-NESS IS CORRECT. PEOPLE CLAIM TO HATE A LOVE TRIANGLE, BUT IN THE END, THEY BUY MORE, TALK MORE AND INVEST MORE AS SOON AS YOU GIVE THEM ONE.
COOOOOOONNNNNNTROVERSY!
THEY LOVE IT.

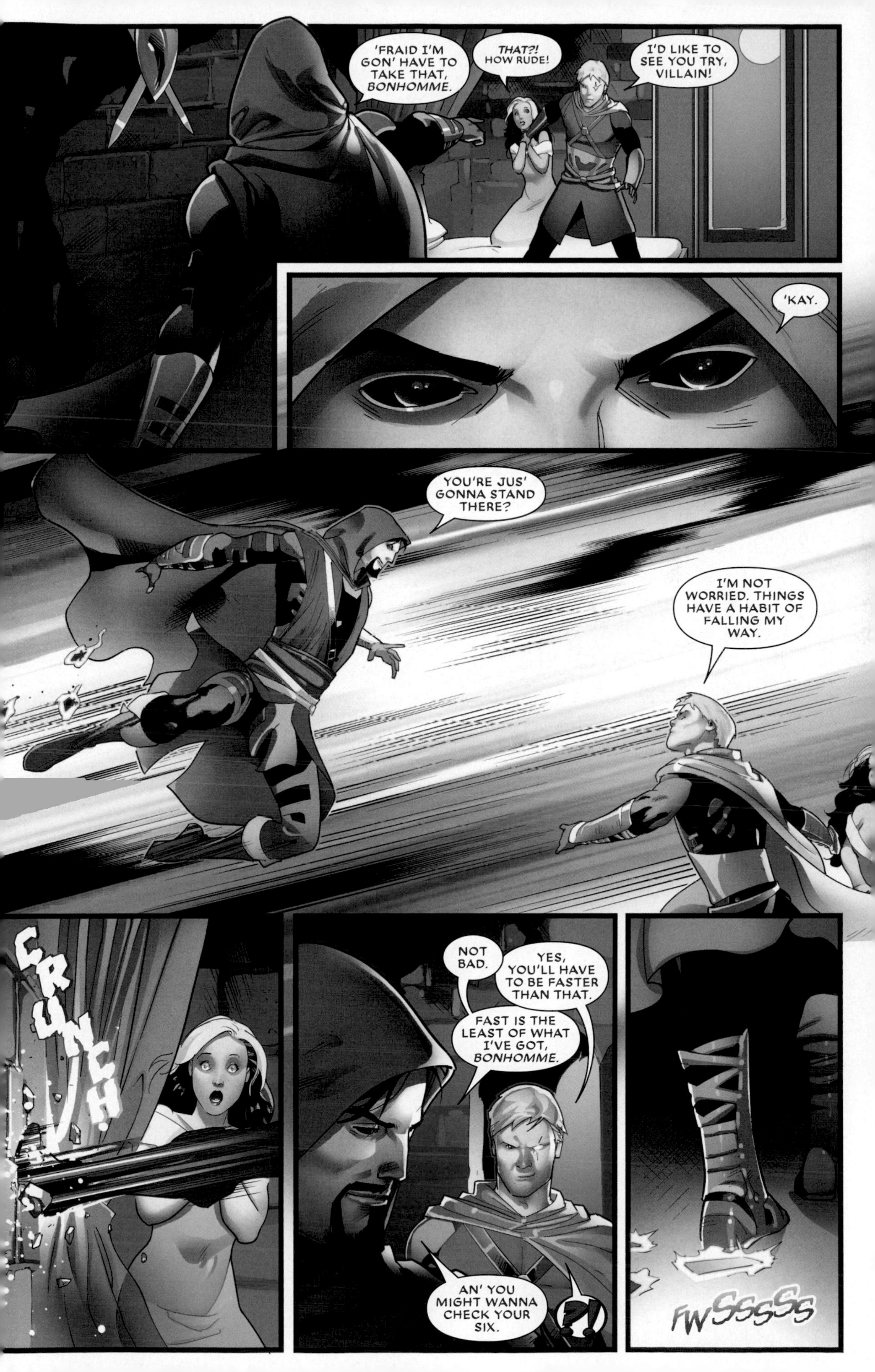

'FRAID I'M GON' HAVE TO TAKE THAT, *BONHOMME*.
THAT?! HOW RUDE!
I'D LIKE TO SEE YOU TRY, VILLAIN!
'KAY.
YOU'RE JUS' GONNA STAND THERE?
I'M NOT WORRIED. THINGS HAVE A HABIT OF FALLING MY WAY.
CRUNCH!
NOT BAD.
YES, YOU'LL HAVE TO BE FASTER THAN THAT.
FAST IS THE LEAST OF WHAT I'VE GOT, *BONHOMME*.
AN' YOU MIGHT WANNA CHECK YOUR SIX.
?!
FWSSSSS

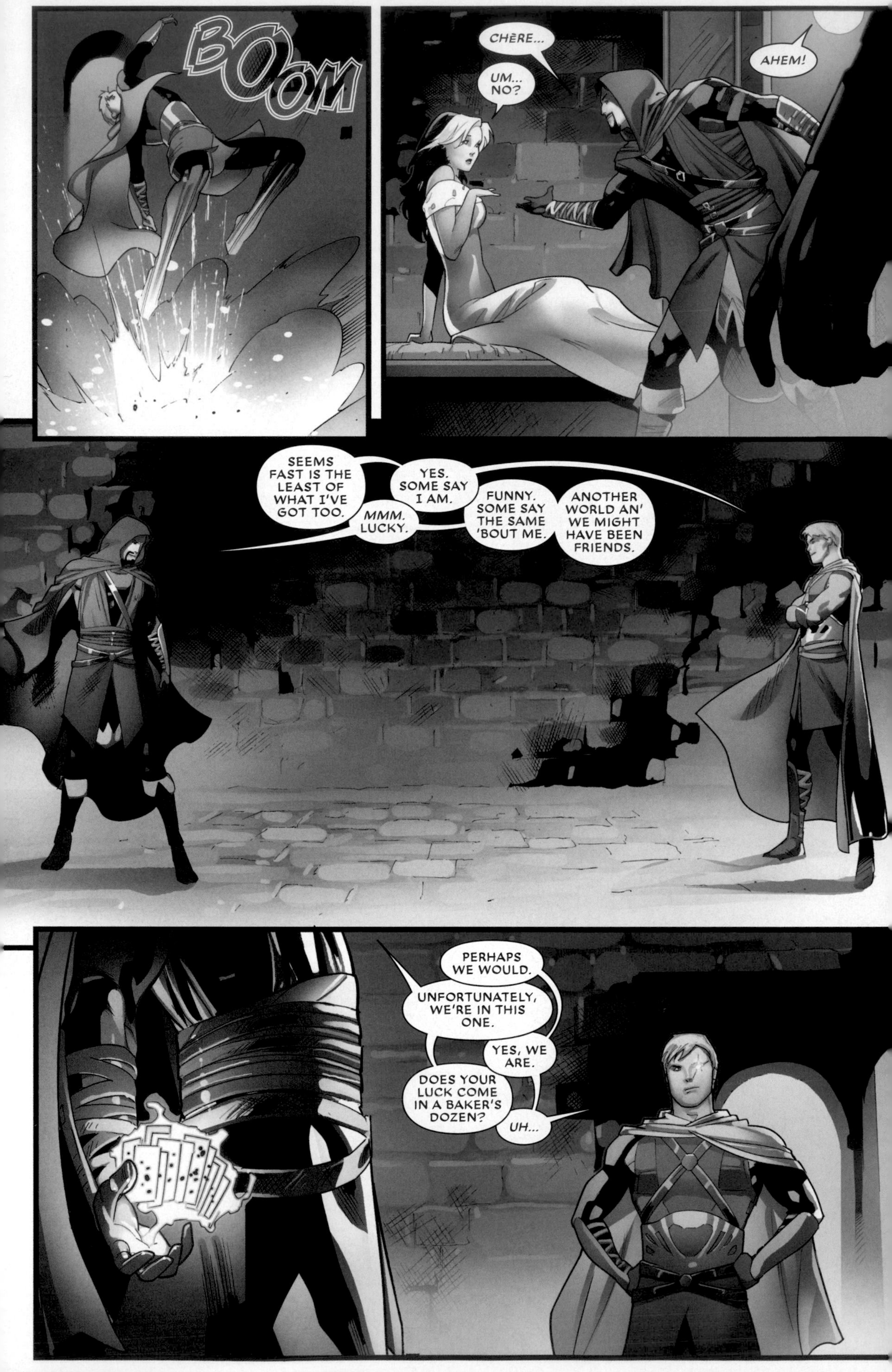
BOOM
CHÈRE...
UM... NO?
AHEM!
SEEMS FAST IS THE LEAST OF WHAT I'VE GOT TOO.
YES. SOME SAY I AM.
MMM. LUCKY.
FUNNY. SOME SAY THE SAME 'BOUT ME.
ANOTHER WORLD AN' WE MIGHT HAVE BEEN FRIENDS.
PERHAPS WE WOULD.
UNFORTUNATELY, WE'RE IN THIS ONE.
YES, WE ARE.
DOES YOUR LUCK COME IN A BAKER'S DOZEN?
UH...

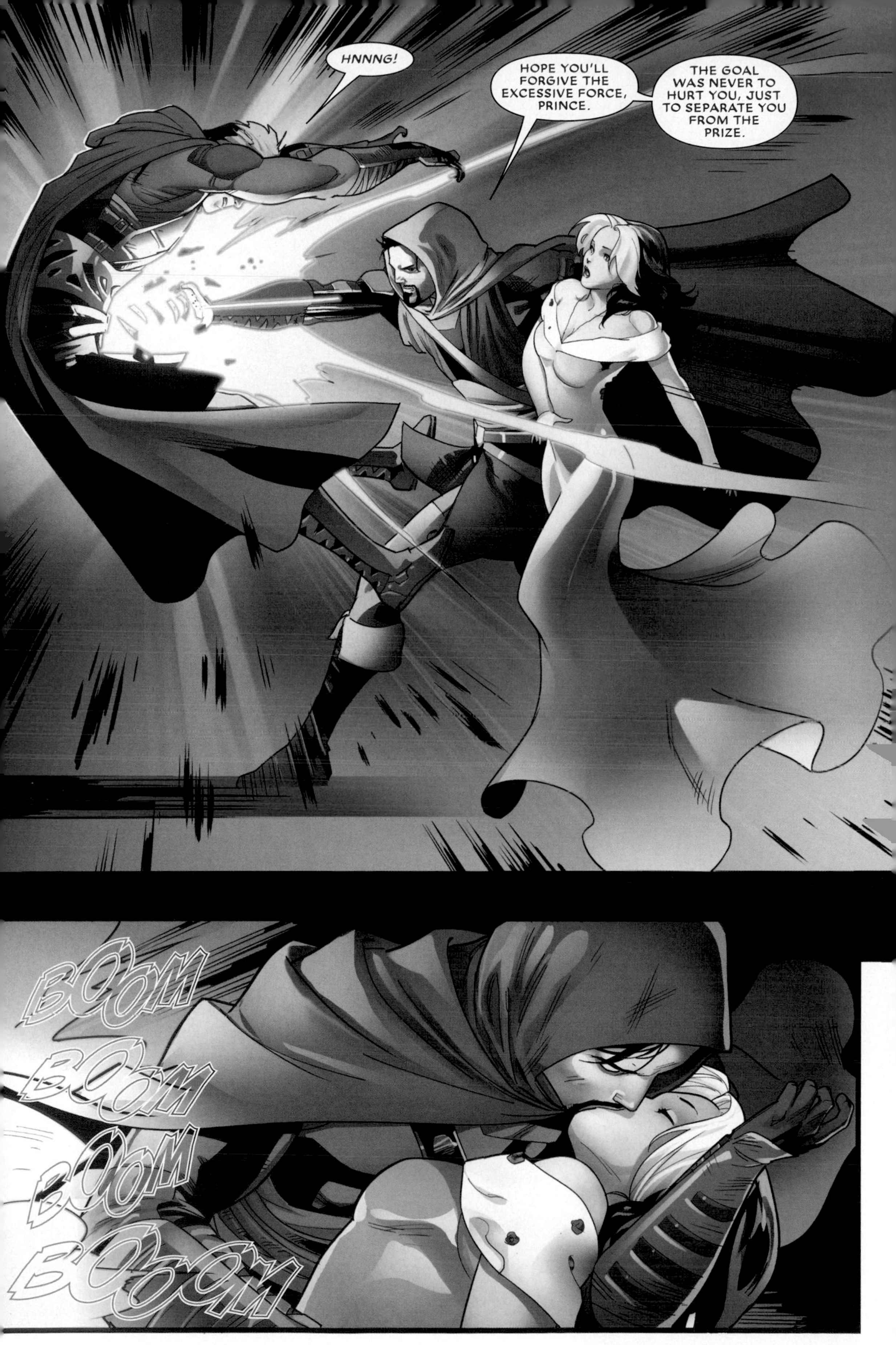
HNNNG!
HOPE YOU'LL FORGIVE THE EXCESSIVE FORCE, PRINCE.
THE GOAL WAS NEVER TO HURT YOU, JUST TO SEPARATE YOU FROM THE PRIZE.
BOOM
BOOM
BOOM
BOOOM

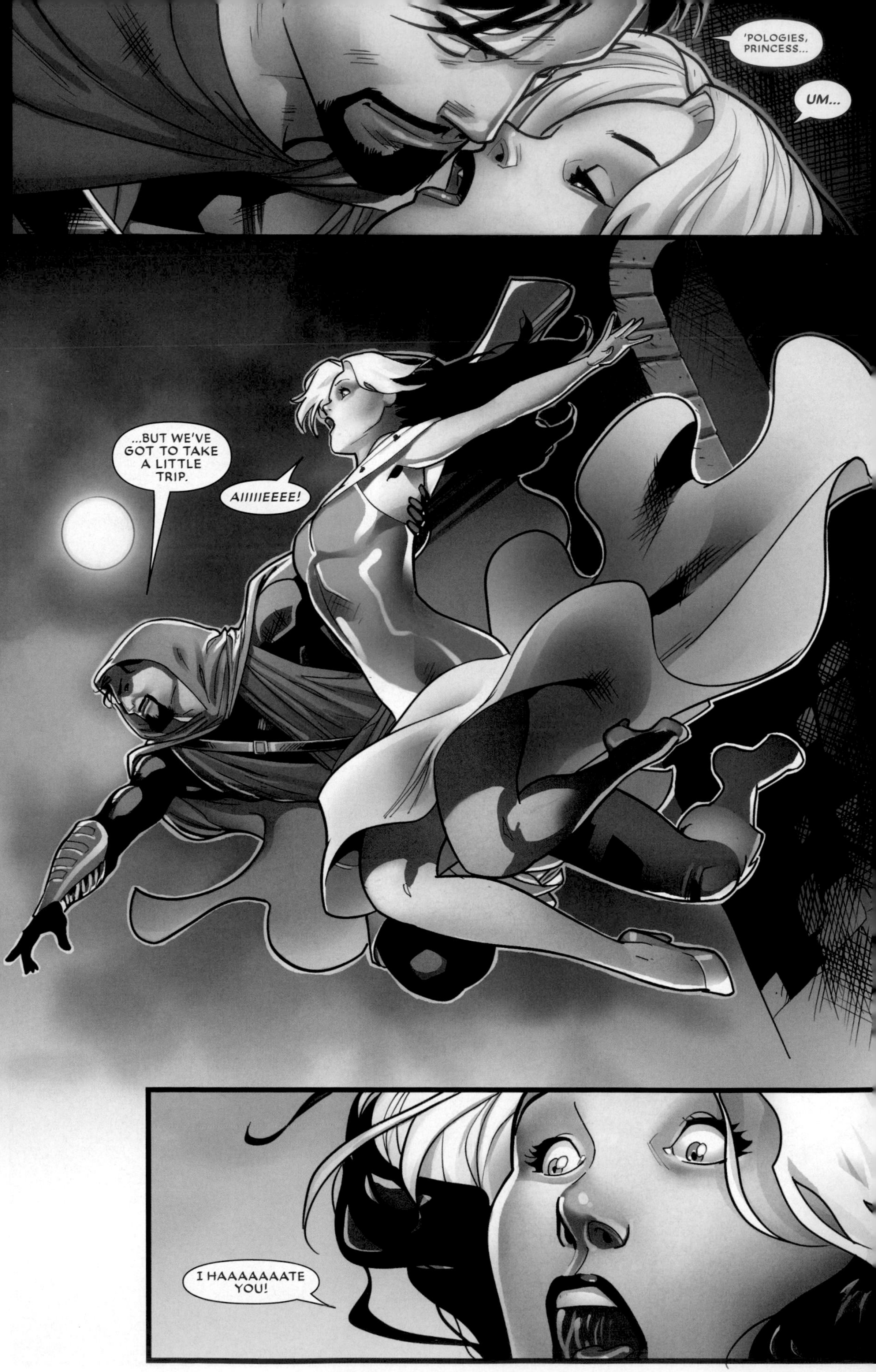
'POLOGIES, PRINCESS...
UM...
...BUT WE'VE GOT TO TAKE A LITTLE TRIP.
AIIIIIEEEE!
I HAAAAAAATE YOU!

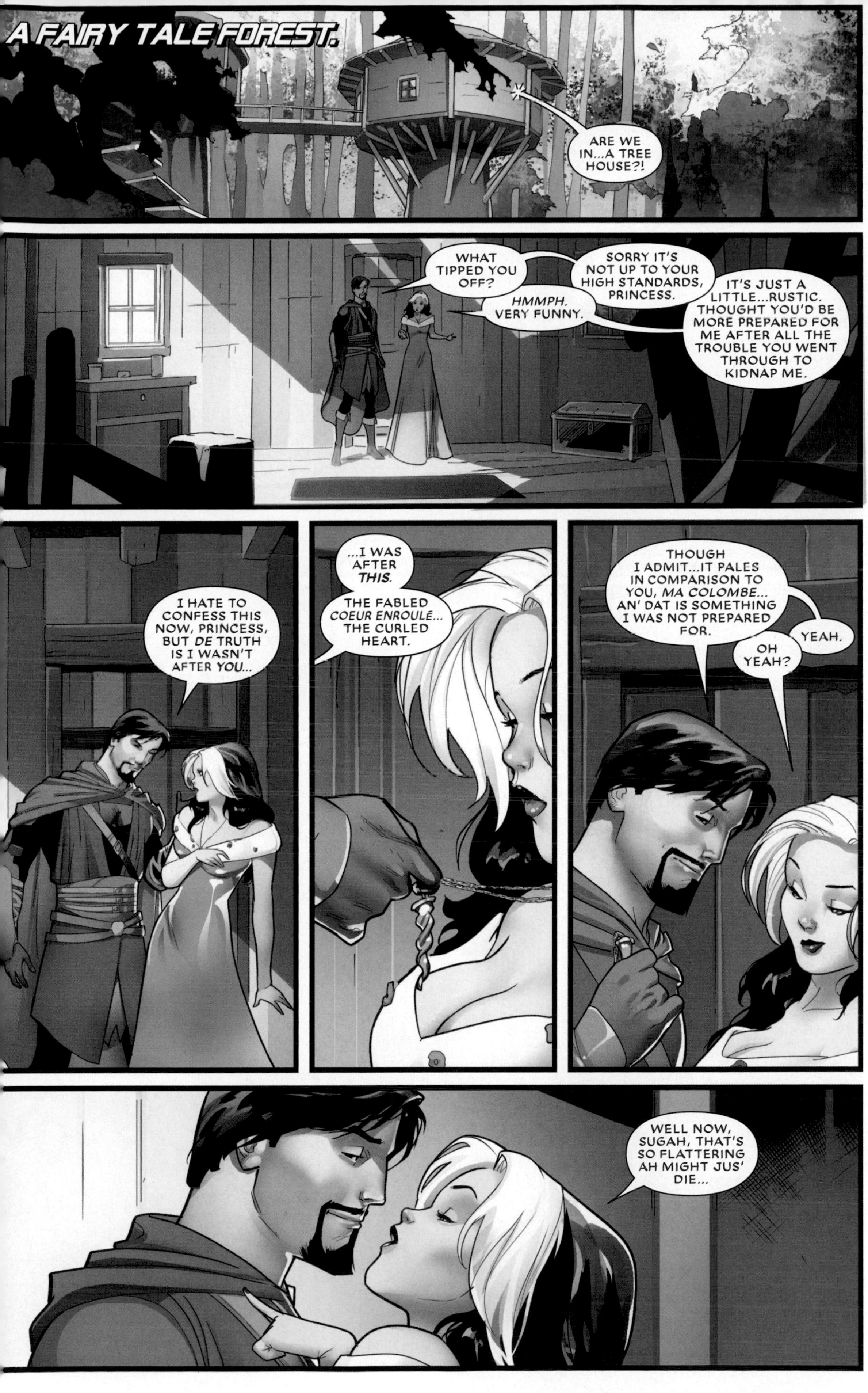
A FAIRY TALE FOREST.
ARE WE IN...A TREE HOUSE?!
SORRY IT'S NOT UP TO YOUR HIGH STANDARDS, PRINCESS.
WHAT TIPPED YOU OFF?
HMMPH. VERY FUNNY.
IT'S JUST A LITTLE...RUSTIC. THOUGHT YOU'D BE MORE PREPARED FOR ME AFTER ALL THE TROUBLE YOU WENT THROUGH TO KIDNAP ME.
I HATE TO CONFESS THIS NOW, PRINCESS, BUT DE TRUTH IS I WASN'T AFTER YOU...
...I WAS AFTER THIS.
THE FABLED COEUR ENROULÉ... THE CURLED HEART.
THOUGH I ADMIT...IT PALES IN COMPARISON TO YOU, MA COLOMBE... AN' DAT IS SOMETHING I WAS NOT PREPARED FOR.
OH YEAH?
YEAH.
WELL NOW, SUGAH, THAT'S SO FLATTERING AH MIGHT JUS' DIE...

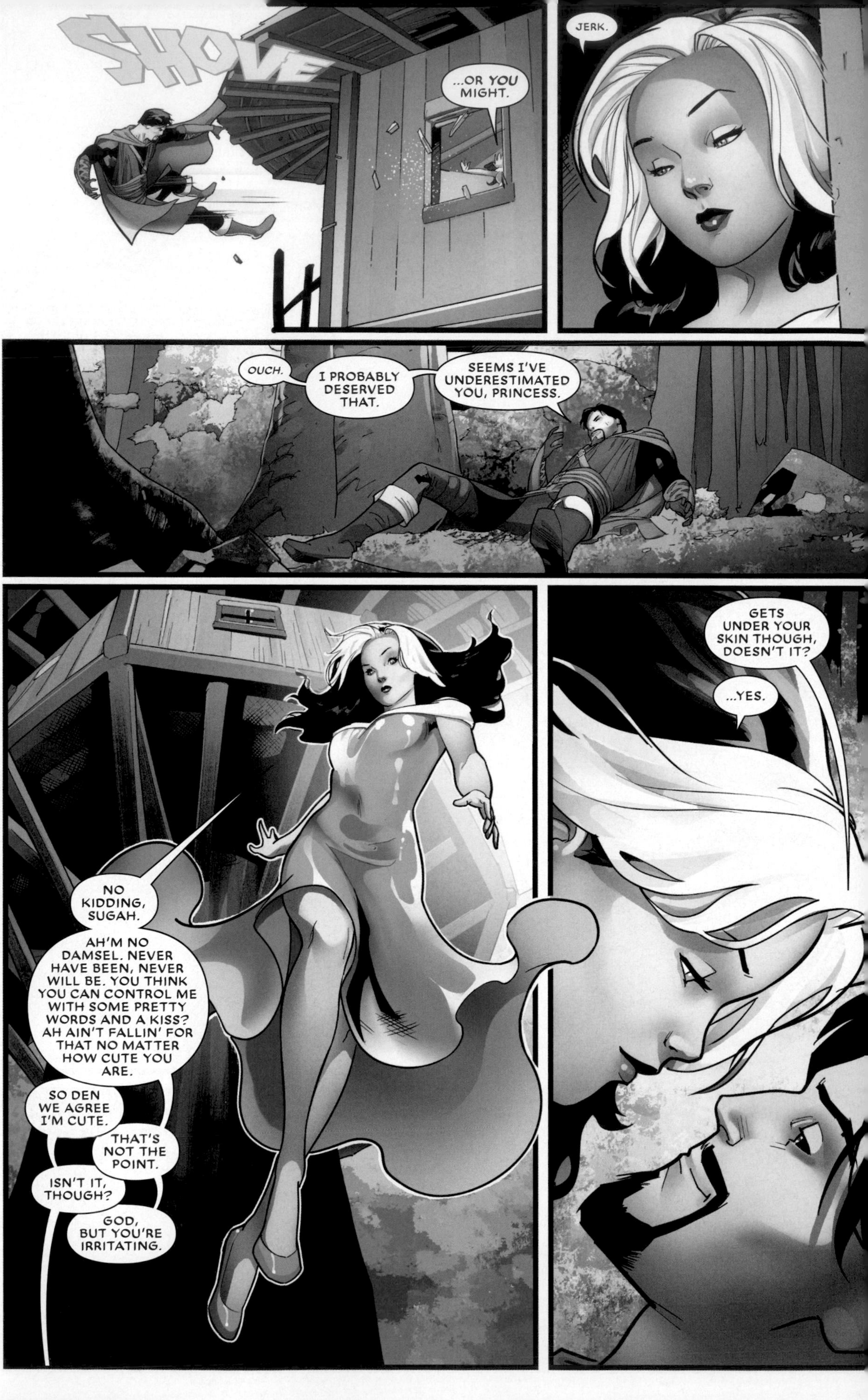
SHOVE
...OR YOU MIGHT.
JERK.
OUCH.
I PROBABLY DESERVED THAT.
SEEMS I'VE UNDERESTIMATED YOU, PRINCESS.
NO KIDDING, SUGAH.
AH'M NO DAMSEL. NEVER HAVE BEEN, NEVER WILL BE. YOU THINK YOU CAN CONTROL ME WITH SOME PRETTY WORDS AND A KISS? AH AIN'T FALLIN' FOR THAT NO MATTER HOW CUTE YOU ARE.
SO DEN WE AGREE I'M CUTE.
THAT'S NOT THE POINT.
ISN'T IT, THOUGH?
GOD, BUT YOU'RE IRRITATING.
GETS UNDER YOUR SKIN THOUGH, DOESN'T IT?
...YES.

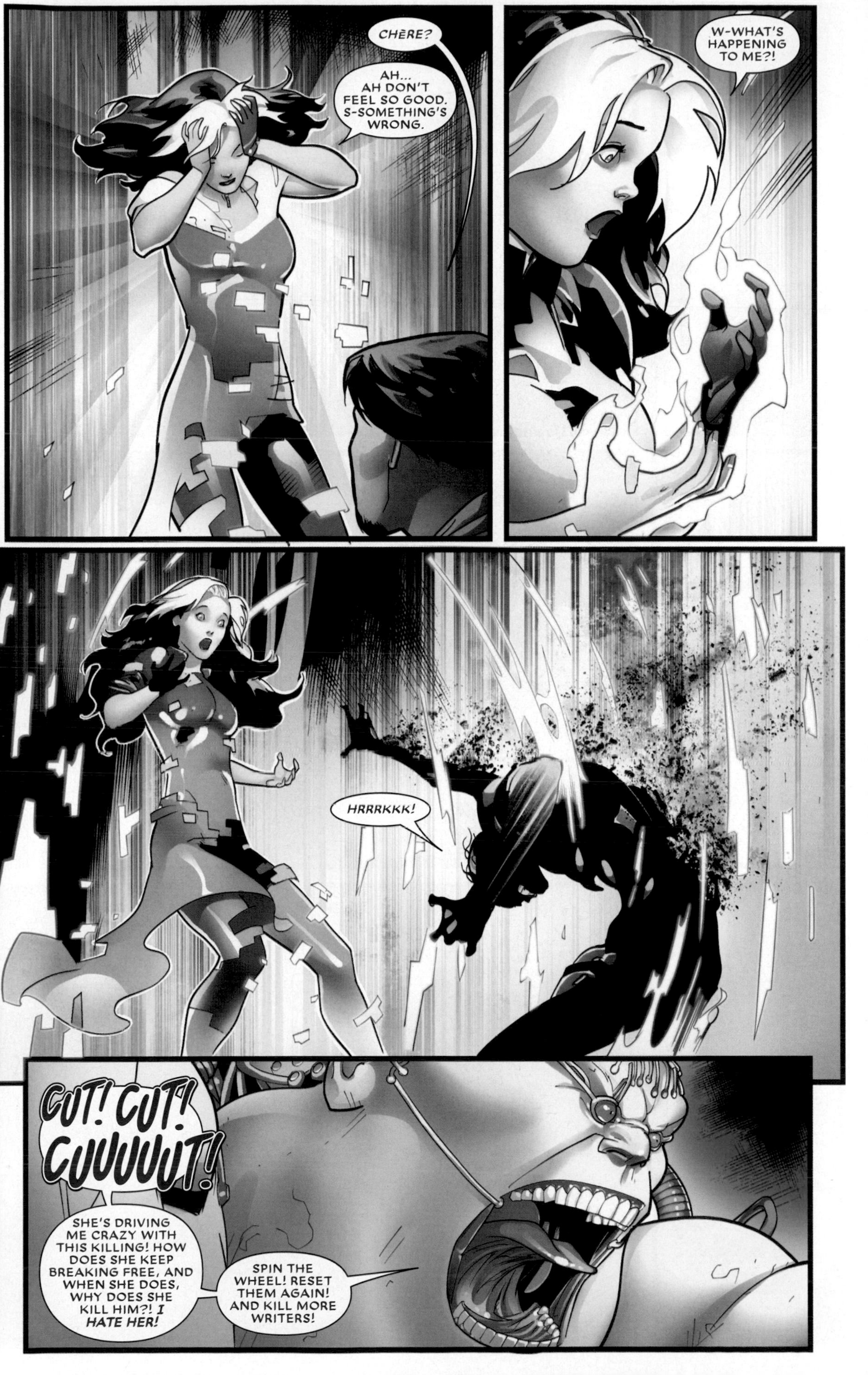
CHÈRE?
AH... AH DON'T FEEL SO GOOD. S-SOMETHING'S WRONG.
W-WHAT'S HAPPENING TO ME?!
HRRRKKK!
CUT! CUT! CUUUUUT!
SHE'S DRIVING ME CRAZY WITH THIS KILLING! HOW DOES SHE KEEP BREAKING FREE, AND WHEN SHE DOES, WHY DOES SHE KILL HIM?! I HATE HER!
SPIN THE WHEEL! RESET THEM AGAIN! AND KILL MORE WRITERS!

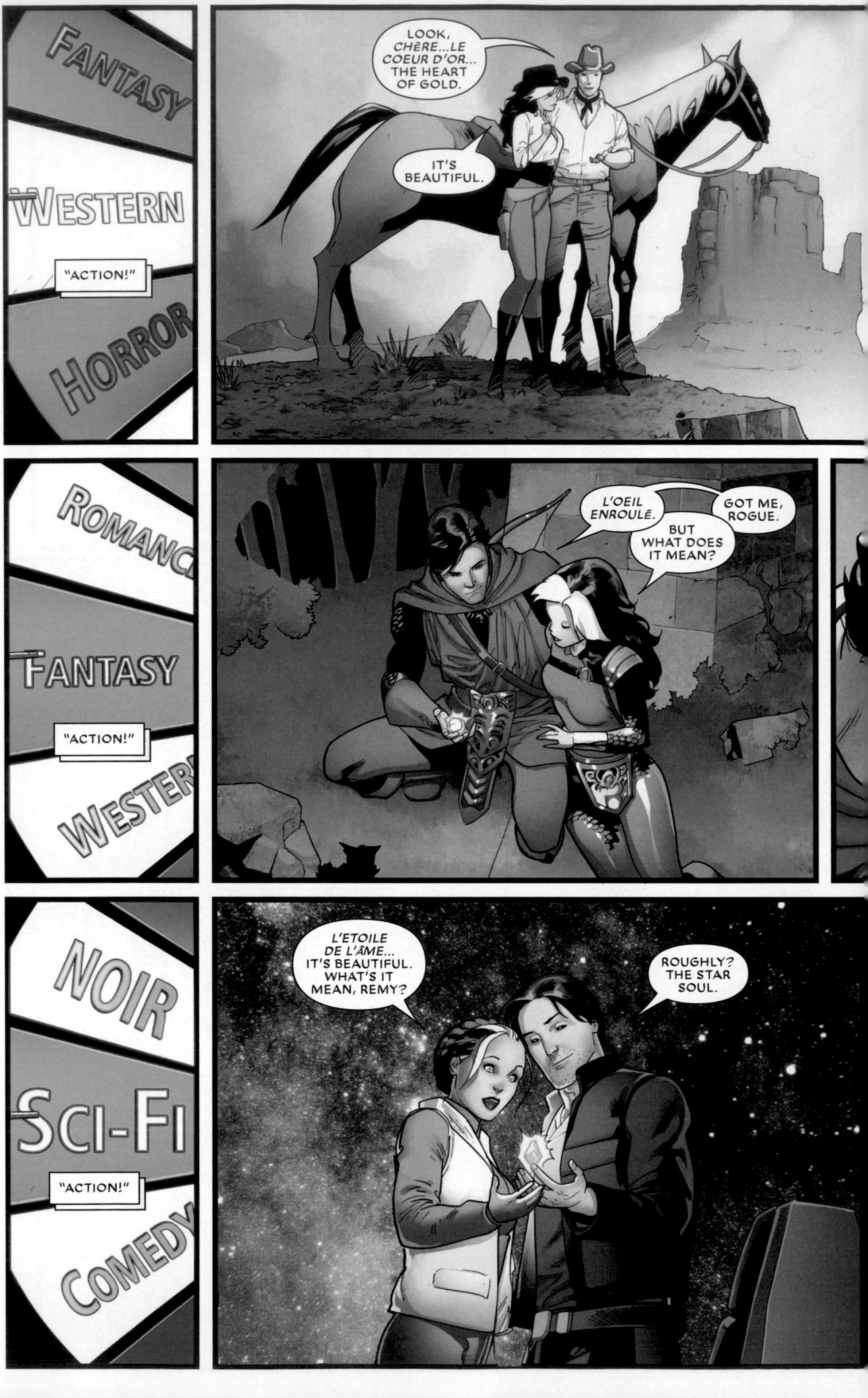
FANTASY
WESTERN
"ACTION!"
HORROR
LOOK, CHÈRE...LE COEUR D'OR... THE HEART OF GOLD.
IT'S BEAUTIFUL.
ROMANCE
FANTASY
"ACTION!"
WESTERN
L'OEIL ENROULÉ.
GOT ME, ROGUE.
BUT WHAT DOES IT MEAN?
NOIR
SCI-FI
"ACTION!"
COMEDY
L'ETOILE DE L'ÂME... IT'S BEAUTIFUL. WHAT'S IT MEAN, REMY?
ROUGHLY? THE STAR SOUL.

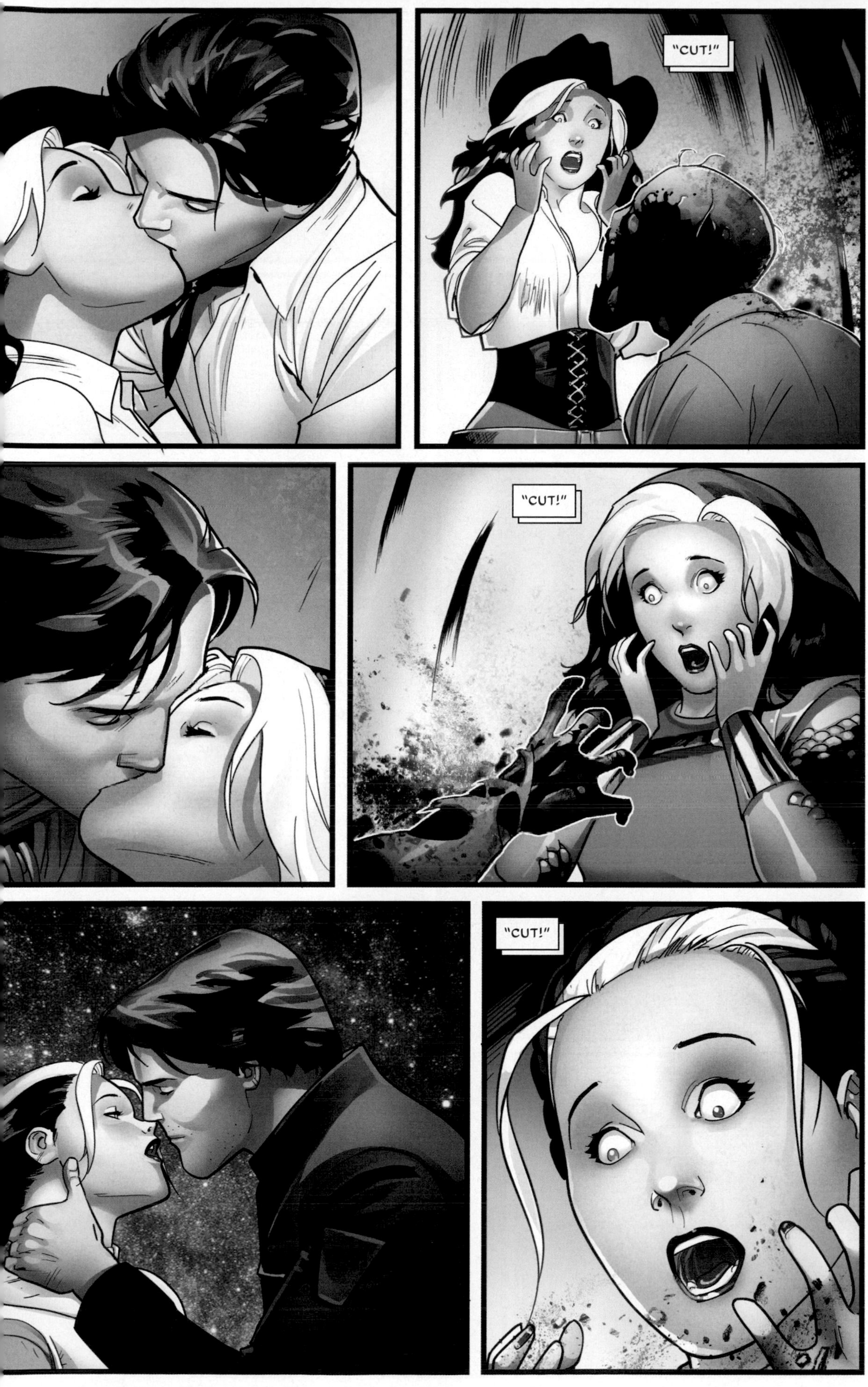
"CUT!"
"CUT!"
"CUT!"

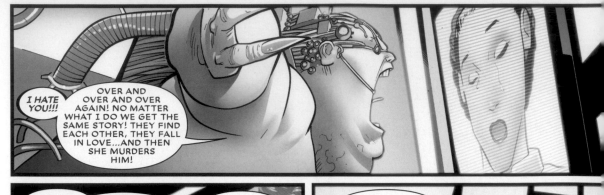

I HATE YOU!!!

OVER AND OVER AND OVER AGAIN! NO MATTER WHAT I DO WE GET THE SAME STORY! THEY FIND EACH OTHER, THEY FALL IN LOVE...AND THEN SHE MURDERS HIM!

I WANT A LOVE STORY, NOT A TRAGEDY!!!

IN FAIRNESS, I'M QUITE CERTAIN THOSE TWO THINGS ARE RELATED.

FINE, FINE, I'M NOT WRITING THIS STUPID ENDING! AND THIS BIZARRE SEARCH FOR AN OBJECT THAT KEEPS COMING UP...*WHAT IS THAT?!*

SPIN MY WHEEL!

AND KILL ALL THE WRITERS!

PERHAPS... INSTEAD OF THAT...I COULD GO INTO THE NEXT SIMULATION AND PUSH THEM IN THE RIGHT DIRECTION? TAKE A CLOSER LOOK AND SEE WHERE THE SNAG IS OCCURRING?

HMMM.

IT MUST BE A MISTAKE IN MAGIC OR TECHNOLOGY...IF I GO INSIDE I MAY BE ABLE TO FIND IT.

FINE! GO! BUT DO NOT FAIL ME, SPIRAL... OR YOU ALONE WILL ANSWER FOR IT!

OH, OF THAT I'M CERTAIN.

HMMM. DOCUMENTARY IS A LITTLE DRY, BUT I DO LOVE...*REALITY TELEVISION!*

COMEDY

DOCUMENTARY

FAIRY TALE

FWAAAASH

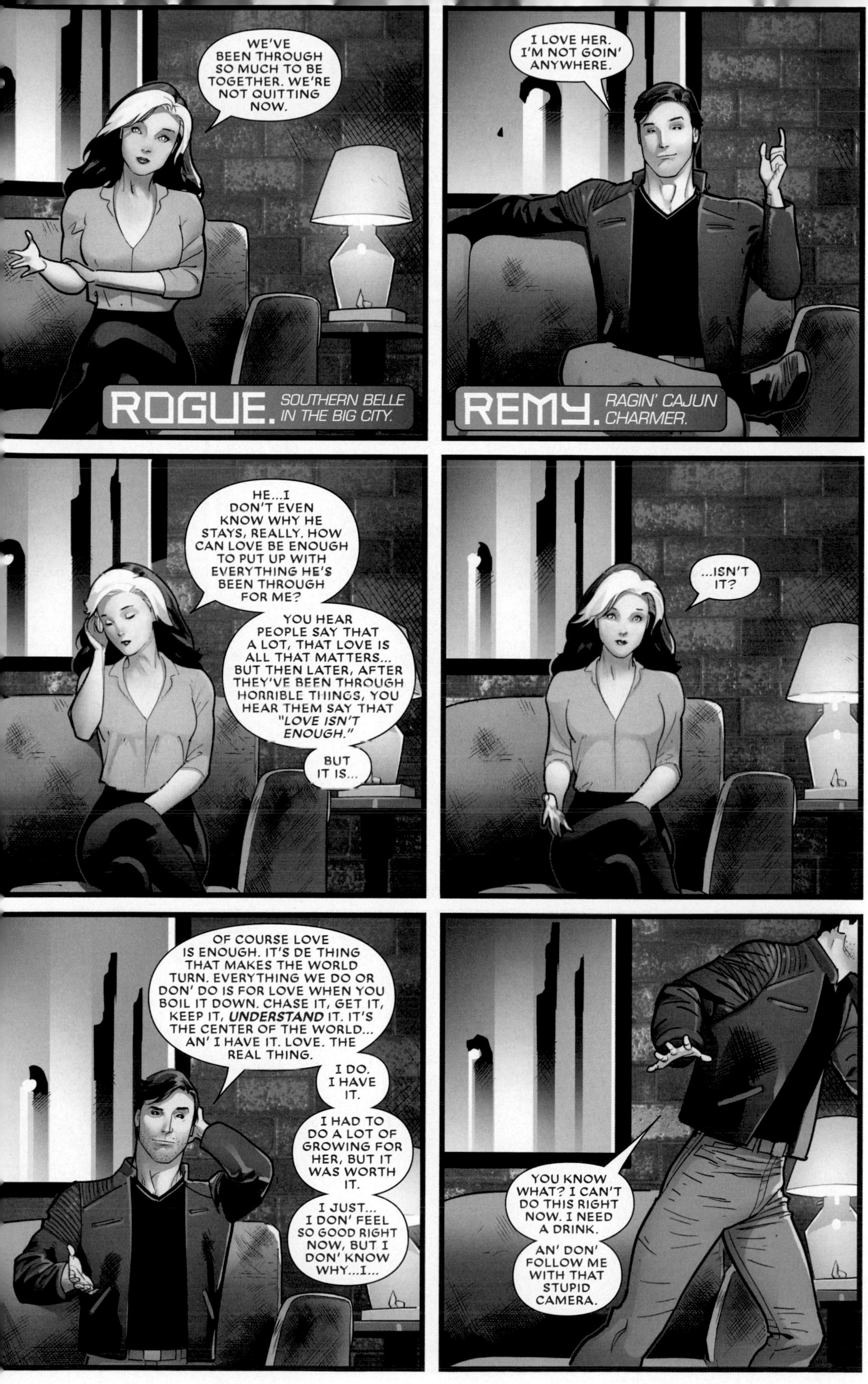
WE'VE BEEN THROUGH SO MUCH TO BE TOGETHER. WE'RE NOT QUITTING NOW.
ROGUE. SOUTHERN BELLE IN THE BIG CITY.
I LOVE HER. I'M NOT GOIN' ANYWHERE.
REMY. RAGIN' CAJUN CHARMER.
HE...I DON'T EVEN KNOW WHY HE STAYS, REALLY. HOW CAN LOVE BE ENOUGH TO PUT UP WITH EVERYTHING HE'S BEEN THROUGH FOR ME?
YOU HEAR PEOPLE SAY THAT A LOT, THAT LOVE IS ALL THAT MATTERS... BUT THEN LATER, AFTER THEY'VE BEEN THROUGH HORRIBLE THINGS, YOU HEAR THEM SAY THAT "LOVE ISN'T ENOUGH."
BUT IT IS...
...ISN'T IT?
OF COURSE LOVE IS ENOUGH. IT'S DE THING THAT MAKES THE WORLD TURN. EVERYTHING WE DO OR DON' DO IS FOR LOVE WHEN YOU BOIL IT DOWN. CHASE IT, GET IT, KEEP IT, UNDERSTAND IT. IT'S THE CENTER OF THE WORLD... AN' I HAVE IT. LOVE. THE REAL THING.
I DO. I HAVE IT.
I HAD TO DO A LOT OF GROWING FOR HER, BUT IT WAS WORTH IT.
I JUST... I DON' FEEL SO GOOD RIGHT NOW, BUT I DON' KNOW WHY...I...
YOU KNOW WHAT? I CAN'T DO THIS RIGHT NOW. I NEED A DRINK.
AN' DON' FOLLOW ME WITH THAT STUPID CAMERA.

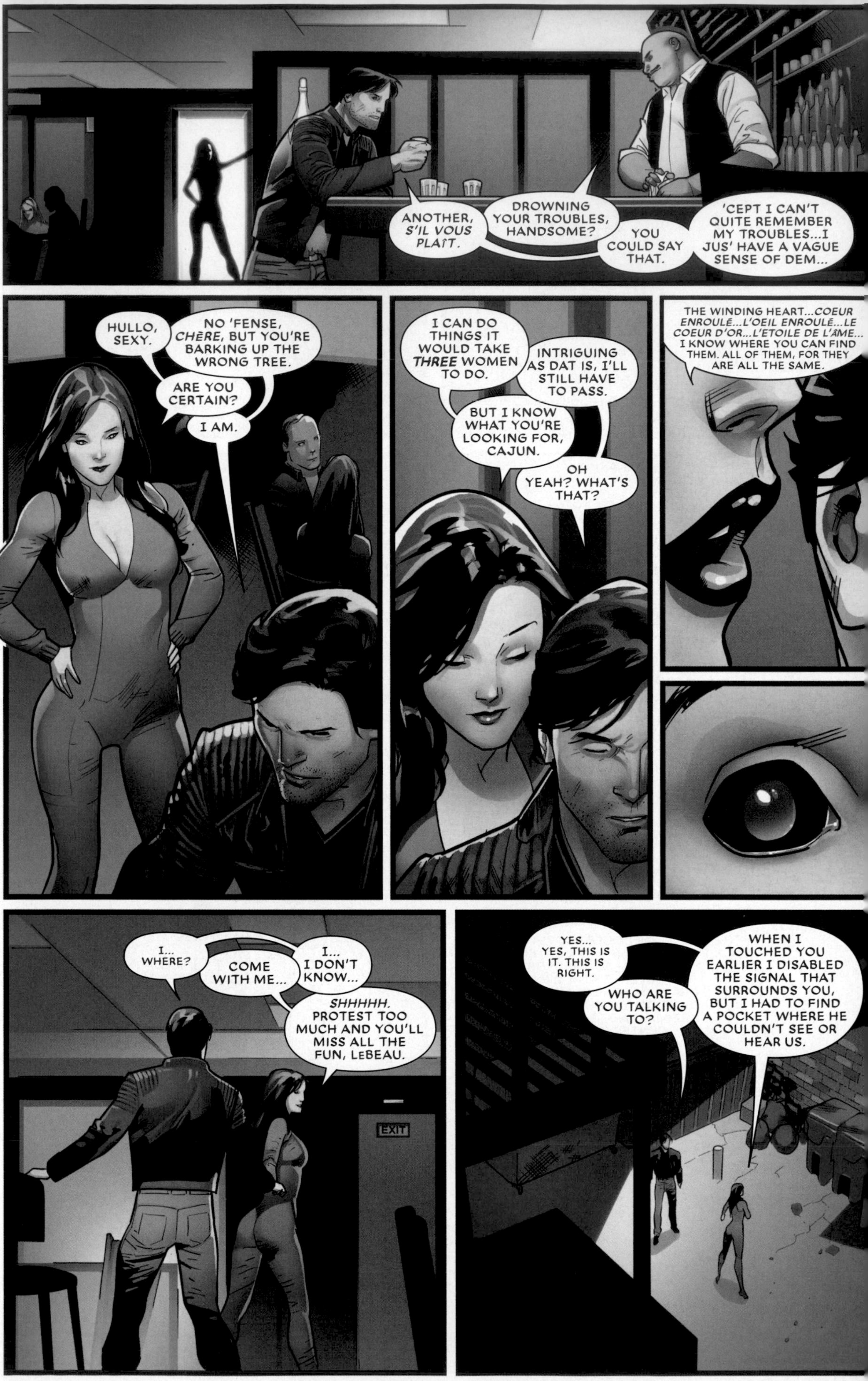

ANOTHER, S'IL VOUS PLAÎT.
DROWNING YOUR TROUBLES, HANDSOME?
YOU COULD SAY THAT.
'CEPT I CAN'T QUITE REMEMBER MY TROUBLES...I JUS' HAVE A VAGUE SENSE OF DEM...
HULLO, SEXY.
NO 'FENSE, CHÈRE, BUT YOU'RE BARKING UP THE WRONG TREE.
ARE YOU CERTAIN?
I AM.
I CAN DO THINGS IT WOULD TAKE THREE WOMEN TO DO.
INTRIGUING AS DAT IS, I'LL STILL HAVE TO PASS.
BUT I KNOW WHAT YOU'RE LOOKING FOR, CAJUN.
OH YEAH? WHAT'S THAT?
THE WINDING HEART...COEUR ENROULÉ...L'OEIL ENROULÉ...LE COEUR D'OR...L'ETOILE DE L'ÂME... I KNOW WHERE YOU CAN FIND THEM. ALL OF THEM, FOR THEY ARE ALL THE SAME.
I... WHERE?
COME WITH ME...
I... I DON'T KNOW...
SHHHHH. PROTEST TOO MUCH AND YOU'LL MISS ALL THE FUN, LEBEAU.
EXIT
YES... YES, THIS IS IT. THIS IS RIGHT.
WHO ARE YOU TALKING TO?
WHEN I TOUCHED YOU EARLIER I DISABLED THE SIGNAL THAT SURROUNDS YOU, BUT I HAD TO FIND A POCKET WHERE HE COULDN'T SEE OR HEAR US.

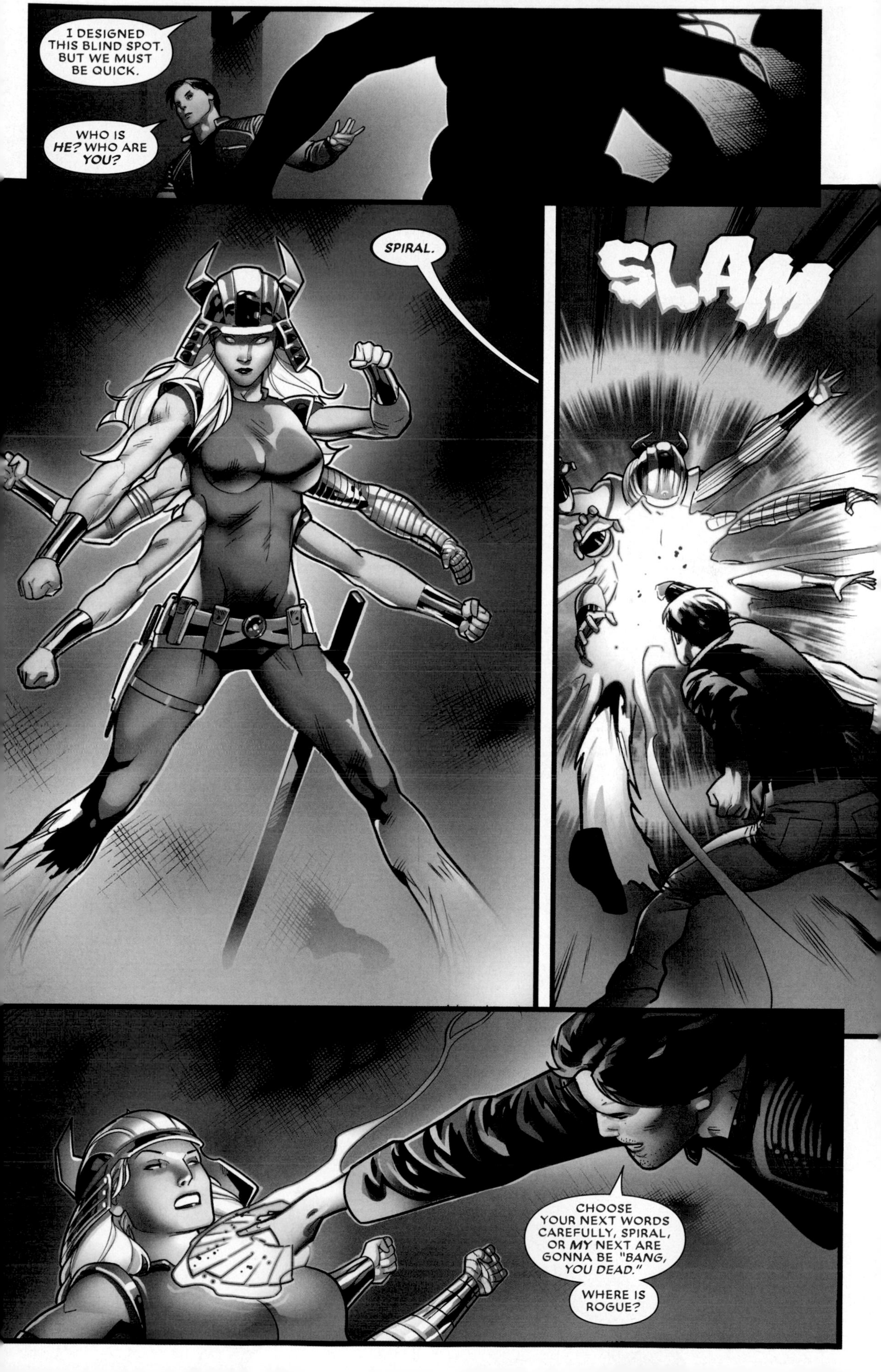
I DESIGNED THIS BLIND SPOT. BUT WE MUST BE QUICK.
WHO IS *HE?* WHO ARE *YOU?*
SPIRAL.
SLAM
CHOOSE YOUR NEXT WORDS CAREFULLY, SPIRAL, OR *MY* NEXT ARE GONNA BE *"BANG, YOU DEAD."*
WHERE IS ROGUE?

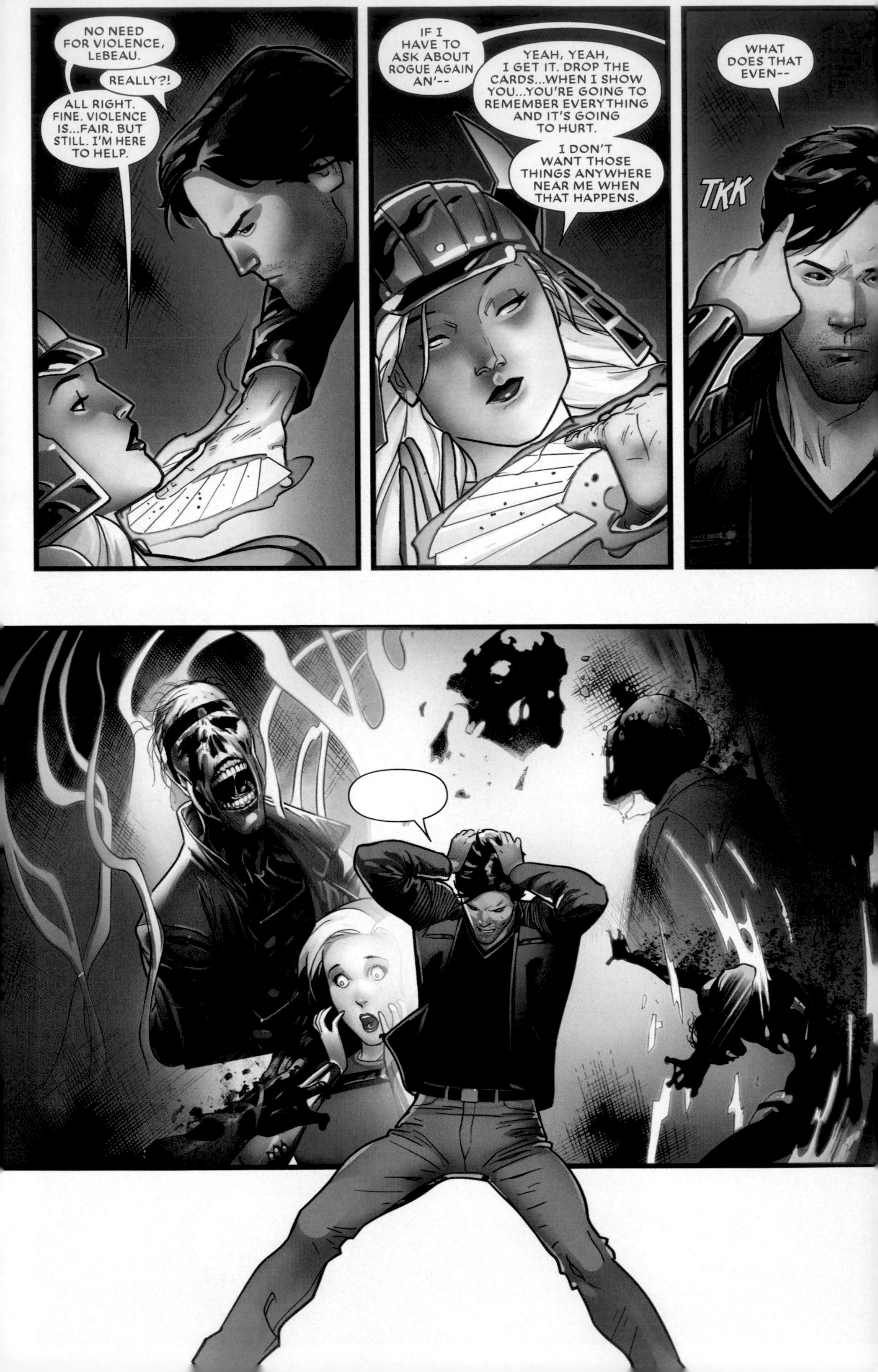
NO NEED FOR VIOLENCE, LEBEAU.
REALLY?!
ALL RIGHT. FINE. VIOLENCE IS...FAIR. BUT STILL. I'M HERE TO HELP.
IF I HAVE TO ASK ABOUT ROGUE AGAIN AN'--
YEAH, YEAH, I GET IT. DROP THE CARDS...WHEN I SHOW YOU...YOU'RE GOING TO REMEMBER EVERYTHING AND IT'S GOING TO HURT.
I DON'T WANT THOSE THINGS ANYWHERE NEAR ME WHEN THAT HAPPENS.
WHAT DOES THAT EVEN--
TKK

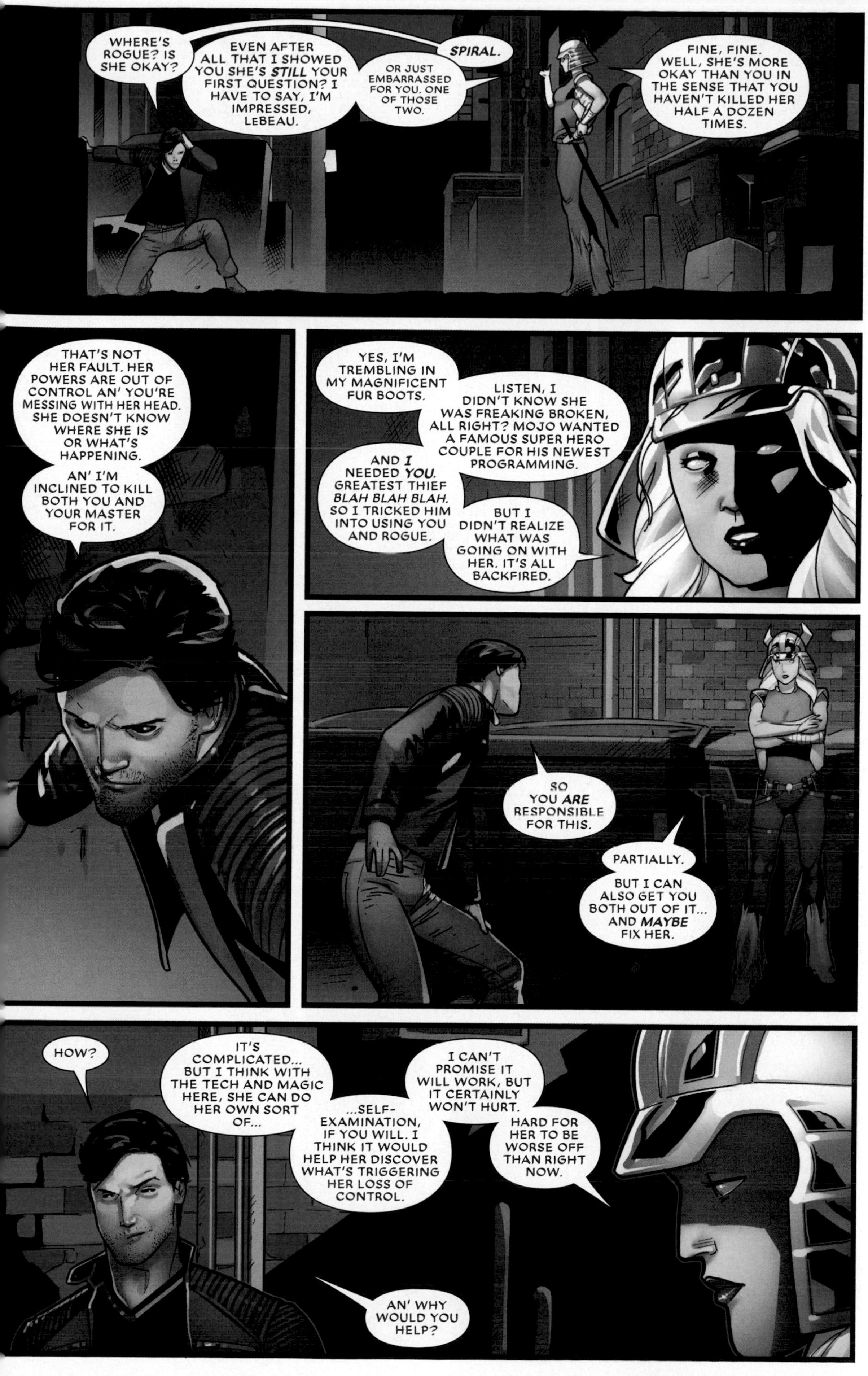
WHERE'S ROGUE? IS SHE OKAY?
EVEN AFTER ALL THAT I SHOWED YOU SHE'S STILL YOUR FIRST QUESTION? I HAVE TO SAY, I'M IMPRESSED, LEBEAU.
SPIRAL.
OR JUST EMBARRASSED FOR YOU. ONE OF THOSE TWO.
FINE, FINE. WELL, SHE'S MORE OKAY THAN YOU IN THE SENSE THAT YOU HAVEN'T KILLED HER HALF A DOZEN TIMES.
THAT'S NOT HER FAULT. HER POWERS ARE OUT OF CONTROL AN' YOU'RE MESSING WITH HER HEAD. SHE DOESN'T KNOW WHERE SHE IS OR WHAT'S HAPPENING.
AN' I'M INCLINED TO KILL BOTH YOU AND YOUR MASTER FOR IT.
YES, I'M TREMBLING IN MY MAGNIFICENT FUR BOOTS.
LISTEN, I DIDN'T KNOW SHE WAS FREAKING BROKEN, ALL RIGHT? MOJO WANTED A FAMOUS SUPER HERO COUPLE FOR HIS NEWEST PROGRAMMING.
AND I NEEDED YOU. GREATEST THIEF BLAH BLAH BLAH. SO I TRICKED HIM INTO USING YOU AND ROGUE.
BUT I DIDN'T REALIZE WHAT WAS GOING ON WITH HER. IT'S ALL BACKFIRED.
SO YOU ARE RESPONSIBLE FOR THIS.
PARTIALLY.
BUT I CAN ALSO GET YOU BOTH OUT OF IT... AND MAYBE FIX HER.
HOW?
IT'S COMPLICATED... BUT I THINK WITH THE TECH AND MAGIC HERE, SHE CAN DO HER OWN SORT OF...
...SELF-EXAMINATION, IF YOU WILL. I THINK IT WOULD HELP HER DISCOVER WHAT'S TRIGGERING HER LOSS OF CONTROL.
I CAN'T PROMISE IT WILL WORK, BUT IT CERTAINLY WON'T HURT.
HARD FOR HER TO BE WORSE OFF THAN RIGHT NOW.
AN' WHY WOULD YOU HELP?

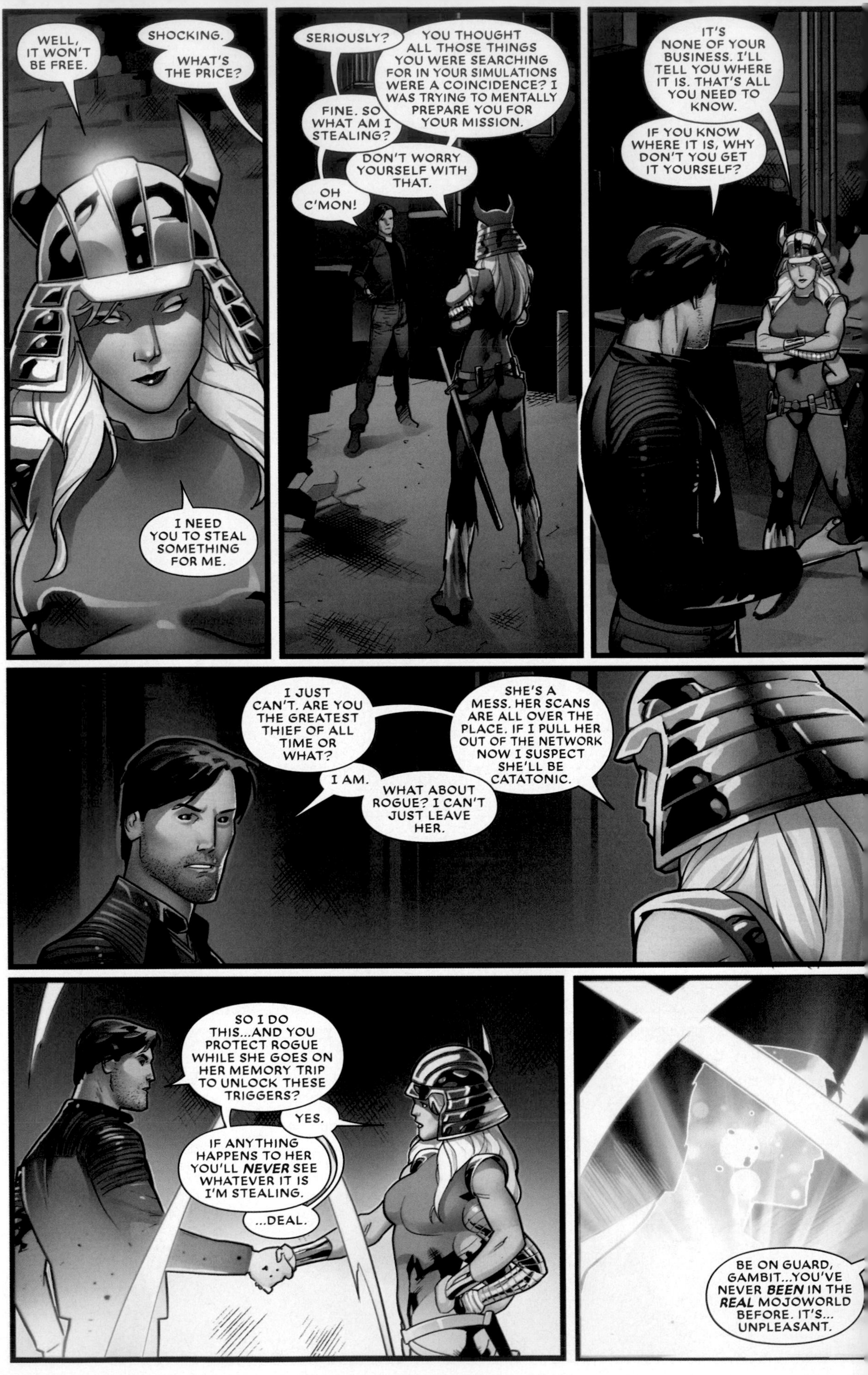
WELL, IT WON'T BE FREE.
SHOCKING.
WHAT'S THE PRICE?
I NEED YOU TO STEAL SOMETHING FOR ME.
SERIOUSLY?
YOU THOUGHT ALL THOSE THINGS YOU WERE SEARCHING FOR IN YOUR SIMULATIONS WERE A COINCIDENCE? I WAS TRYING TO MENTALLY PREPARE YOU FOR YOUR MISSION.
FINE. SO WHAT AM I STEALING?
DON'T WORRY YOURSELF WITH THAT.
OH C'MON!
IT'S NONE OF YOUR BUSINESS. I'LL TELL YOU WHERE IT IS. THAT'S ALL YOU NEED TO KNOW.
IF YOU KNOW WHERE IT IS, WHY DON'T YOU GET IT YOURSELF?
I JUST CAN'T. ARE YOU THE GREATEST THIEF OF ALL TIME OR WHAT?
I AM.
WHAT ABOUT ROGUE? I CAN'T JUST LEAVE HER.
SHE'S A MESS. HER SCANS ARE ALL OVER THE PLACE. IF I PULL HER OUT OF THE NETWORK NOW I SUSPECT SHE'LL BE CATATONIC.
SO I DO THIS...AND YOU PROTECT ROGUE WHILE SHE GOES ON HER MEMORY TRIP TO UNLOCK THESE TRIGGERS?
YES.
IF ANYTHING HAPPENS TO HER YOU'LL *NEVER* SEE WHATEVER IT IS I'M STEALING.
...DEAL.
BE ON GUARD, GAMBIT...YOU'VE NEVER *BEEN* IN THE *REAL* MOJOWORLD BEFORE. IT'S... UNPLEASANT.

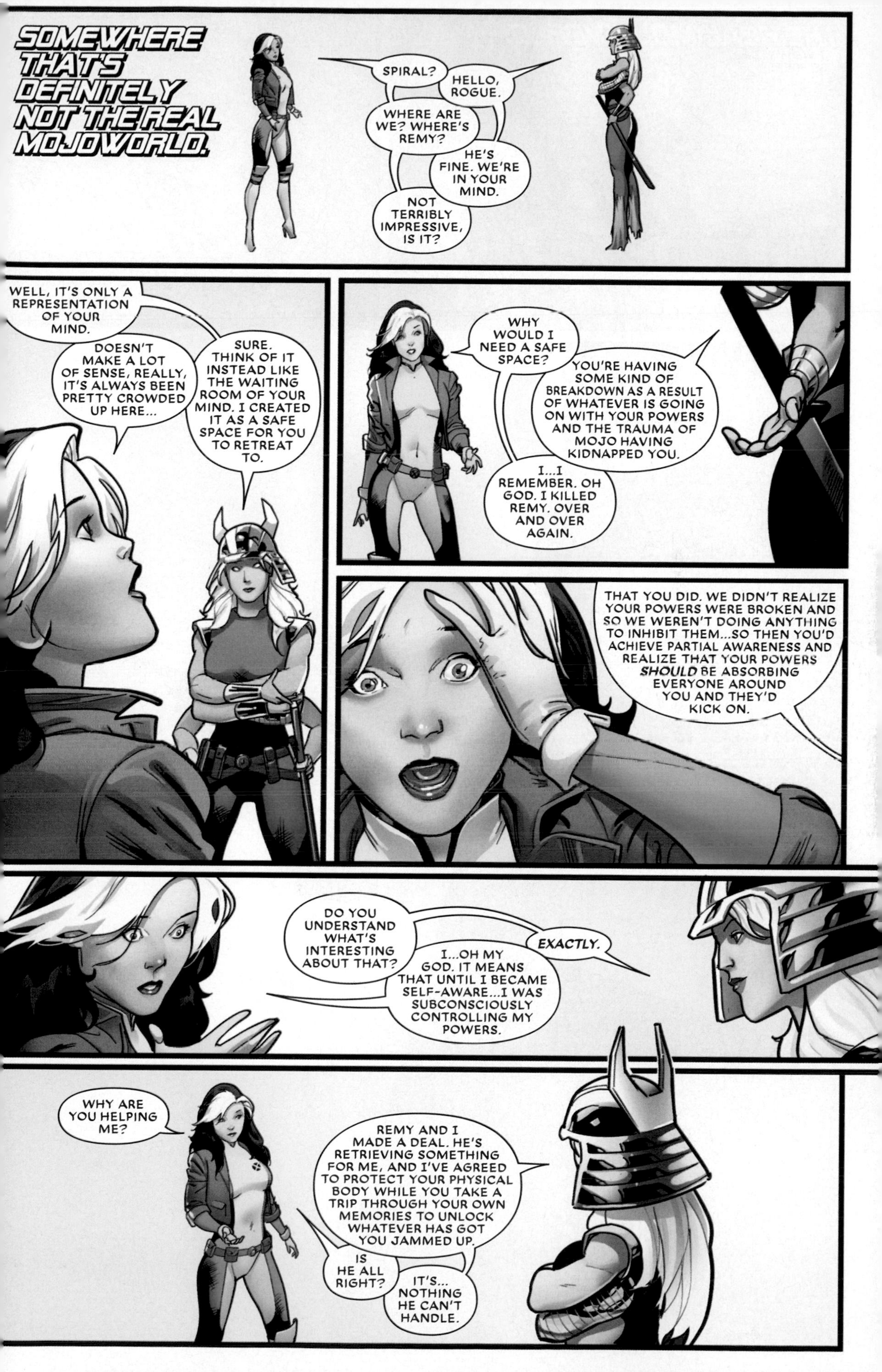
SOMEWHERE THAT'S DEFINITELY NOT THE REAL MOJOWORLD.
SPIRAL?
HELLO, ROGUE.
WHERE ARE WE? WHERE'S REMY?
HE'S FINE. WE'RE IN YOUR MIND.
NOT TERRIBLY IMPRESSIVE, IS IT?
WELL, IT'S ONLY A REPRESENTATION OF YOUR MIND.
DOESN'T MAKE A LOT OF SENSE, REALLY, IT'S ALWAYS BEEN PRETTY CROWDED UP HERE...
SURE. THINK OF IT INSTEAD LIKE THE WAITING ROOM OF YOUR MIND. I CREATED IT AS A SAFE SPACE FOR YOU TO RETREAT TO.
WHY WOULD I NEED A SAFE SPACE?
YOU'RE HAVING SOME KIND OF BREAKDOWN AS A RESULT OF WHATEVER IS GOING ON WITH YOUR POWERS AND THE TRAUMA OF MOJO HAVING KIDNAPPED YOU.
I...I REMEMBER. OH GOD. I KILLED REMY. OVER AND OVER AGAIN.
THAT YOU DID. WE DIDN'T REALIZE YOUR POWERS WERE BROKEN AND SO WE WEREN'T DOING ANYTHING TO INHIBIT THEM...SO THEN YOU'D ACHIEVE PARTIAL AWARENESS AND REALIZE THAT YOUR POWERS *SHOULD* BE ABSORBING EVERYONE AROUND YOU AND THEY'D KICK ON.
DO YOU UNDERSTAND WHAT'S INTERESTING ABOUT THAT?
I...OH MY GOD. IT MEANS THAT UNTIL I BECAME SELF-AWARE...I WAS SUBCONSCIOUSLY CONTROLLING MY POWERS.
EXACTLY.
WHY ARE YOU HELPING ME?
REMY AND I MADE A DEAL. HE'S RETRIEVING SOMETHING FOR ME, AND I'VE AGREED TO PROTECT YOUR PHYSICAL BODY WHILE YOU TAKE A TRIP THROUGH YOUR OWN MEMORIES TO UNLOCK WHATEVER HAS GOT YOU JAMMED UP.
IS HE ALL RIGHT?
IT'S... NOTHING HE CAN'T HANDLE.

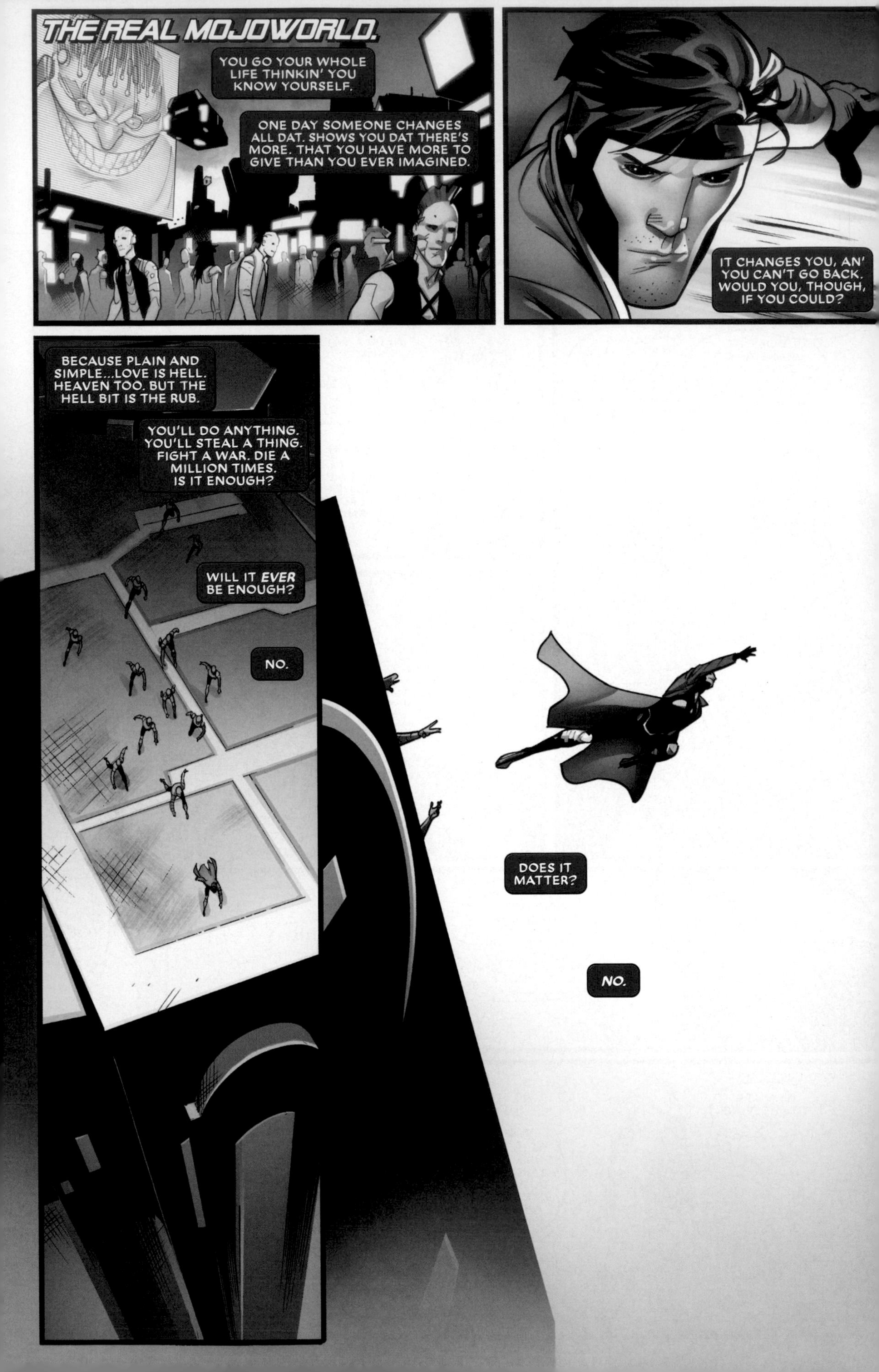
THE REAL MOJOWORLD.
YOU GO YOUR WHOLE LIFE THINKIN' YOU KNOW YOURSELF.
ONE DAY SOMEONE CHANGES ALL DAT. SHOWS YOU DAT THERE'S MORE. THAT YOU HAVE MORE TO GIVE THAN YOU EVER IMAGINED.
IT CHANGES YOU, AN' YOU CAN'T GO BACK. WOULD YOU, THOUGH, IF YOU COULD?
BECAUSE PLAIN AND SIMPLE...LOVE IS HELL. HEAVEN TOO. BUT THE HELL BIT IS THE RUB.
YOU'LL DO ANYTHING. YOU'LL STEAL A THING. FIGHT A WAR. DIE A MILLION TIMES. IS IT ENOUGH?
WILL IT *EVER* BE ENOUGH?
NO.
DOES IT MATTER?
NO.

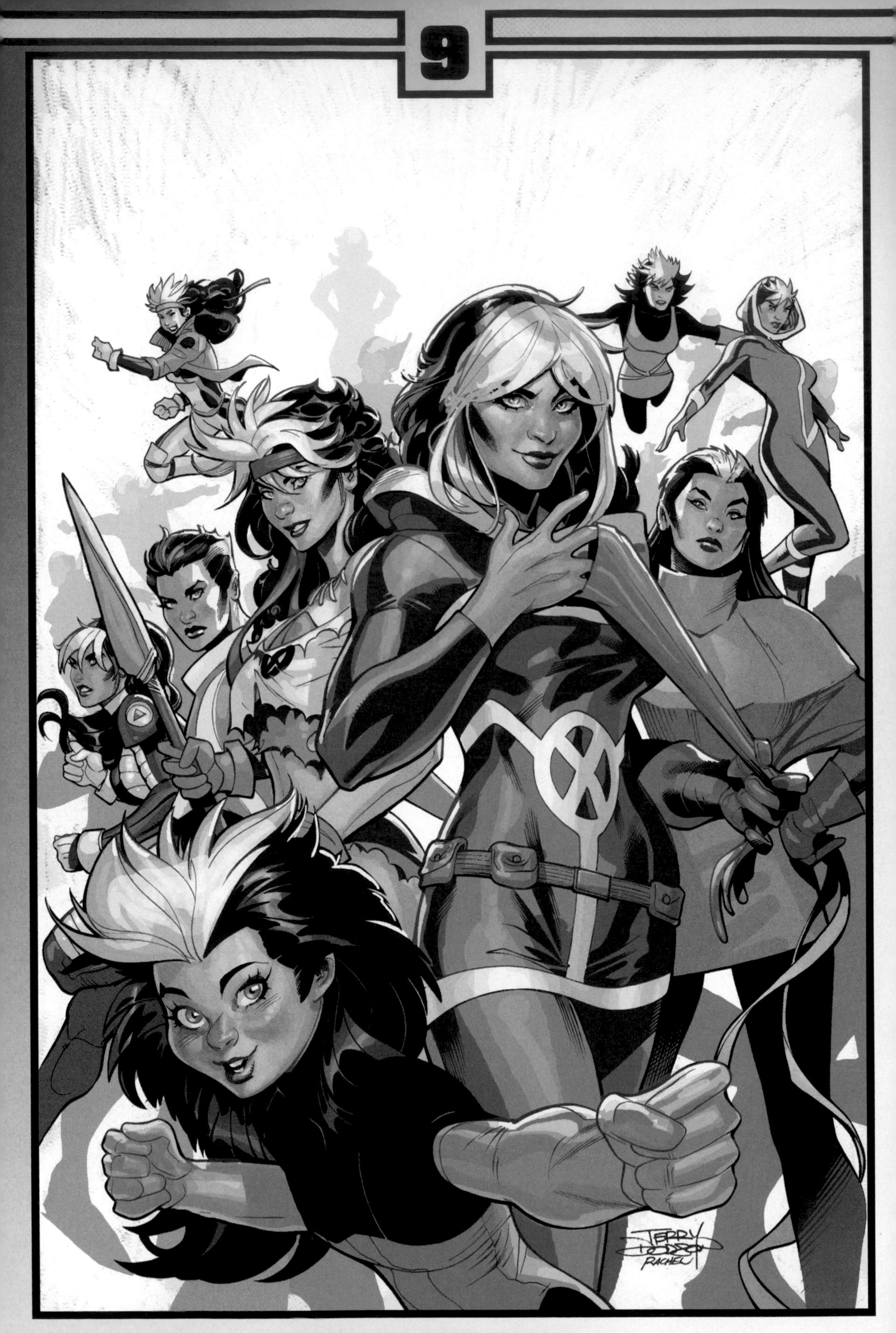
TERRY DODSON RACHEL

GAMBIT AND ROGUE FOREVER PART 3

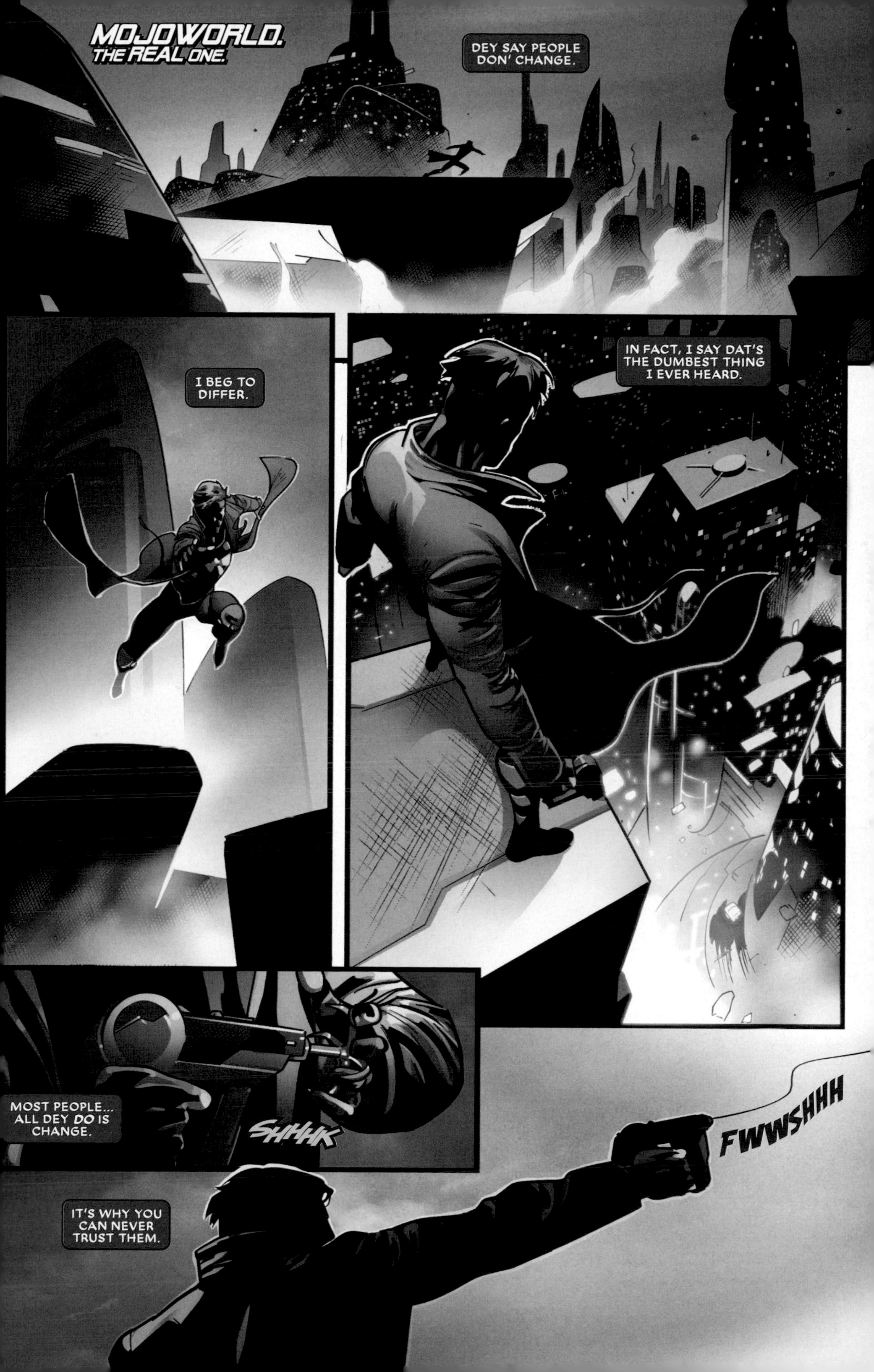
MOJOWORLD.
THE REAL ONE.
DEY SAY PEOPLE DON' CHANGE.
I BEG TO DIFFER.
IN FACT, I SAY DAT'S THE DUMBEST THING I EVER HEARD.
MOST PEOPLE... ALL DEY DO IS CHANGE.
SHHHK
FWWSHHH
IT'S WHY YOU CAN NEVER TRUST THEM.

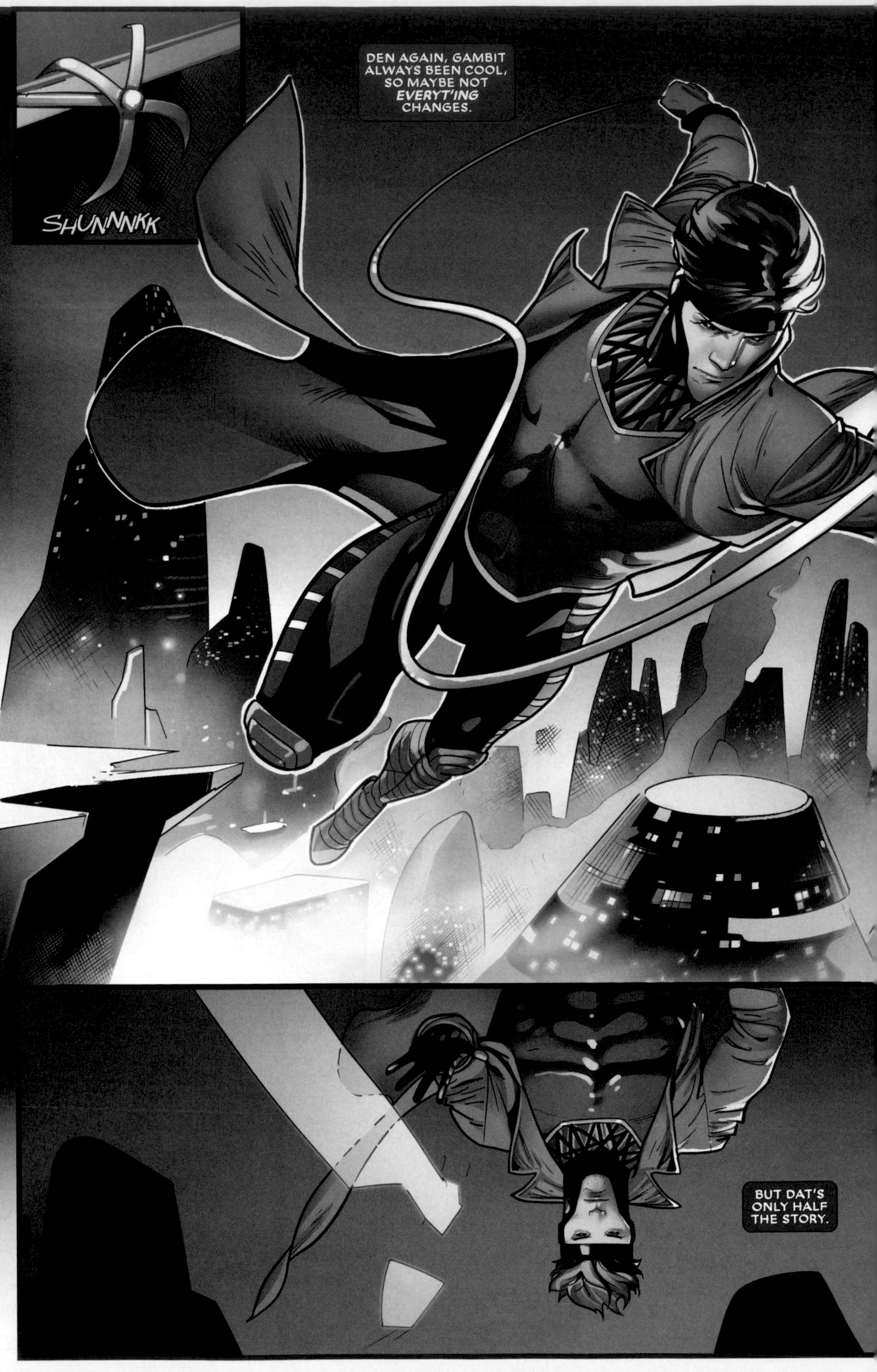
SHUNNNKK
DEN AGAIN, GAMBIT ALWAYS BEEN COOL, SO MAYBE NOT *EVERYT'ING* CHANGES.
BUT DAT'S ONLY HALF THE STORY.

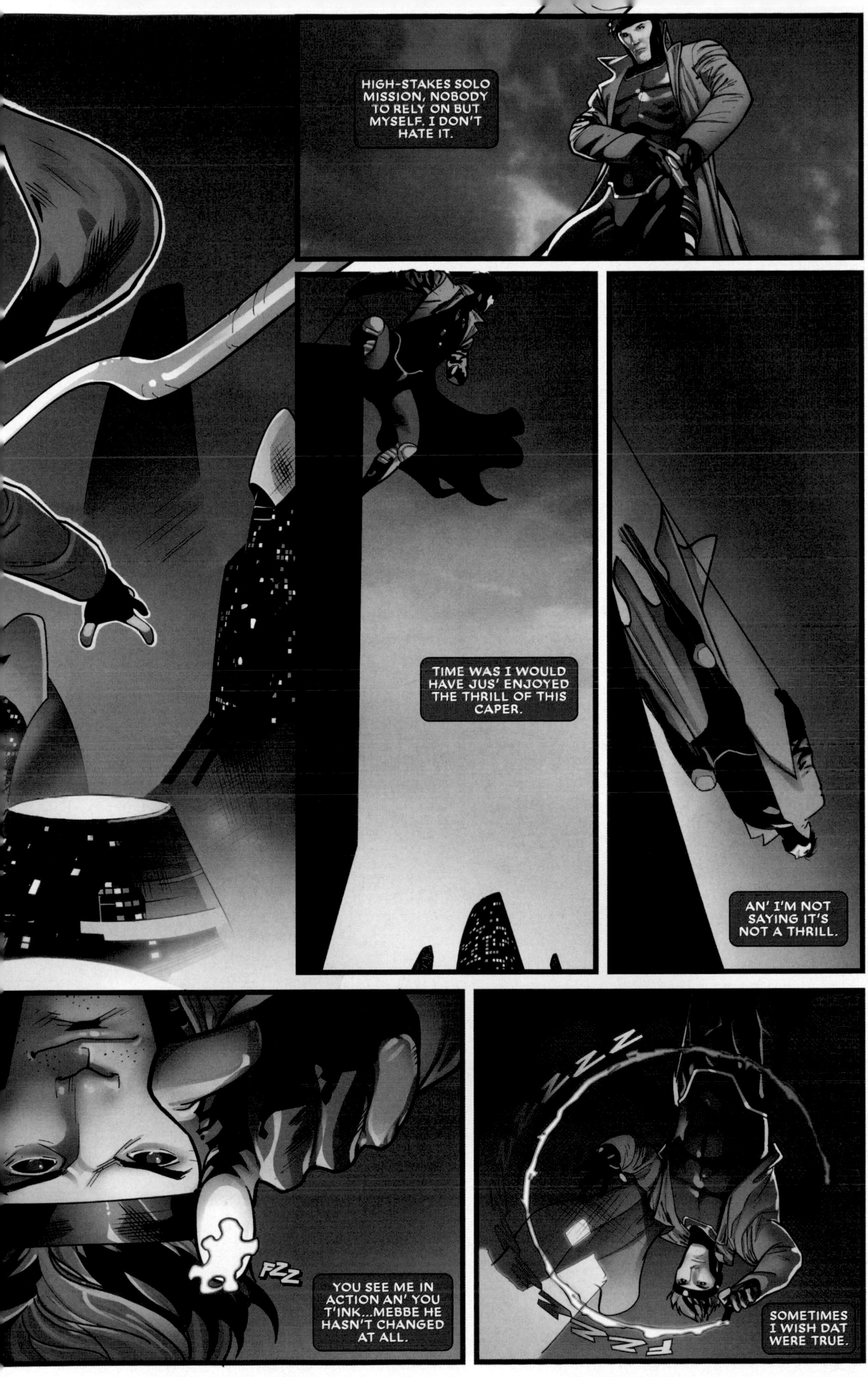
HIGH-STAKES SOLO MISSION, NOBODY TO RELY ON BUT MYSELF. I DON'T HATE IT.
TIME WAS I WOULD HAVE JUS' ENJOYED THE THRILL OF THIS CAPER.
AN' I'M NOT SAYING IT'S NOT A THRILL.
FZZ
YOU SEE ME IN ACTION AN' YOU T'INK...MEBBE HE HASN'T CHANGED AT ALL.
ZZZ
FZZ
SOMETIMES I WISH DAT WERE TRUE.

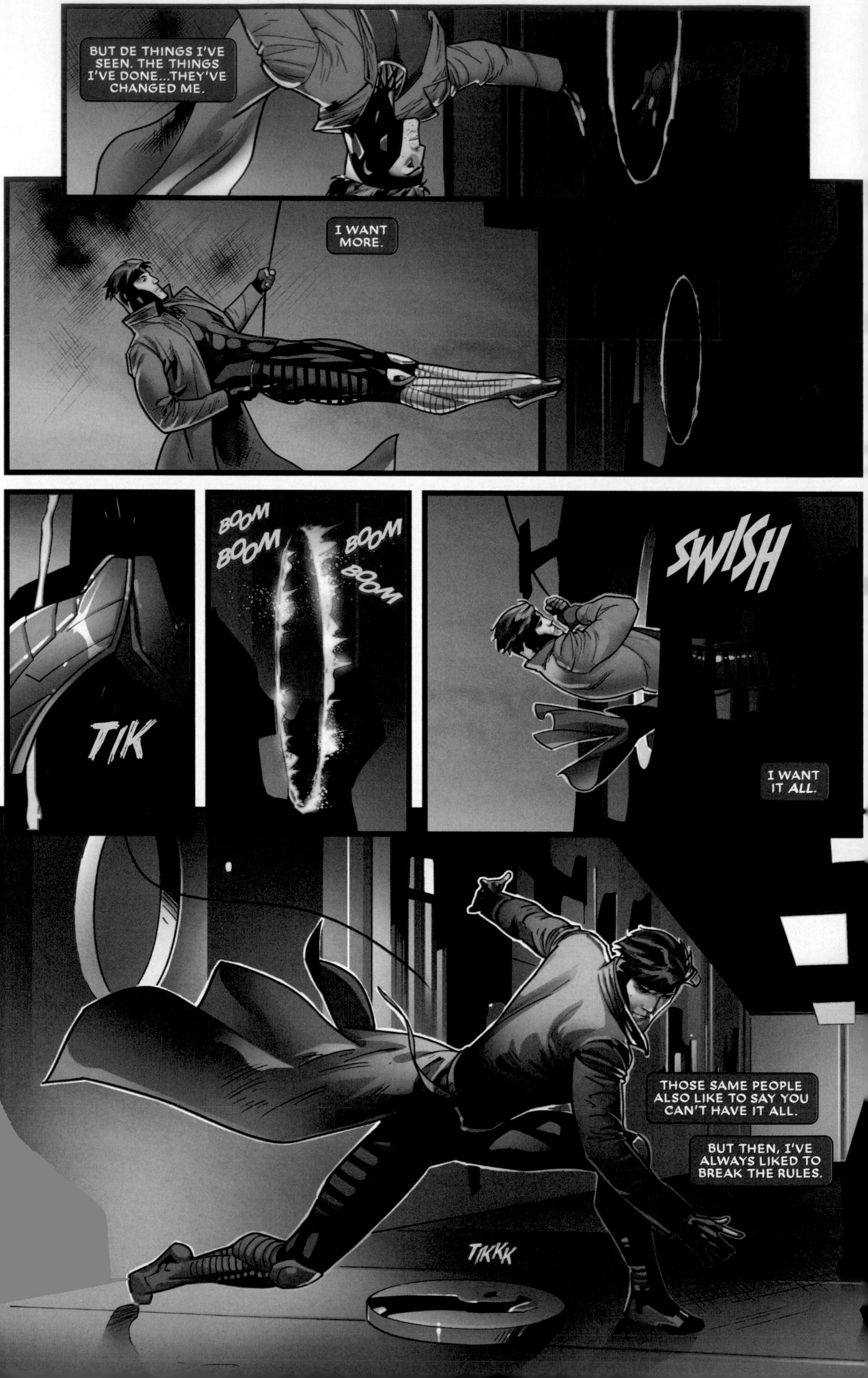

BUT DE THINGS I'VE SEEN. THE THINGS I'VE DONE...THEY'VE CHANGED ME.
I WANT MORE.
TIK
BOOM BOOM
BOOM BOOM
SWISH
I WANT IT ALL.
THOSE SAME PEOPLE ALSO LIKE TO SAY YOU CAN'T HAVE IT ALL.
BUT THEN, I'VE ALWAYS LIKED TO BREAK THE RULES.
TIKKK

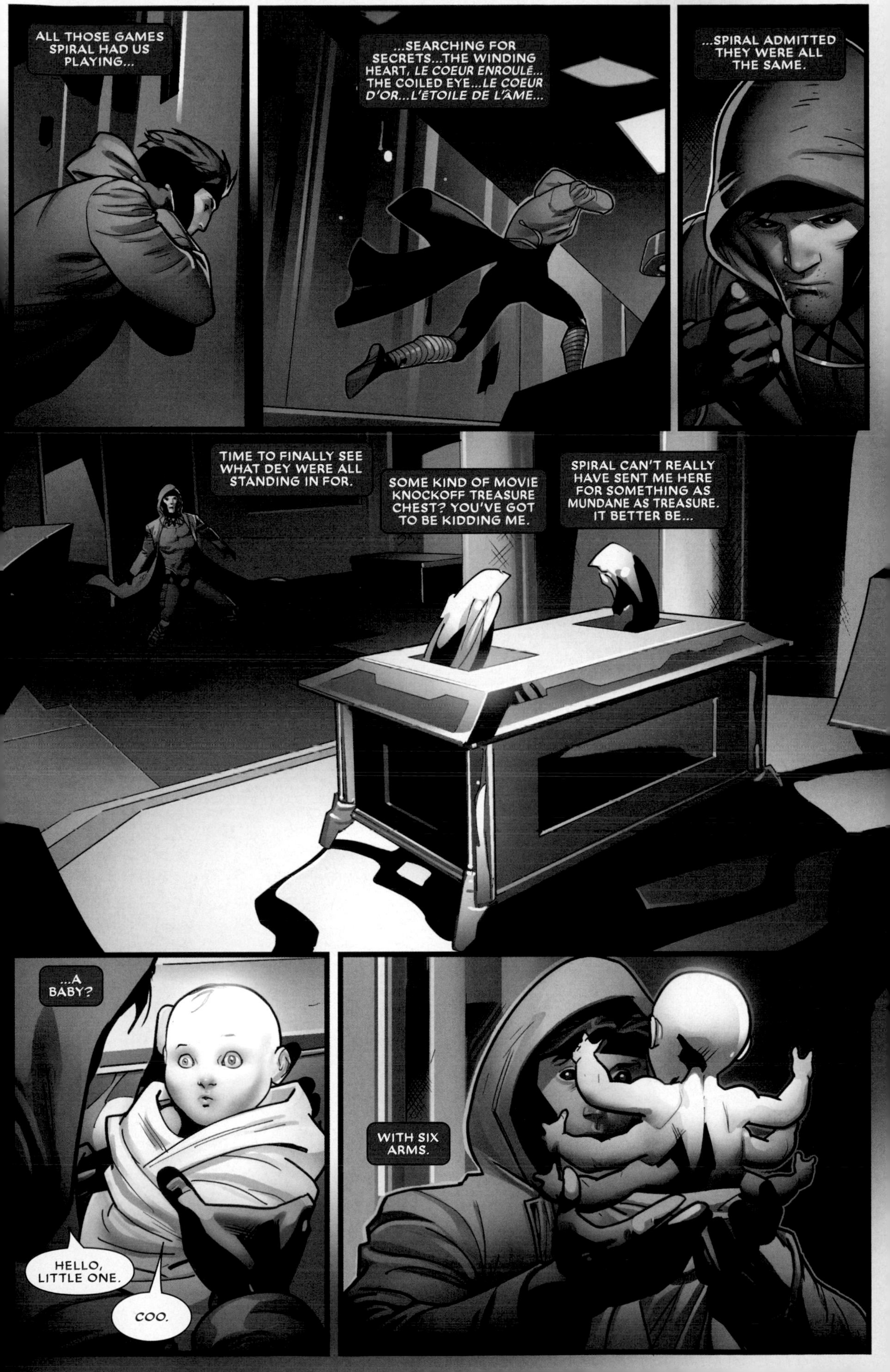
ALL THOSE GAMES SPIRAL HAD US PLAYING...
...SEARCHING FOR SECRETS...THE WINDING HEART, *LE COEUR ENROULÉ*... THE COILED EYE...*LE COEUR D'OR*...*L'ÉTOILE DE L'ÂME*...
...SPIRAL ADMITTED THEY WERE ALL THE SAME.
TIME TO FINALLY SEE WHAT DEY WERE ALL STANDING IN FOR.
SOME KIND OF MOVIE KNOCKOFF TREASURE CHEST? YOU'VE GOT TO BE KIDDING ME.
SPIRAL CAN'T REALLY HAVE SENT ME HERE FOR SOMETHING AS MUNDANE AS TREASURE. IT BETTER BE...
...A BABY?
HELLO, LITTLE ONE.
COO.
WITH SIX ARMS.

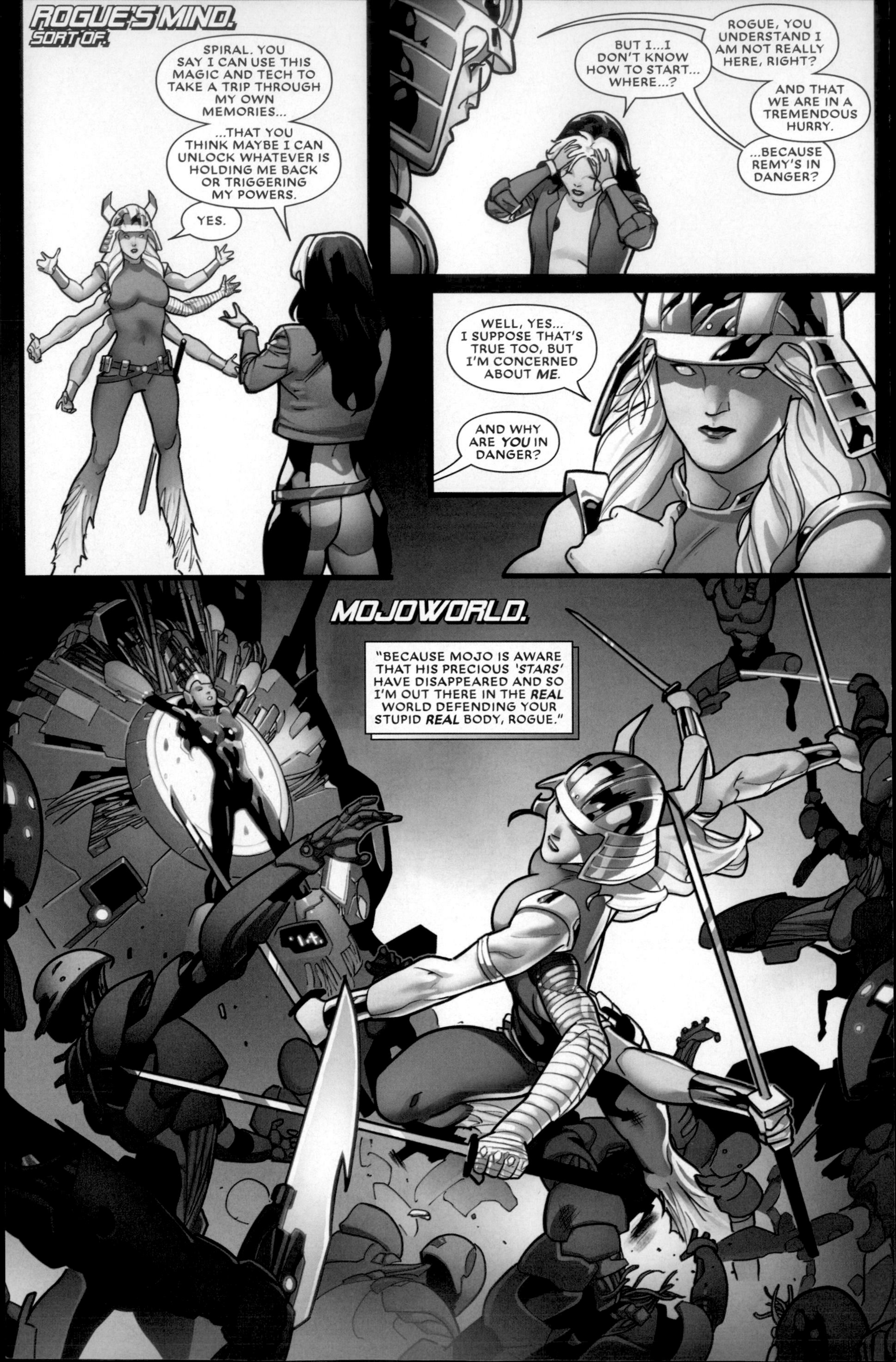
ROGUE'S MIND. SORT OF.
SPIRAL. YOU SAY I CAN USE THIS MAGIC AND TECH TO TAKE A TRIP THROUGH MY OWN MEMORIES...
...THAT YOU THINK MAYBE I CAN UNLOCK WHATEVER IS HOLDING ME BACK OR TRIGGERING MY POWERS.
YES.
ROGUE, YOU UNDERSTAND I AM NOT REALLY HERE, RIGHT?
BUT I...I DON'T KNOW HOW TO START... WHERE...?
AND THAT WE ARE IN A TREMENDOUS HURRY.
...BECAUSE REMY'S IN DANGER?
WELL, YES... I SUPPOSE THAT'S TRUE TOO, BUT I'M CONCERNED ABOUT *ME*.
AND WHY ARE *YOU* IN DANGER?
MOJOWORLD.
"BECAUSE MOJO IS AWARE THAT HIS PRECIOUS *'STARS'* HAVE DISAPPEARED AND SO I'M OUT THERE IN THE *REAL* WORLD DEFENDING YOUR STUPID *REAL* BODY, ROGUE."

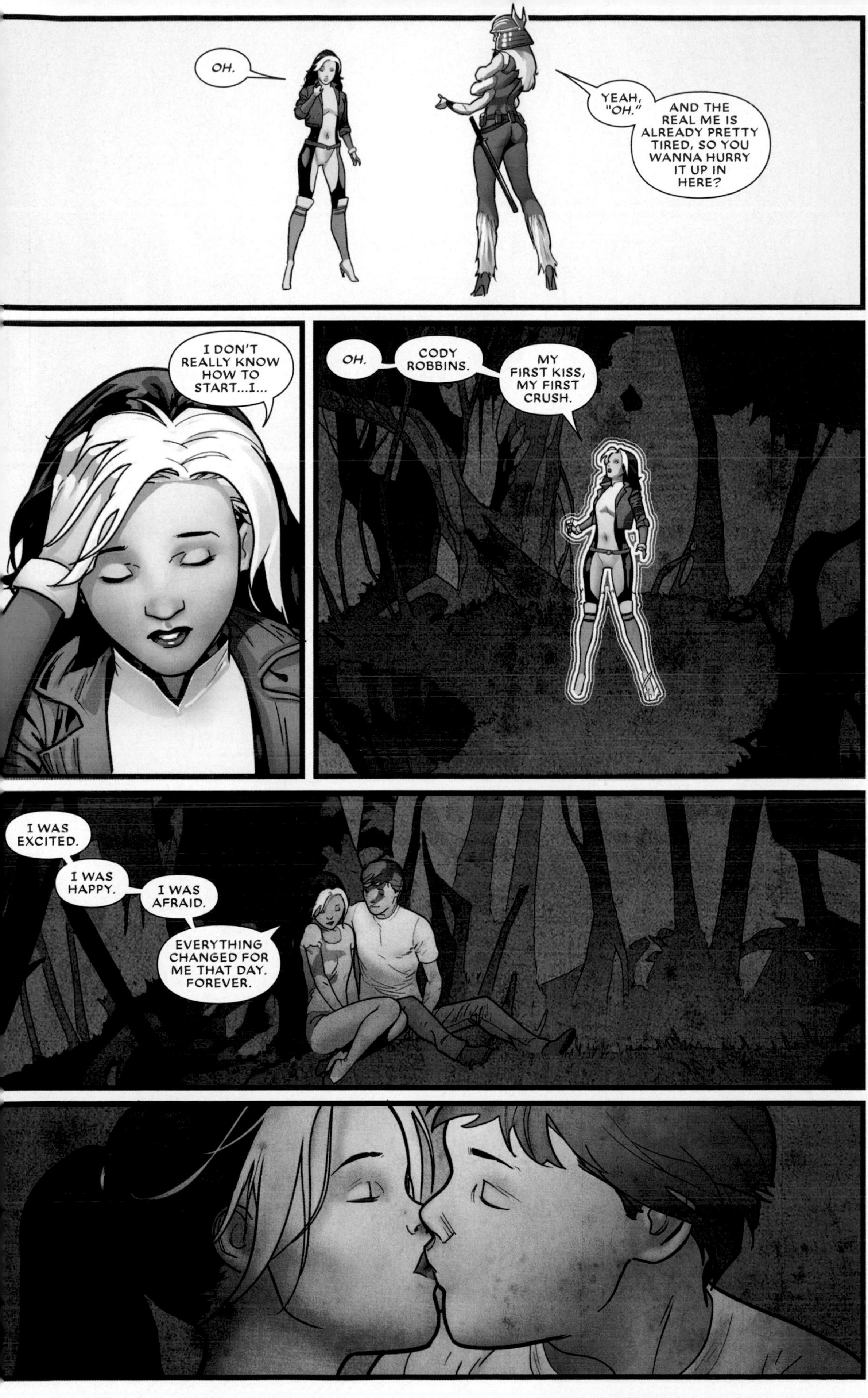
OH.
YEAH, "OH."
AND THE REAL ME IS ALREADY PRETTY TIRED, SO YOU WANNA HURRY IT UP IN HERE?
I DON'T REALLY KNOW HOW TO START...I...
OH.
CODY ROBBINS.
MY FIRST KISS, MY FIRST CRUSH.
I WAS EXCITED.
I WAS HAPPY.
I WAS AFRAID.
EVERYTHING CHANGED FOR ME THAT DAY. FOREVER.

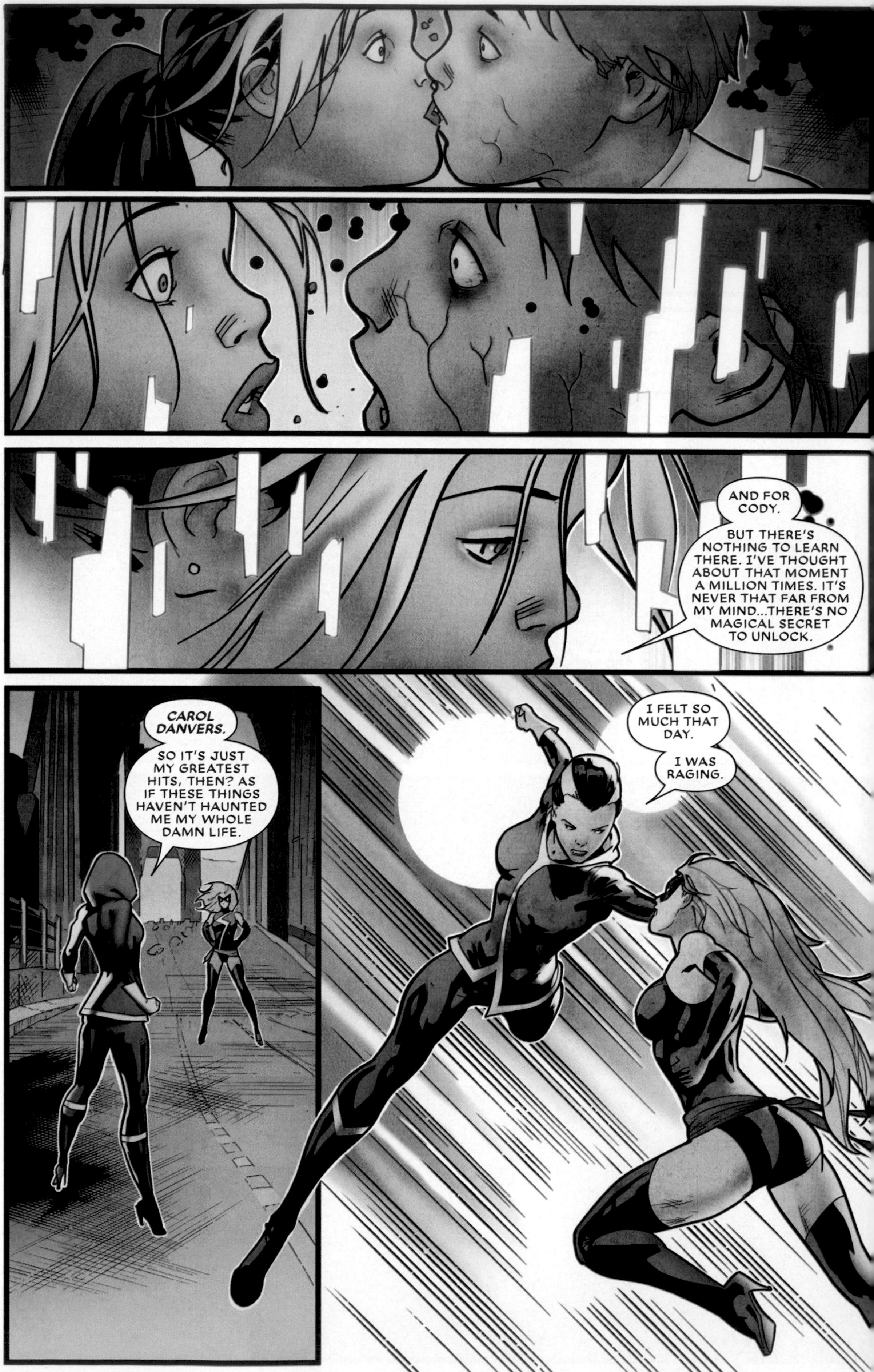
AND FOR CODY.
BUT THERE'S NOTHING TO LEARN THERE. I'VE THOUGHT ABOUT THAT MOMENT A MILLION TIMES. IT'S NEVER THAT FAR FROM MY MIND...THERE'S NO MAGICAL SECRET TO UNLOCK.
CAROL DANVERS.
SO IT'S JUST MY GREATEST HITS, THEN? AS IF THESE THINGS HAVEN'T HAUNTED ME MY WHOLE DAMN LIFE.
I FELT SO MUCH THAT DAY.
I WAS RAGING.

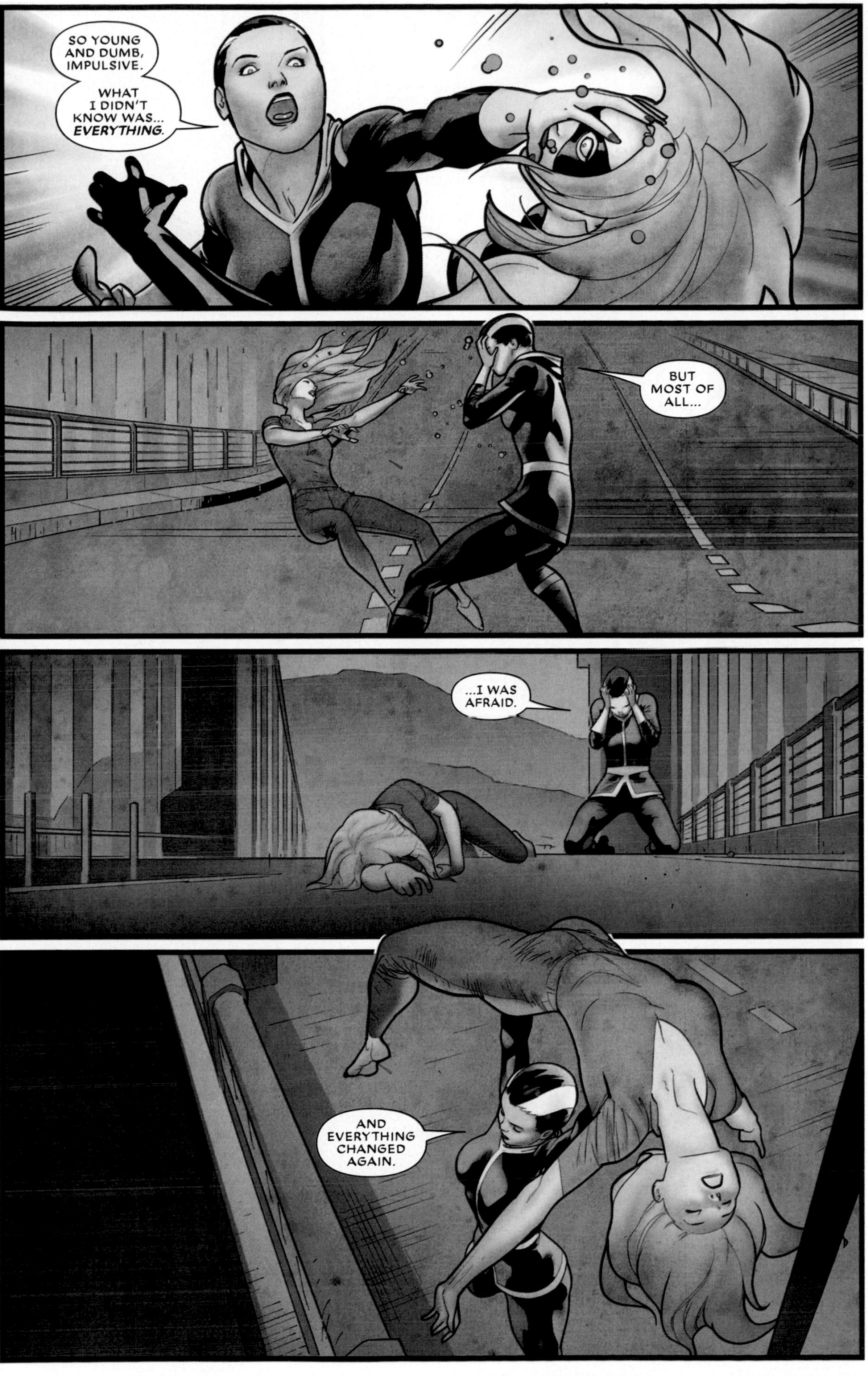
SO YOUNG AND DUMB, IMPULSIVE.
WHAT I DIDN'T KNOW WAS... *EVERYTHING.*
BUT MOST OF ALL...
...I WAS AFRAID.
AND EVERYTHING CHANGED AGAIN.

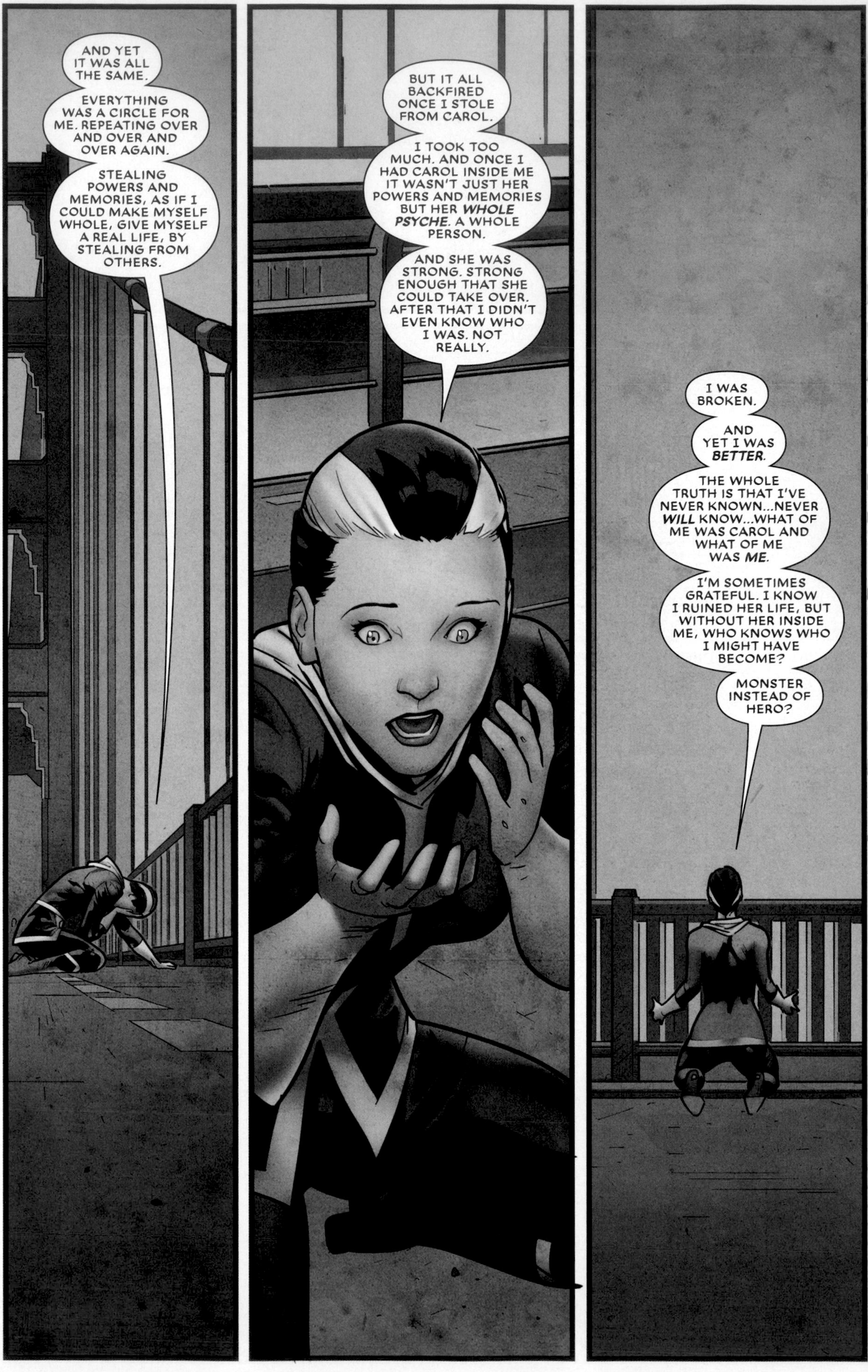
AND YET IT WAS ALL THE SAME.
EVERYTHING WAS A CIRCLE FOR ME. REPEATING OVER AND OVER AND OVER AGAIN.
STEALING POWERS AND MEMORIES, AS IF I COULD MAKE MYSELF WHOLE, GIVE MYSELF A REAL LIFE, BY STEALING FROM OTHERS.
BUT IT ALL BACKFIRED ONCE I STOLE FROM CAROL.
I TOOK TOO MUCH. AND ONCE I HAD CAROL INSIDE ME IT WASN'T JUST HER POWERS AND MEMORIES BUT HER *WHOLE PSYCHE*. A WHOLE PERSON.
AND SHE WAS STRONG. STRONG ENOUGH THAT SHE COULD TAKE OVER. AFTER THAT I DIDN'T EVEN KNOW WHO I WAS. NOT REALLY.
I WAS BROKEN.
AND YET I WAS *BETTER*.
THE WHOLE TRUTH IS THAT I'VE NEVER KNOWN...NEVER *WILL* KNOW...WHAT OF ME WAS CAROL AND WHAT OF ME WAS *ME*.
I'M SOMETIMES GRATEFUL. I KNOW I RUINED HER LIFE, BUT WITHOUT HER INSIDE ME, WHO KNOWS WHO I MIGHT HAVE BECOME?
MONSTER INSTEAD OF HERO?

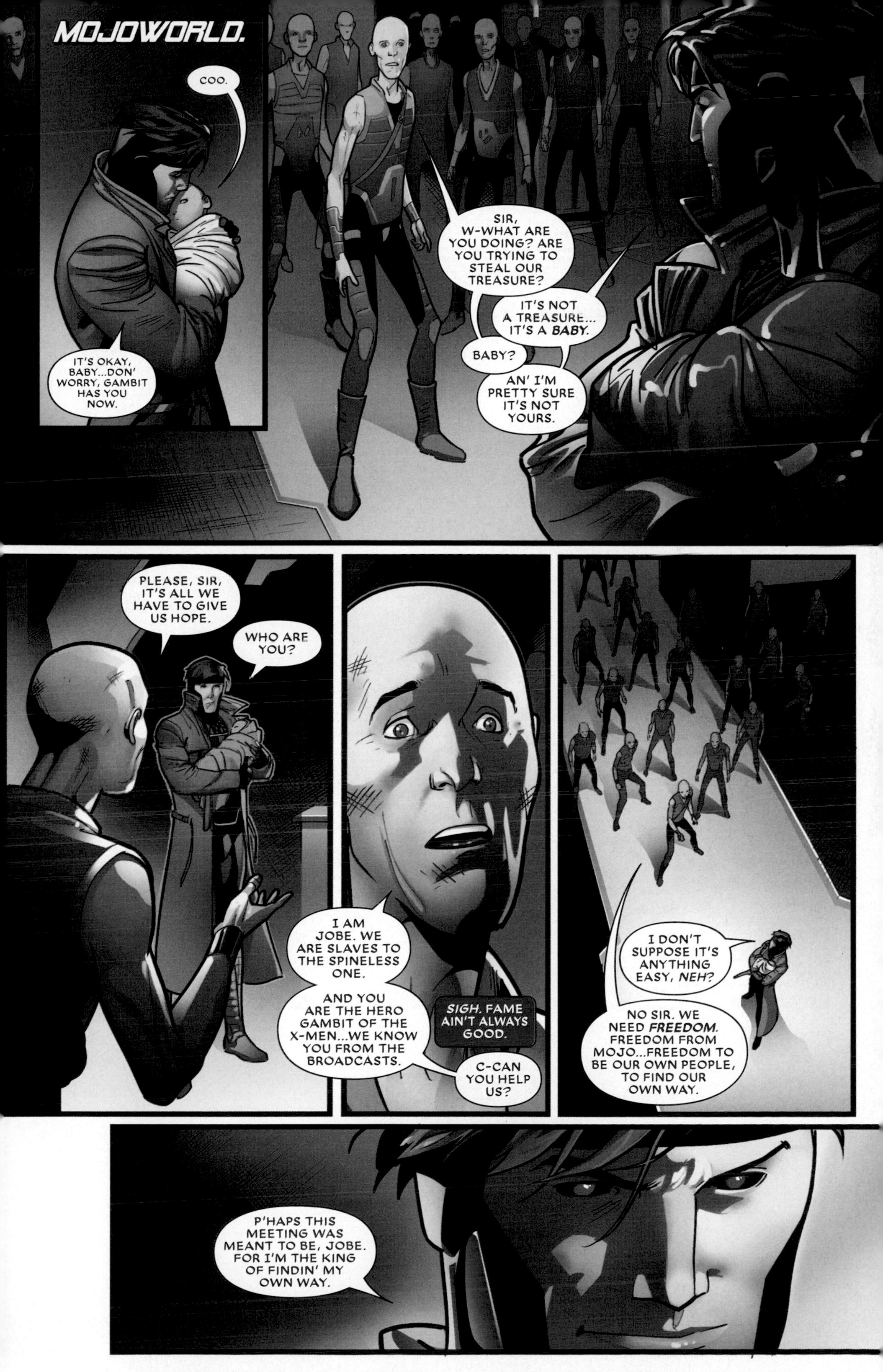
MOJOWORLD.
COO.
IT'S OKAY, BABY...DON' WORRY, GAMBIT HAS YOU NOW.
SIR, W-WHAT ARE YOU DOING? ARE YOU TRYING TO STEAL OUR TREASURE?
IT'S NOT A TREASURE... IT'S A BABY.
BABY?
AN' I'M PRETTY SURE IT'S NOT YOURS.
PLEASE, SIR, IT'S ALL WE HAVE TO GIVE US HOPE.
WHO ARE YOU?
I AM JOBE. WE ARE SLAVES TO THE SPINELESS ONE.
AND YOU ARE THE HERO GAMBIT OF THE X-MEN...WE KNOW YOU FROM THE BROADCASTS.
SIGH. FAME AIN'T ALWAYS GOOD.
C-CAN YOU HELP US?
I DON'T SUPPOSE IT'S ANYTHING EASY, NEH?
NO SIR. WE NEED FREEDOM. FREEDOM FROM MOJO...FREEDOM TO BE OUR OWN PEOPLE, TO FIND OUR OWN WAY.
P'HAPS THIS MEETING WAS MEANT TO BE, JOBE. FOR I'M THE KING OF FINDIN' MY OWN WAY.

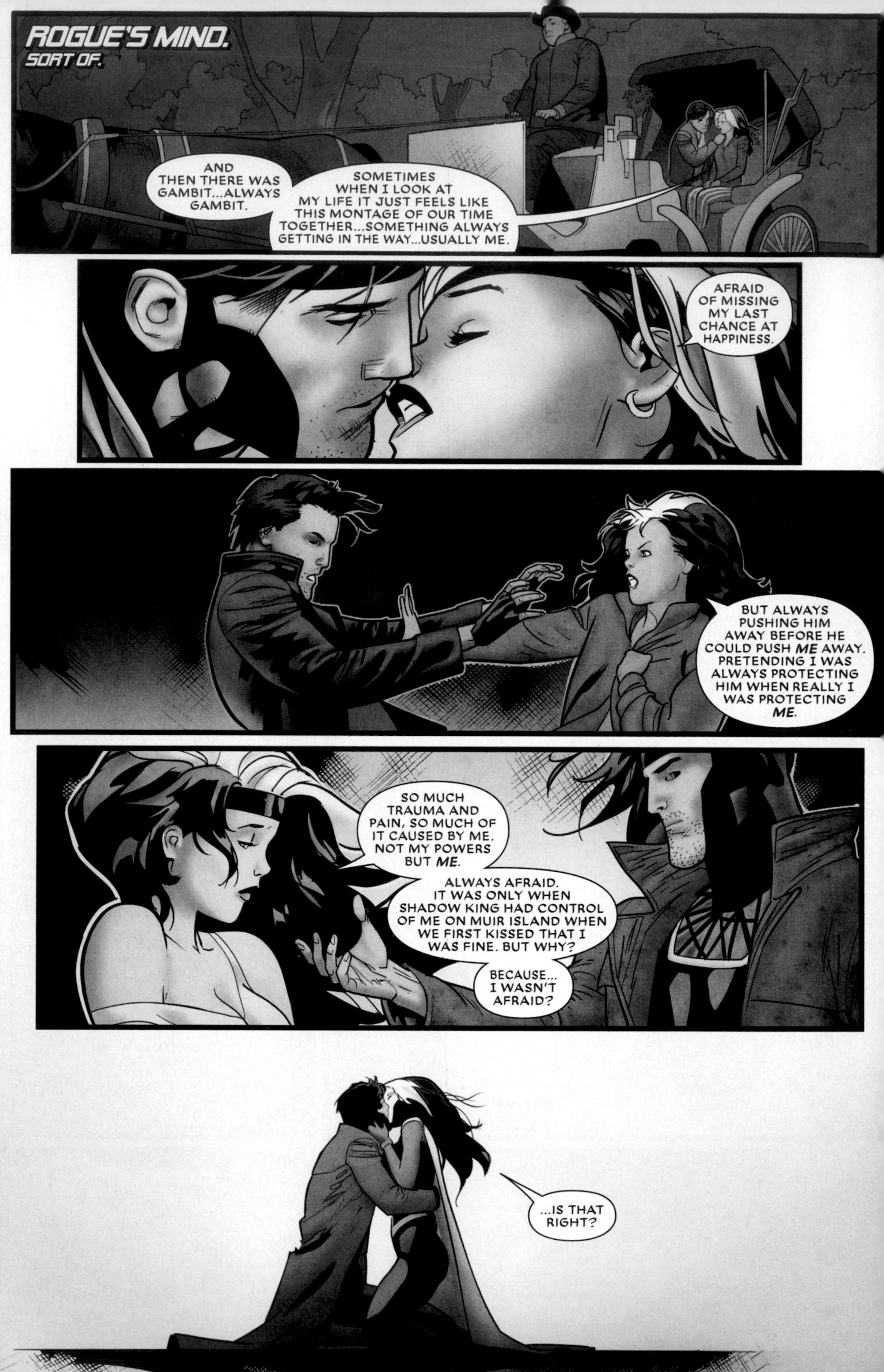
ROGUE'S MIND. SORT OF.
AND THEN THERE WAS GAMBIT...ALWAYS GAMBIT.
SOMETIMES WHEN I LOOK AT MY LIFE IT JUST FEELS LIKE THIS MONTAGE OF OUR TIME TOGETHER...SOMETHING ALWAYS GETTING IN THE WAY...USUALLY ME.
AFRAID OF MISSING MY LAST CHANCE AT HAPPINESS.
BUT ALWAYS PUSHING HIM AWAY BEFORE HE COULD PUSH ME AWAY. PRETENDING I WAS ALWAYS PROTECTING HIM WHEN REALLY I WAS PROTECTING ME.
SO MUCH TRAUMA AND PAIN, SO MUCH OF IT CAUSED BY ME. NOT MY POWERS BUT ME.
ALWAYS AFRAID. IT WAS ONLY WHEN SHADOW KING HAD CONTROL OF ME ON MUIR ISLAND WHEN WE FIRST KISSED THAT I WAS FINE. BUT WHY?
BECAUSE... I WASN'T AFRAID?
...IS THAT RIGHT?

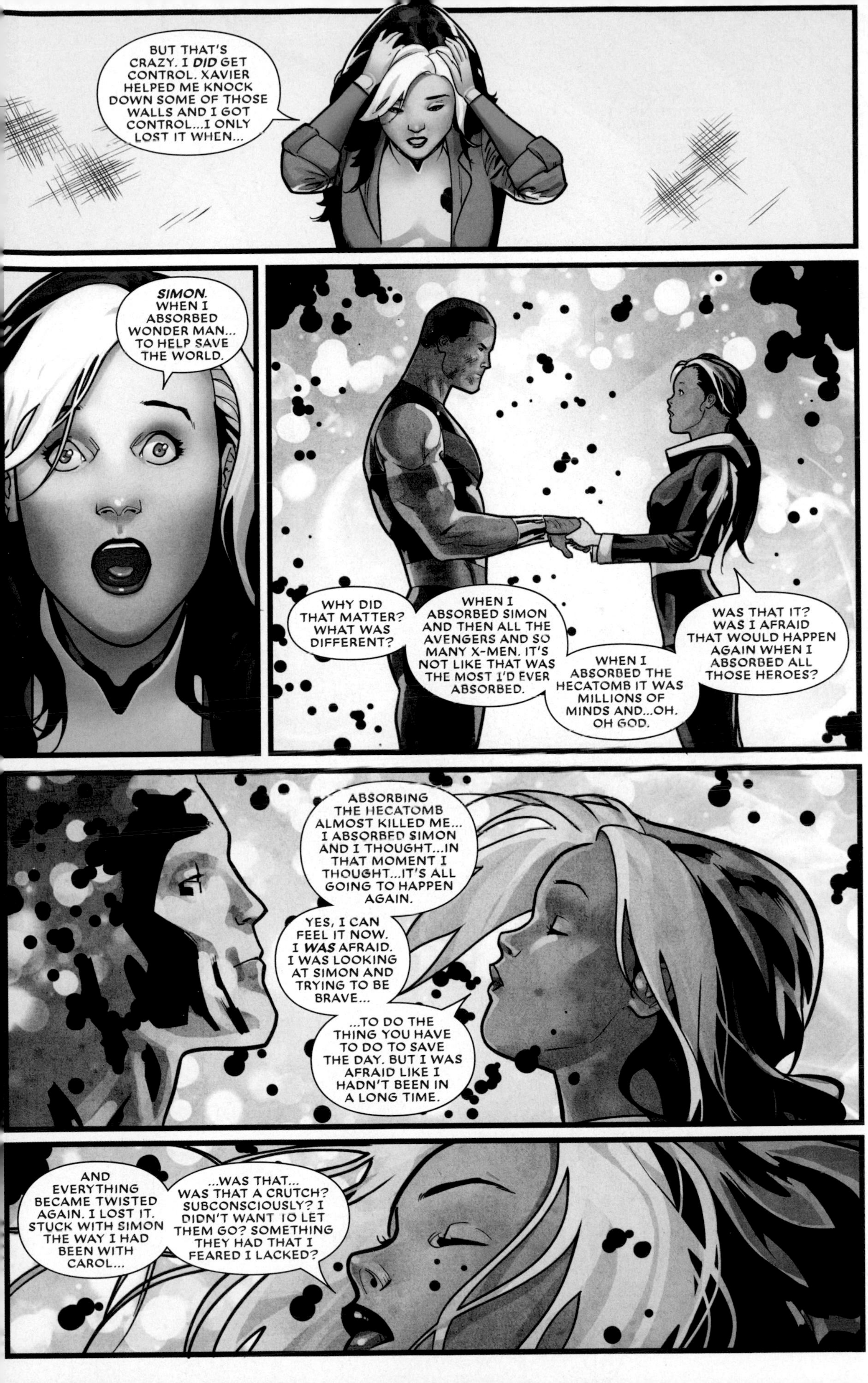
BUT THAT'S CRAZY. I *DID* GET CONTROL. XAVIER HELPED ME KNOCK DOWN SOME OF THOSE WALLS AND I GOT CONTROL...I ONLY LOST IT WHEN...
SIMON. WHEN I ABSORBED WONDER MAN... TO HELP SAVE THE WORLD.
WHY DID THAT MATTER? WHAT WAS DIFFERENT?
WHEN I ABSORBED SIMON AND THEN ALL THE AVENGERS AND SO MANY X-MEN. IT'S NOT LIKE THAT WAS THE MOST I'D EVER ABSORBED.
WHEN I ABSORBED THE HECATOMB IT WAS MILLIONS OF MINDS AND...OH. OH GOD.
WAS THAT IT? WAS I AFRAID THAT WOULD HAPPEN AGAIN WHEN I ABSORBED ALL THOSE HEROES?
ABSORBING THE HECATOMB ALMOST KILLED ME... I ABSORBED SIMON AND I THOUGHT...IN THAT MOMENT I THOUGHT...IT'S ALL GOING TO HAPPEN AGAIN.
YES, I CAN FEEL IT NOW. I *WAS* AFRAID. I WAS LOOKING AT SIMON AND TRYING TO BE BRAVE...
...TO DO THE THING YOU HAVE TO DO TO SAVE THE DAY. BUT I WAS AFRAID LIKE I HADN'T BEEN IN A LONG TIME.
AND EVERYTHING BECAME TWISTED AGAIN. I LOST IT. STUCK WITH SIMON THE WAY I HAD BEEN WITH CAROL...
...WAS THAT... WAS THAT A CRUTCH? SUBCONSCIOUSLY? I DIDN'T WANT TO LET THEM GO? SOMETHING THEY HAD THAT I FEARED I LACKED?

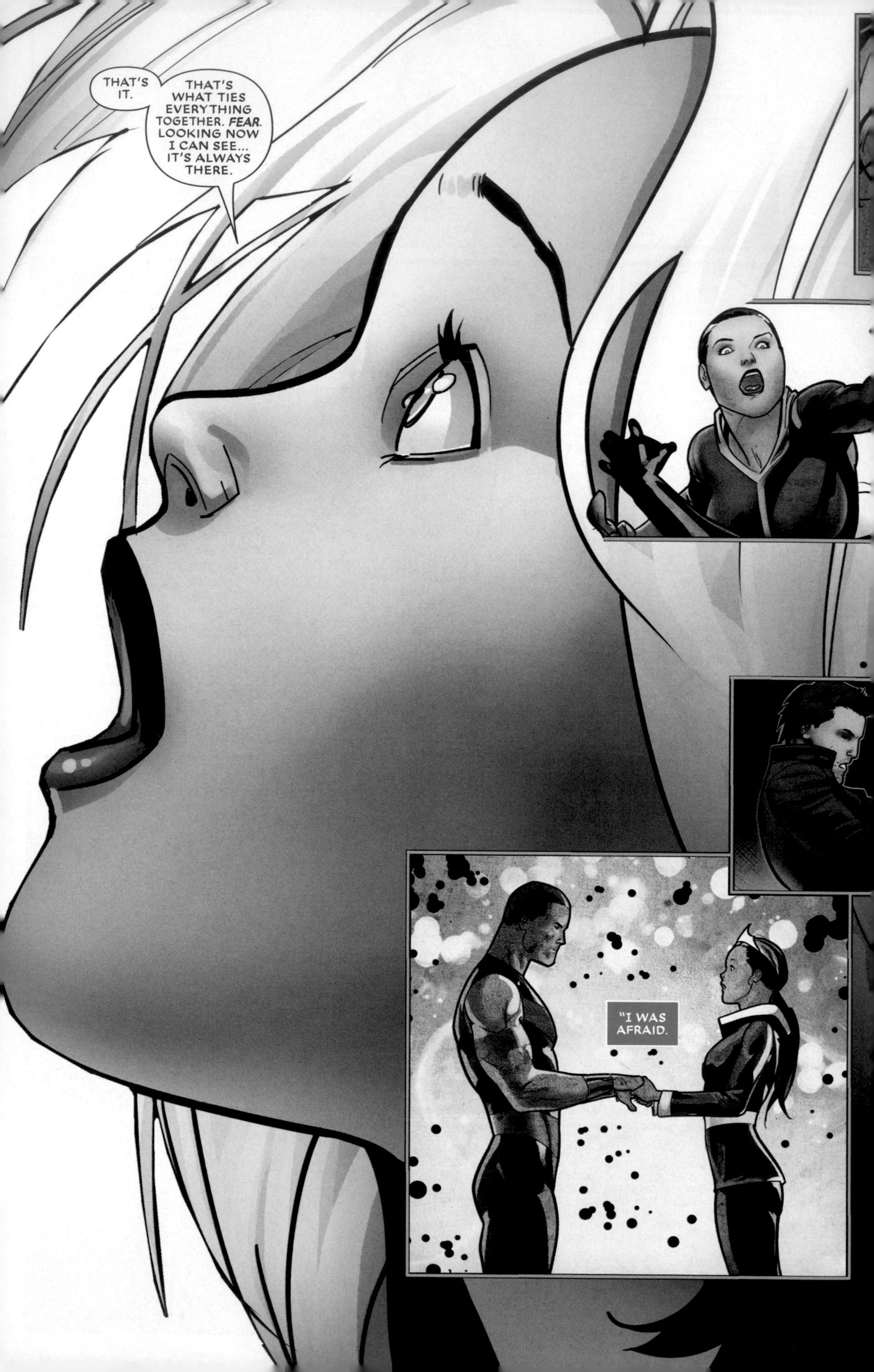
THAT'S IT.
THAT'S WHAT TIES EVERYTHING TOGETHER. FEAR. LOOKING NOW I CAN SEE... IT'S ALWAYS THERE.
"I WAS AFRAID.

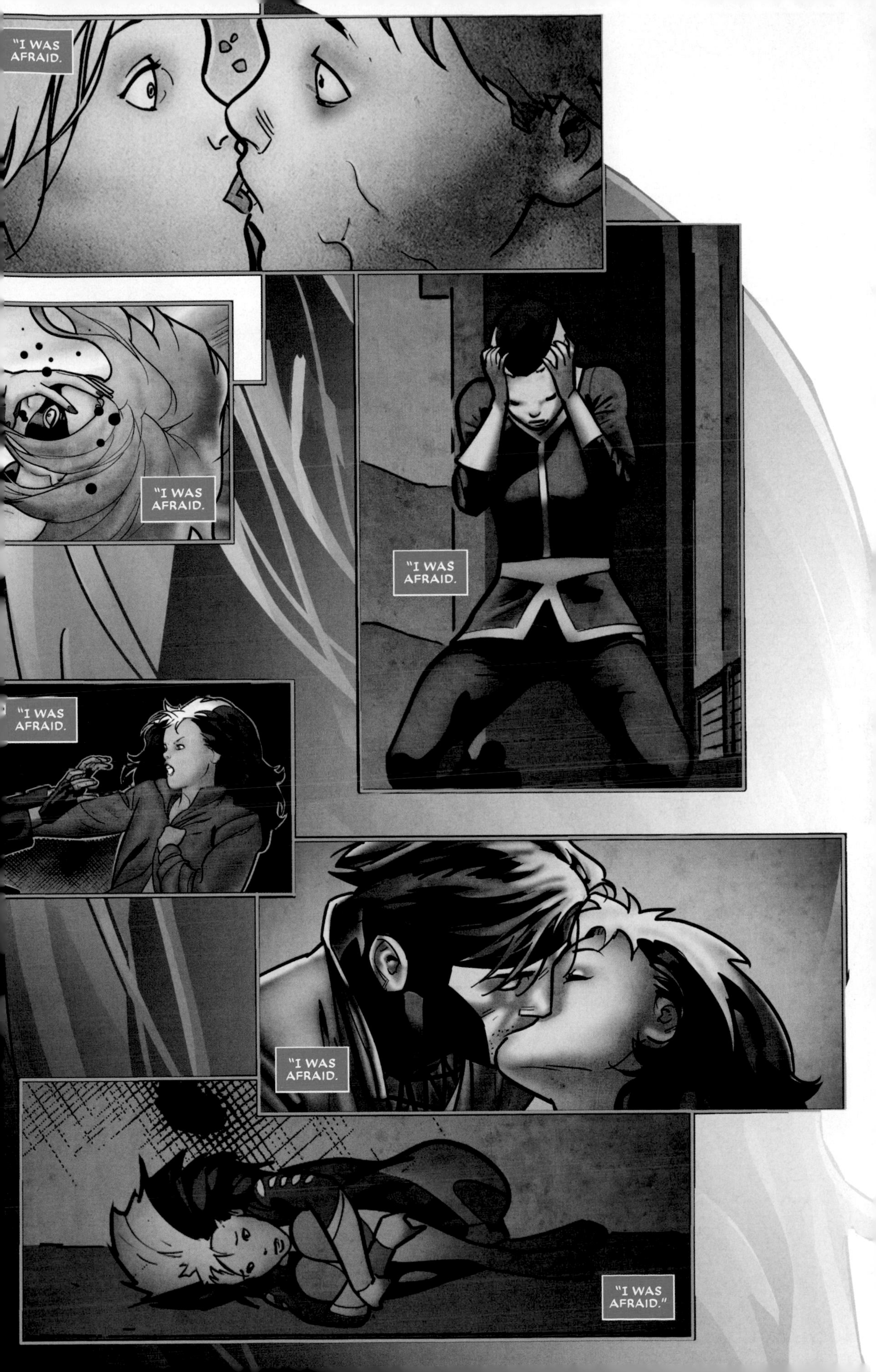
"I WAS AFRAID.
"I WAS AFRAID.
"I WAS AFRAID.
"I WAS AFRAID.
"I WAS AFRAID.
"I WAS AFRAID."

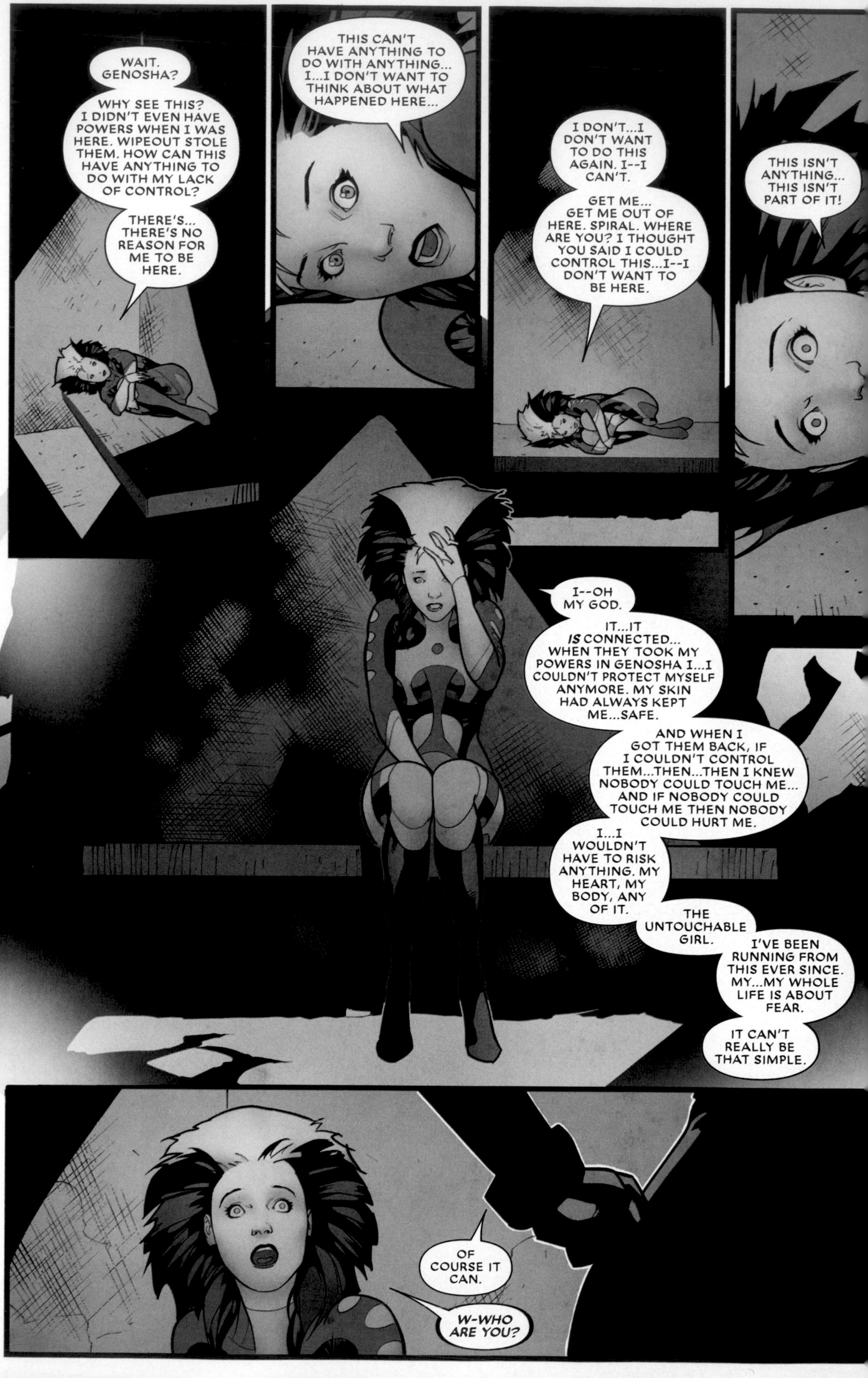
WAIT. GENOSHA?
WHY SEE THIS? I DIDN'T EVEN HAVE POWERS WHEN I WAS HERE. WIPEOUT STOLE THEM. HOW CAN THIS HAVE ANYTHING TO DO WITH MY LACK OF CONTROL?
THERE'S... THERE'S NO REASON FOR ME TO BE HERE.
THIS CAN'T HAVE ANYTHING TO DO WITH ANYTHING... I...I DON'T WANT TO THINK ABOUT WHAT HAPPENED HERE...
I DON'T...I DON'T WANT TO DO THIS AGAIN. I--I CAN'T.
GET ME... GET ME OUT OF HERE. SPIRAL. WHERE ARE YOU? I THOUGHT YOU SAID I COULD CONTROL THIS...I--I DON'T WANT TO BE HERE.
THIS ISN'T ANYTHING... THIS ISN'T PART OF IT!
I--OH MY GOD.
IT...IT *IS* CONNECTED... WHEN THEY TOOK MY POWERS IN GENOSHA I...I COULDN'T PROTECT MYSELF ANYMORE. MY SKIN HAD ALWAYS KEPT ME...SAFE.
AND WHEN I GOT THEM BACK, IF I COULDN'T CONTROL THEM...THEN...THEN I KNEW NOBODY COULD TOUCH ME... AND IF NOBODY COULD TOUCH ME THEN NOBODY COULD HURT ME.
I...I WOULDN'T HAVE TO RISK ANYTHING. MY HEART, MY BODY, ANY OF IT.
THE UNTOUCHABLE GIRL.
I'VE BEEN RUNNING FROM THIS EVER SINCE. MY...MY WHOLE LIFE IS ABOUT FEAR.
IT CAN'T REALLY BE THAT SIMPLE.
OF COURSE IT CAN.
W-WHO ARE YOU?

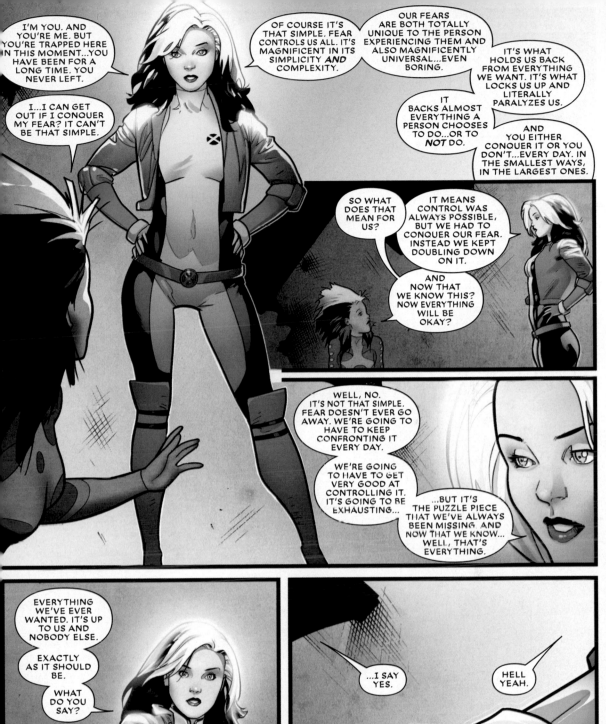

I'M YOU. AND YOU'RE ME. BUT YOU'RE TRAPPED HERE IN THIS MOMENT...YOU HAVE BEEN FOR A LONG TIME. YOU NEVER LEFT.

I...I CAN GET OUT IF I CONQUER MY FEAR? IT CAN'T BE THAT SIMPLE.

OF COURSE IT'S THAT SIMPLE. FEAR CONTROLS US ALL. IT'S MAGNIFICENT IN ITS SIMPLICITY **AND** COMPLEXITY.

OUR FEARS ARE BOTH TOTALLY UNIQUE TO THE PERSON EXPERIENCING THEM AND ALSO MAGNIFICENTLY UNIVERSAL...EVEN BORING.

IT'S WHAT HOLDS US BACK FROM EVERYTHING WE WANT. IT'S WHAT LOCKS US UP AND LITERALLY PARALYZES US.

IT BACKS ALMOST EVERYTHING A PERSON CHOOSES TO DO...OR TO **NOT DO**.

AND YOU EITHER CONQUER IT OR YOU DON'T...EVERY DAY. IN THE SMALLEST WAYS, IN THE LARGEST ONES.

SO WHAT DOES THAT MEAN FOR US?

IT MEANS CONTROL WAS ALWAYS POSSIBLE, BUT WE HAD TO CONQUER OUR FEAR. INSTEAD WE KEPT DOUBLING DOWN ON IT.

AND NOW THAT WE KNOW THIS? NOW EVERYTHING WILL BE OKAY?

WELL, NO. IT'S NOT THAT SIMPLE. FEAR DOESN'T EVER GO AWAY. WE'RE GOING TO HAVE TO KEEP CONFRONTING IT EVERY DAY.

WE'RE GOING TO HAVE TO GET VERY GOOD AT CONTROLLING IT. IT'S GOING TO BE EXHAUSTING...

...BUT IT'S THE PUZZLE PIECE THAT WE'VE ALWAYS BEEN MISSING. AND NOW THAT WE KNOW... WELL, THAT'S EVERYTHING.

EVERYTHING WE'VE EVER WANTED. IT'S UP TO US AND NOBODY ELSE.

EXACTLY AS IT SHOULD BE.

WHAT DO YOU SAY?

...I SAY YES.

HELL YEAH.

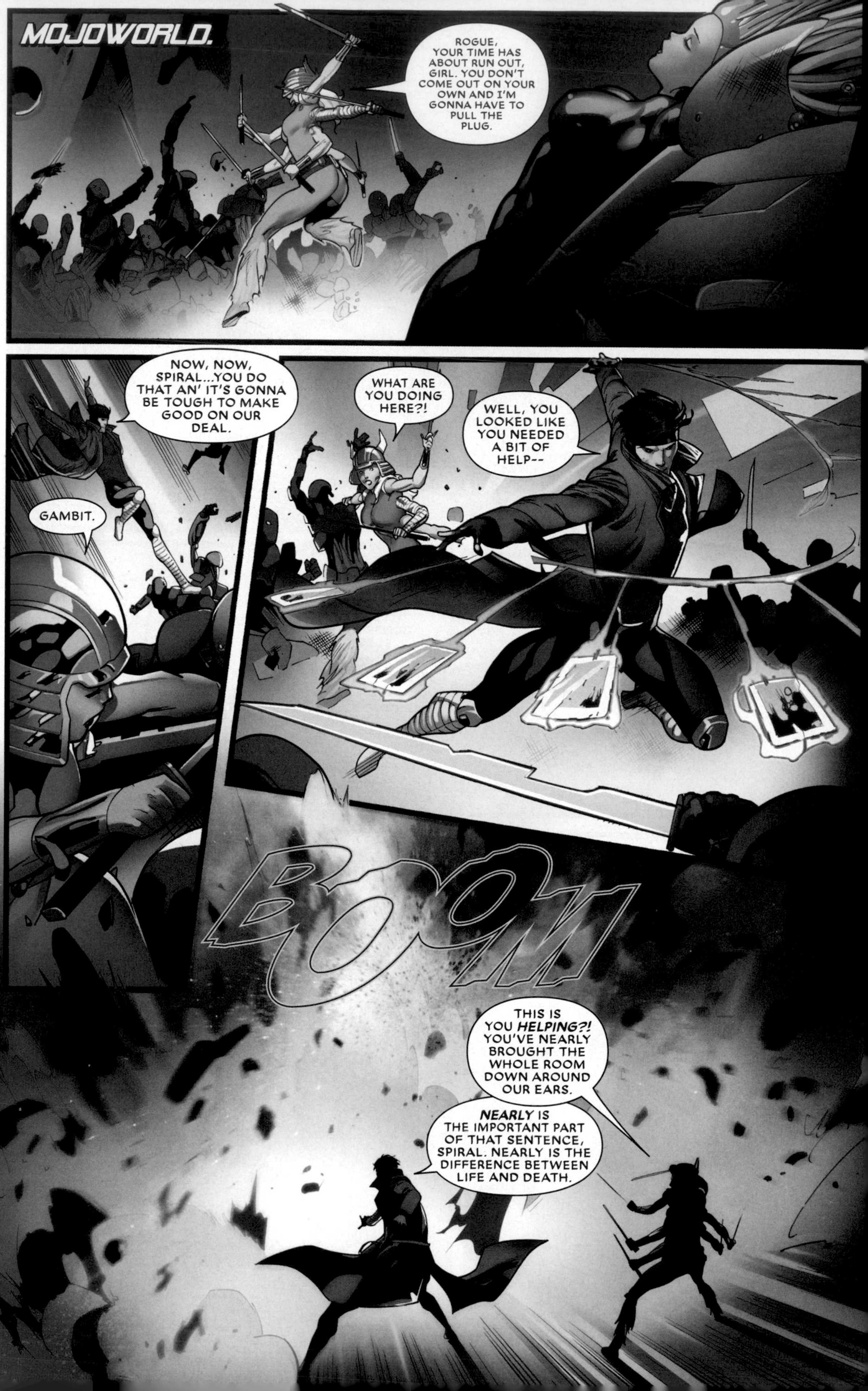
MOJOWORLD.
ROGUE, YOUR TIME HAS ABOUT RUN OUT, GIRL. YOU DON'T COME OUT ON YOUR OWN AND I'M GONNA HAVE TO PULL THE PLUG.
NOW, NOW, SPIRAL...YOU DO THAT AN' IT'S GONNA BE TOUGH TO MAKE GOOD ON OUR DEAL.
GAMBIT.
WHAT ARE YOU DOING HERE?!
WELL, YOU LOOKED LIKE YOU NEEDED A BIT OF HELP--
BOOM
THIS IS YOU *HELPING?!* YOU'VE NEARLY BROUGHT THE WHOLE ROOM DOWN AROUND OUR EARS.
NEARLY IS THE IMPORTANT PART OF THAT SENTENCE, SPIRAL. NEARLY IS THE DIFFERENCE BETWEEN LIFE AND DEATH.

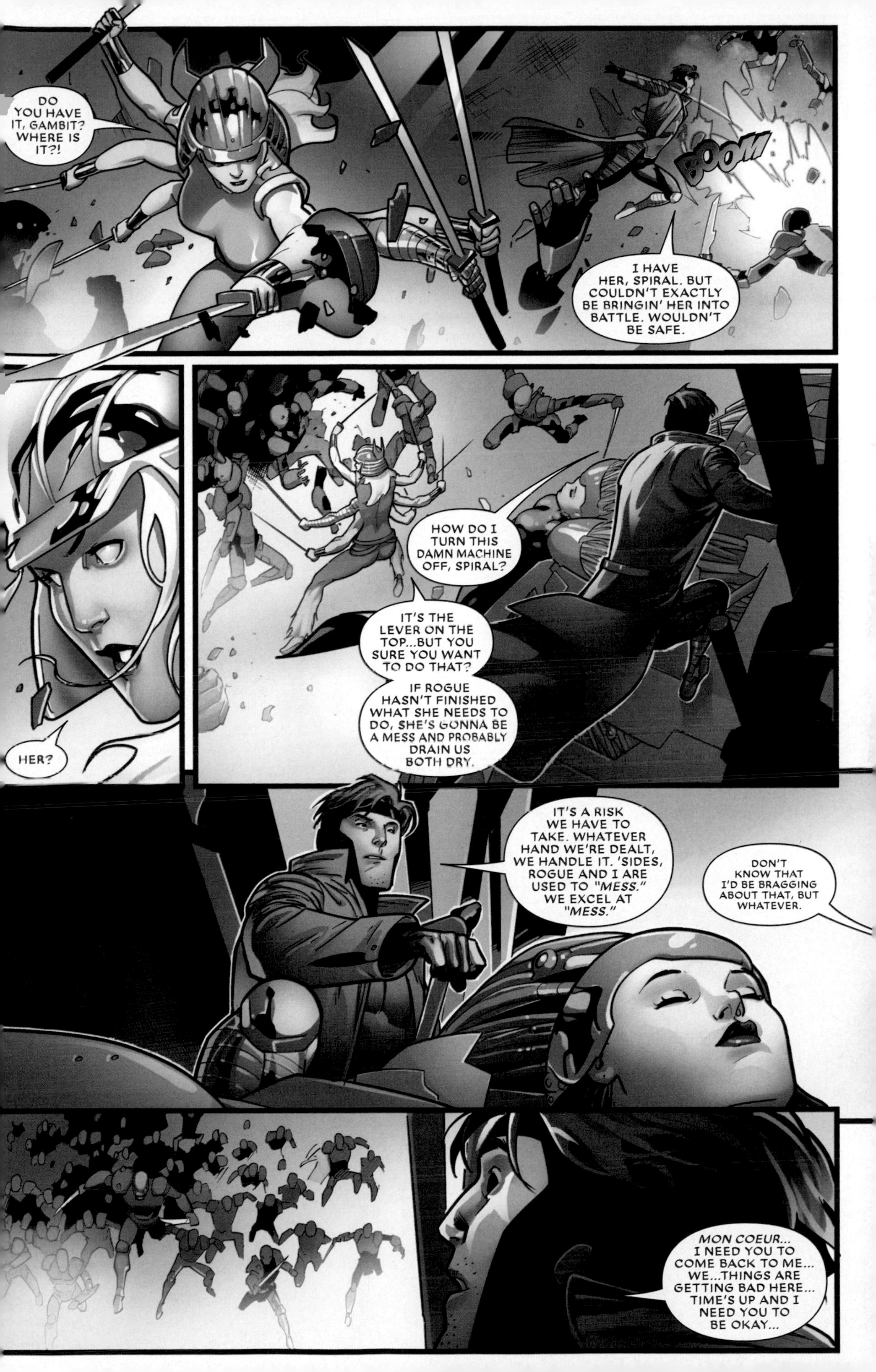
DO YOU HAVE IT, GAMBIT? WHERE IS IT?!
BOOM
I HAVE HER, SPIRAL. BUT COULDN'T EXACTLY BE BRINGIN' HER INTO BATTLE. WOULDN'T BE SAFE.
HER?
HOW DO I TURN THIS DAMN MACHINE OFF, SPIRAL?
IT'S THE LEVER ON THE TOP...BUT YOU SURE YOU WANT TO DO THAT?
IF ROGUE HASN'T FINISHED WHAT SHE NEEDS TO DO, SHE'S GONNA BE A MESS AND PROBABLY DRAIN US BOTH DRY.
IT'S A RISK WE HAVE TO TAKE. WHATEVER HAND WE'RE DEALT, WE HANDLE IT. 'SIDES, ROGUE AND I ARE USED TO "MESS." WE EXCEL AT "MESS."
DON'T KNOW THAT I'D BE BRAGGING ABOUT THAT, BUT WHATEVER.
MON COEUR... I NEED YOU TO COME BACK TO ME... WE...THINGS ARE GETTING BAD HERE... TIME'S UP AND I NEED YOU TO BE OKAY...

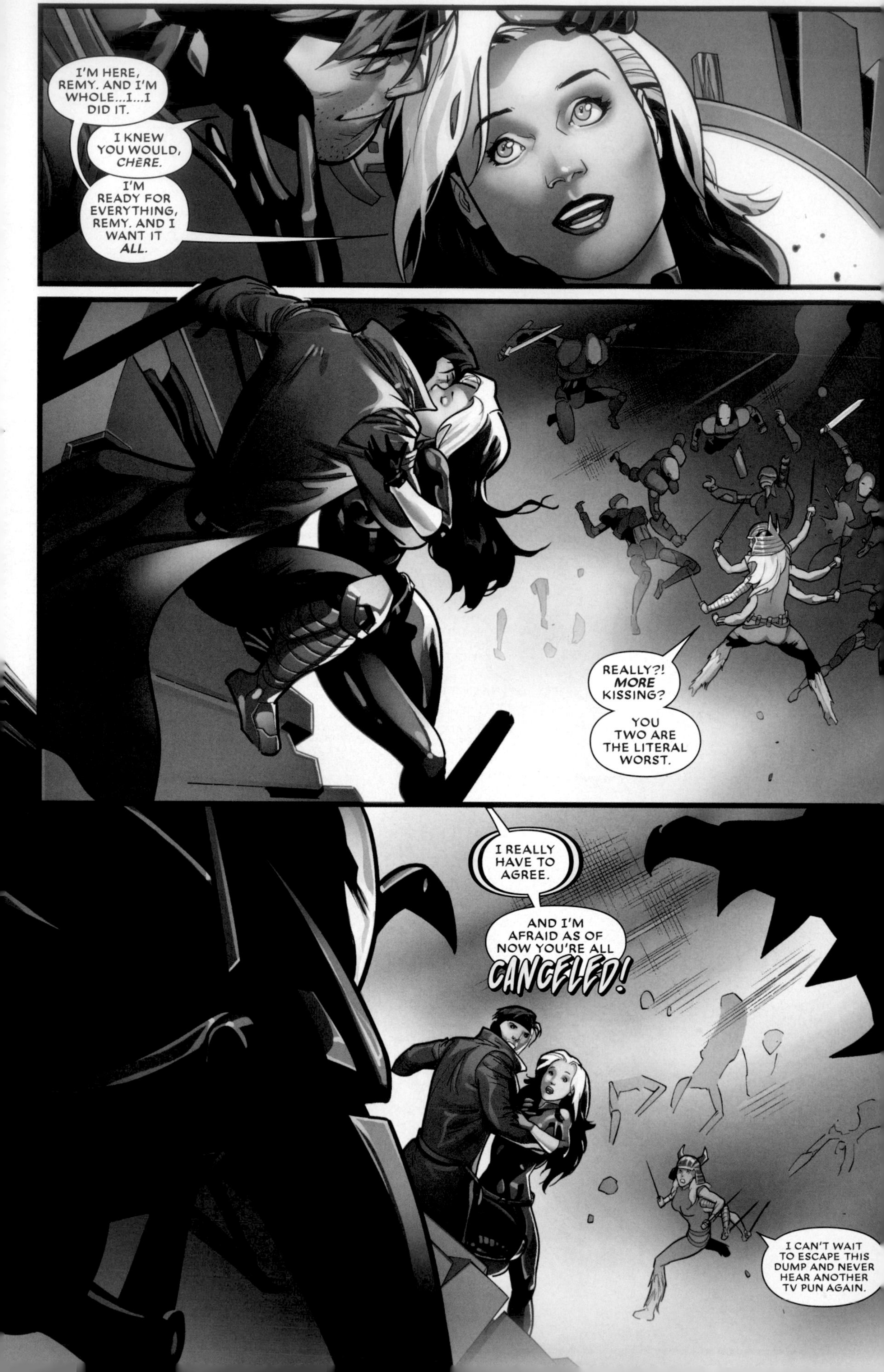
I'M HERE, REMY. AND I'M WHOLE...I...I DID IT.
I KNEW YOU WOULD, *CHÈRE*.
I'M READY FOR EVERYTHING, REMY. AND I WANT IT *ALL*.
REALLY?! *MORE* KISSING?
YOU TWO ARE THE LITERAL WORST.
I REALLY HAVE TO AGREE.
AND I'M AFRAID AS OF NOW YOU'RE ALL
CANCELED!
I CAN'T WAIT TO ESCAPE THIS DUMP AND NEVER HEAR ANOTHER TV PUN AGAIN.

10

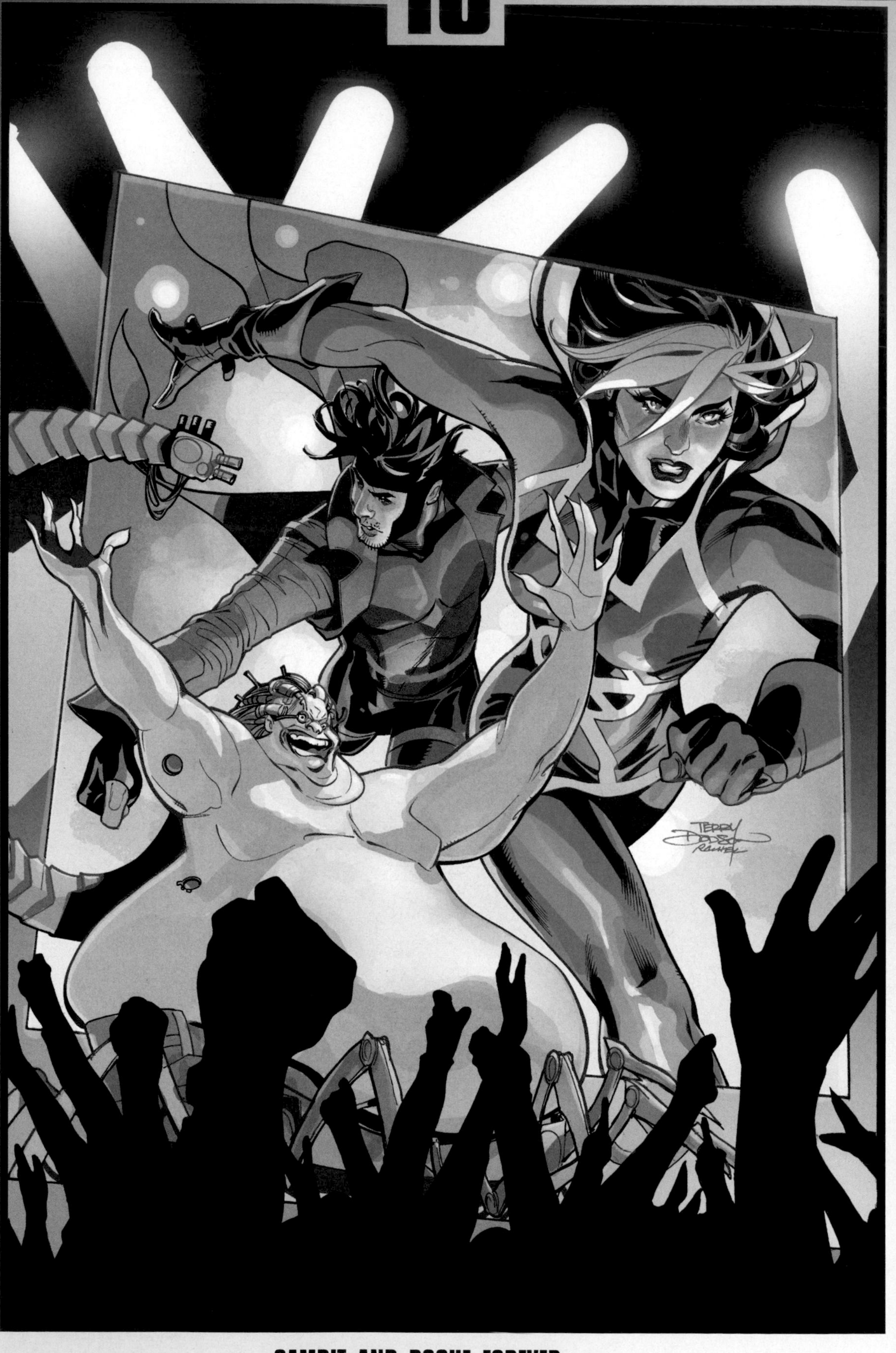

GAMBIT AND ROGUE FOREVER PART 4

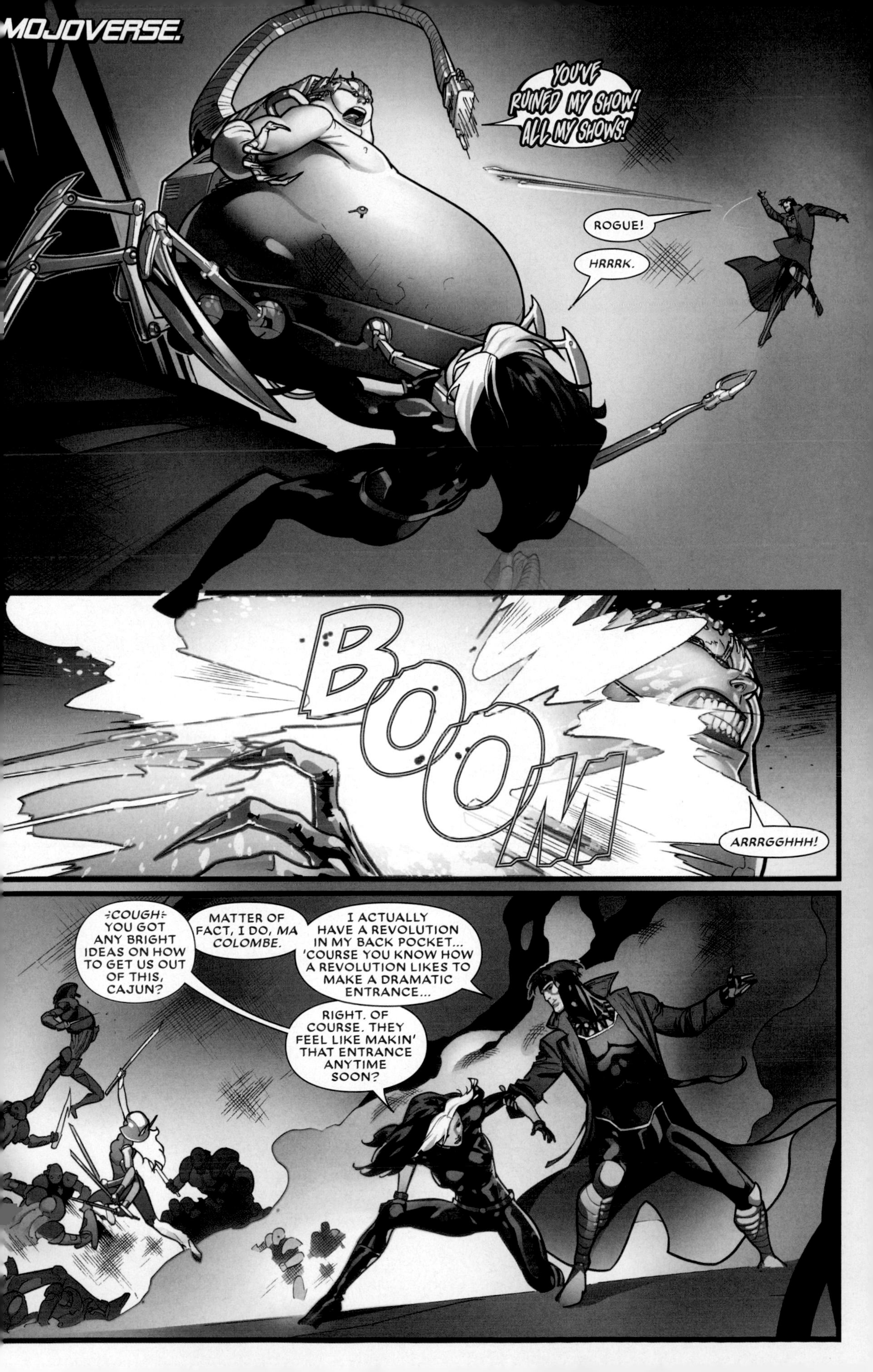

MOJOVERSE.
YOU'VE RUINED MY SHOW! ALL MY SHOWS!
ROGUE!
HRRRK.
BOOOM
ARRRGGHHH!
¬COUGH¬ YOU GOT ANY BRIGHT IDEAS ON HOW TO GET US OUT OF THIS, CAJUN?
MATTER OF FACT, I DO, MA COLOMBE.
I ACTUALLY HAVE A REVOLUTION IN MY BACK POCKET... 'COURSE YOU KNOW HOW A REVOLUTION LIKES TO MAKE A DRAMATIC ENTRANCE...
RIGHT. OF COURSE. THEY FEEL LIKE MAKIN' THAT ENTRANCE ANYTIME SOON?

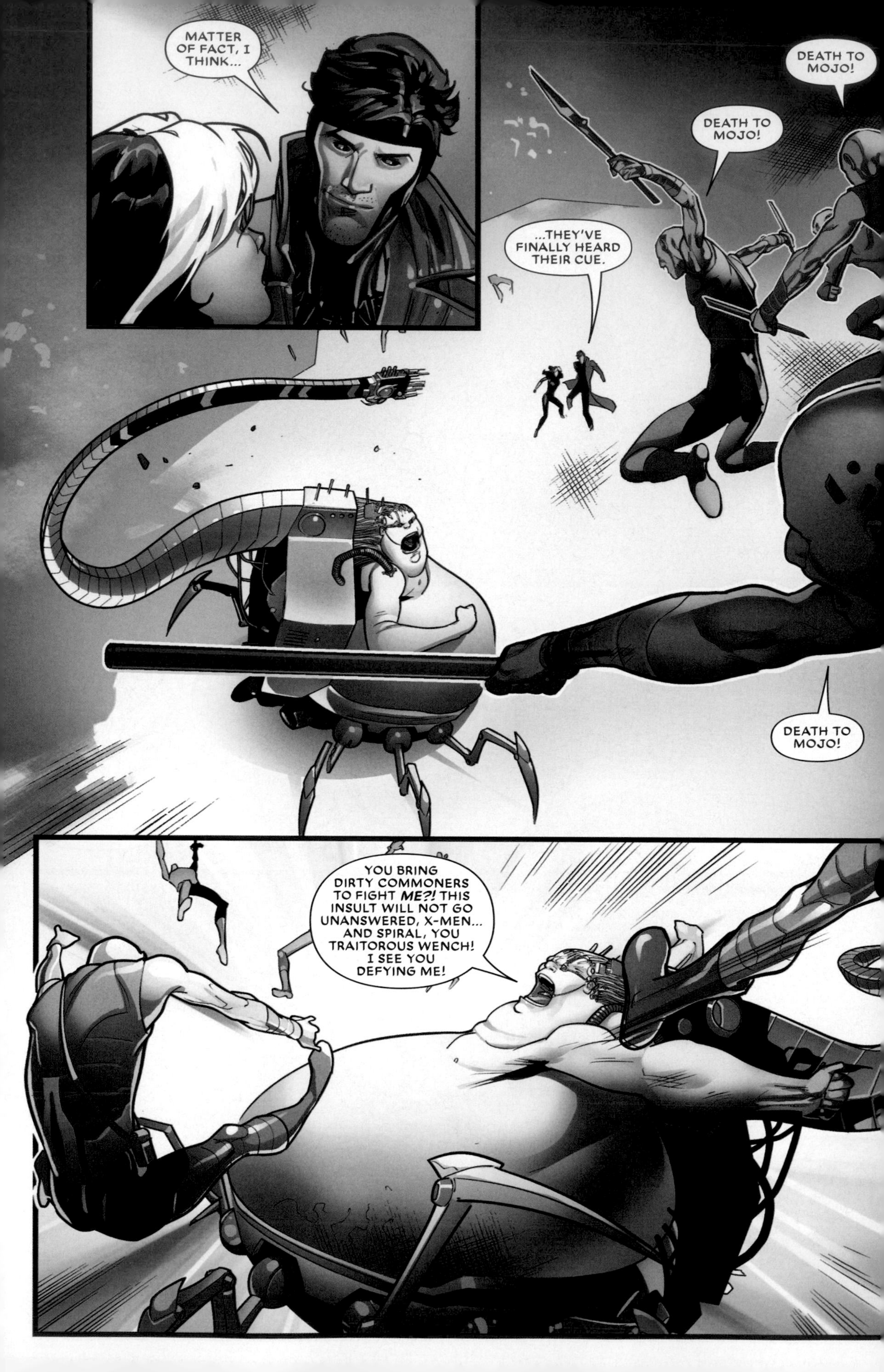
MATTER OF FACT, I THINK...
DEATH TO MOJO!
DEATH TO MOJO!
...THEY'VE FINALLY HEARD THEIR CUE.
DEATH TO MOJO!
YOU BRING DIRTY COMMONERS TO FIGHT ME?! THIS INSULT WILL NOT GO UNANSWERED, X-MEN... AND SPIRAL, YOU TRAITOROUS WENCH! I SEE YOU DEFYING ME!

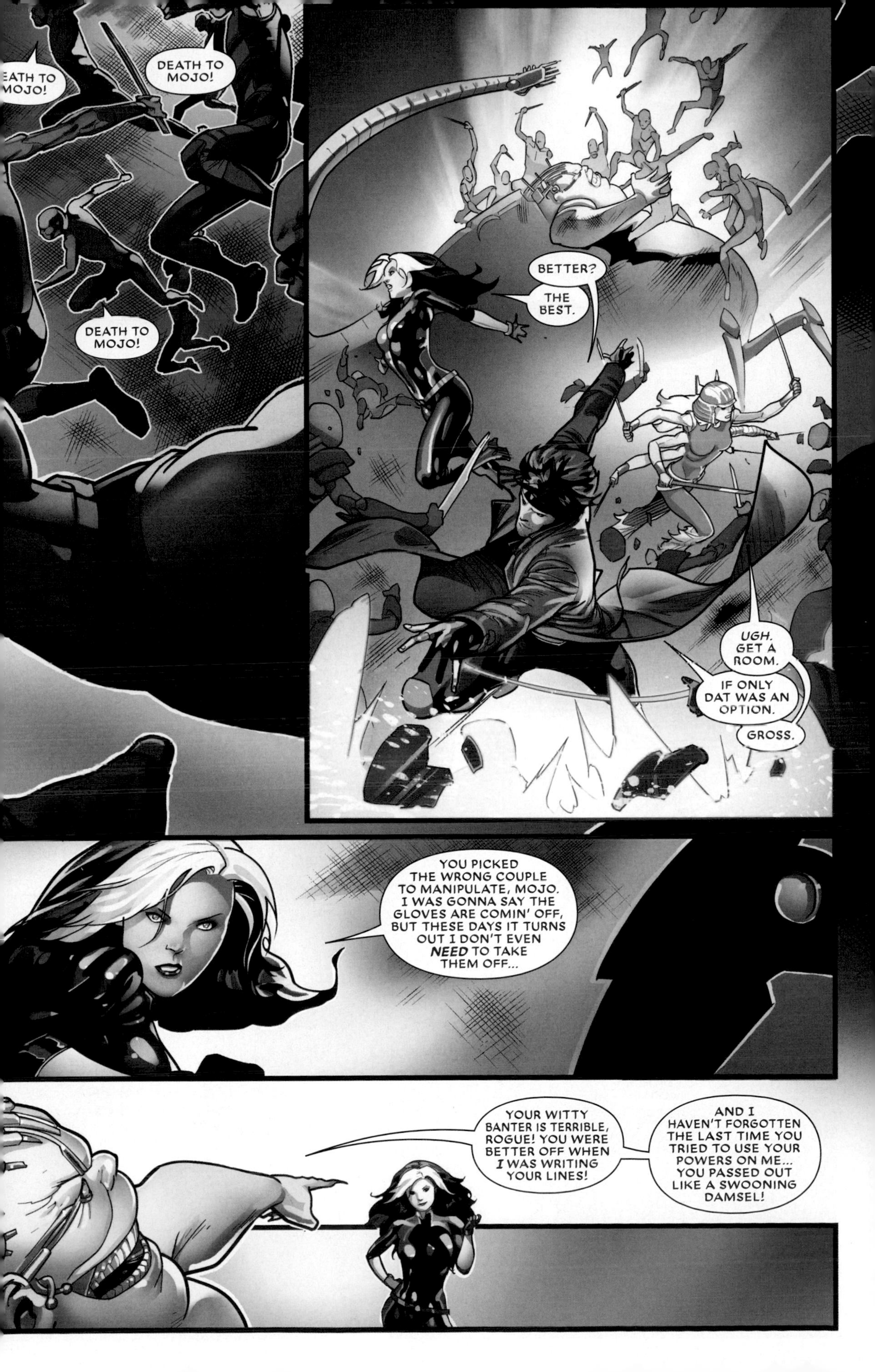
EATH TO MOJO!
DEATH TO MOJO!
DEATH TO MOJO!
BETTER?
THE BEST.
UGH. GET A ROOM.
IF ONLY DAT WAS AN OPTION.
GROSS.
YOU PICKED THE WRONG COUPLE TO MANIPULATE, MOJO. I WAS GONNA SAY THE GLOVES ARE COMIN' OFF, BUT THESE DAYS IT TURNS OUT I DON'T EVEN ***NEED*** TO TAKE THEM OFF...
YOUR WITTY BANTER IS TERRIBLE, ROGUE! YOU WERE BETTER OFF WHEN *I* WAS WRITING YOUR LINES!
AND I HAVEN'T FORGOTTEN THE LAST TIME YOU TRIED TO USE YOUR POWERS ON ME... YOU PASSED OUT LIKE A SWOONING DAMSEL!

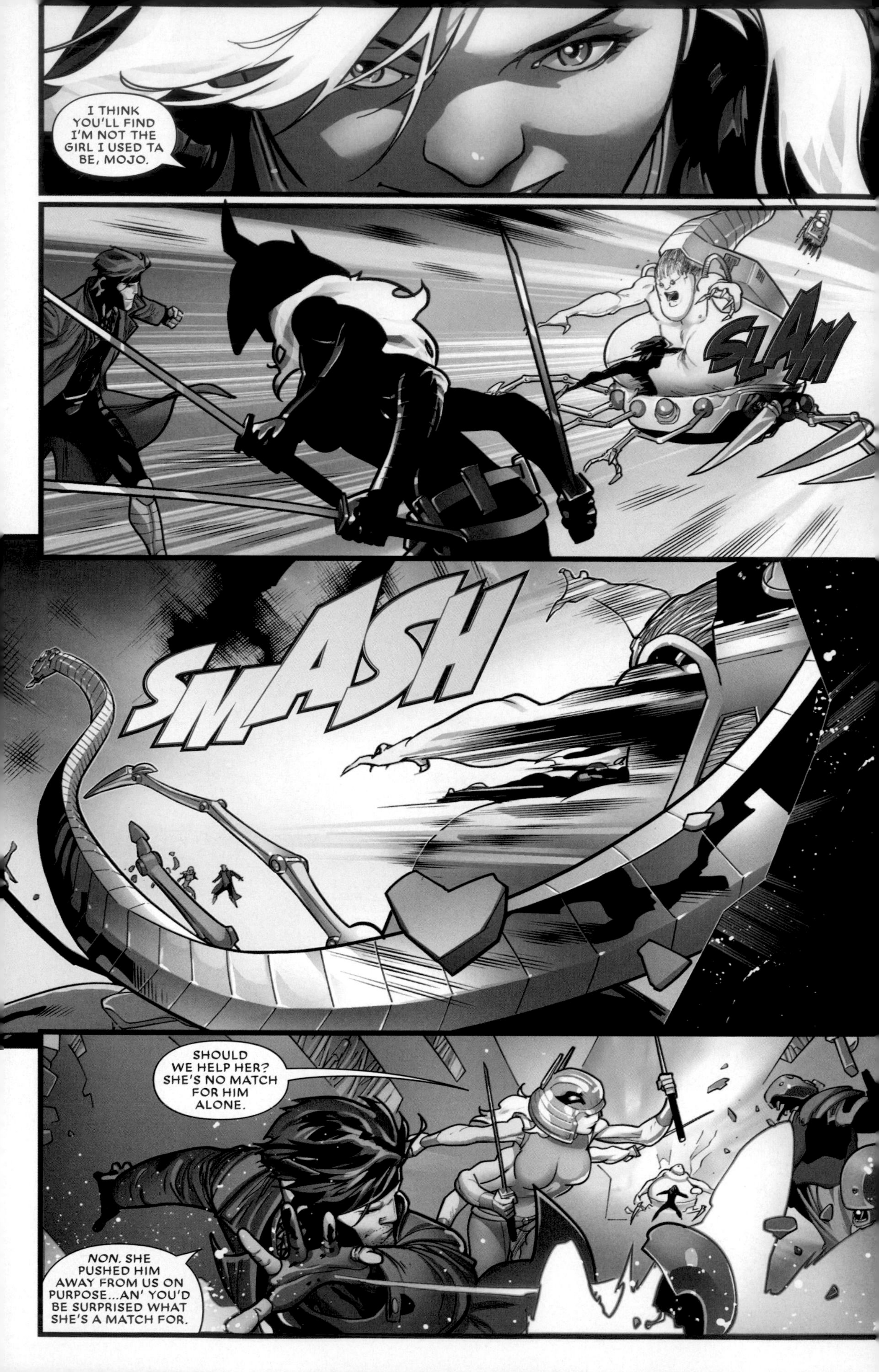
I THINK YOU'LL FIND I'M NOT THE GIRL I USED TA BE, MOJO.
SLAM
SMASH
SHOULD WE HELP HER? SHE'S NO MATCH FOR HIM ALONE.
NON. SHE PUSHED HIM AWAY FROM US ON PURPOSE...AN' YOU'D BE SURPRISED WHAT SHE'S A MATCH FOR.

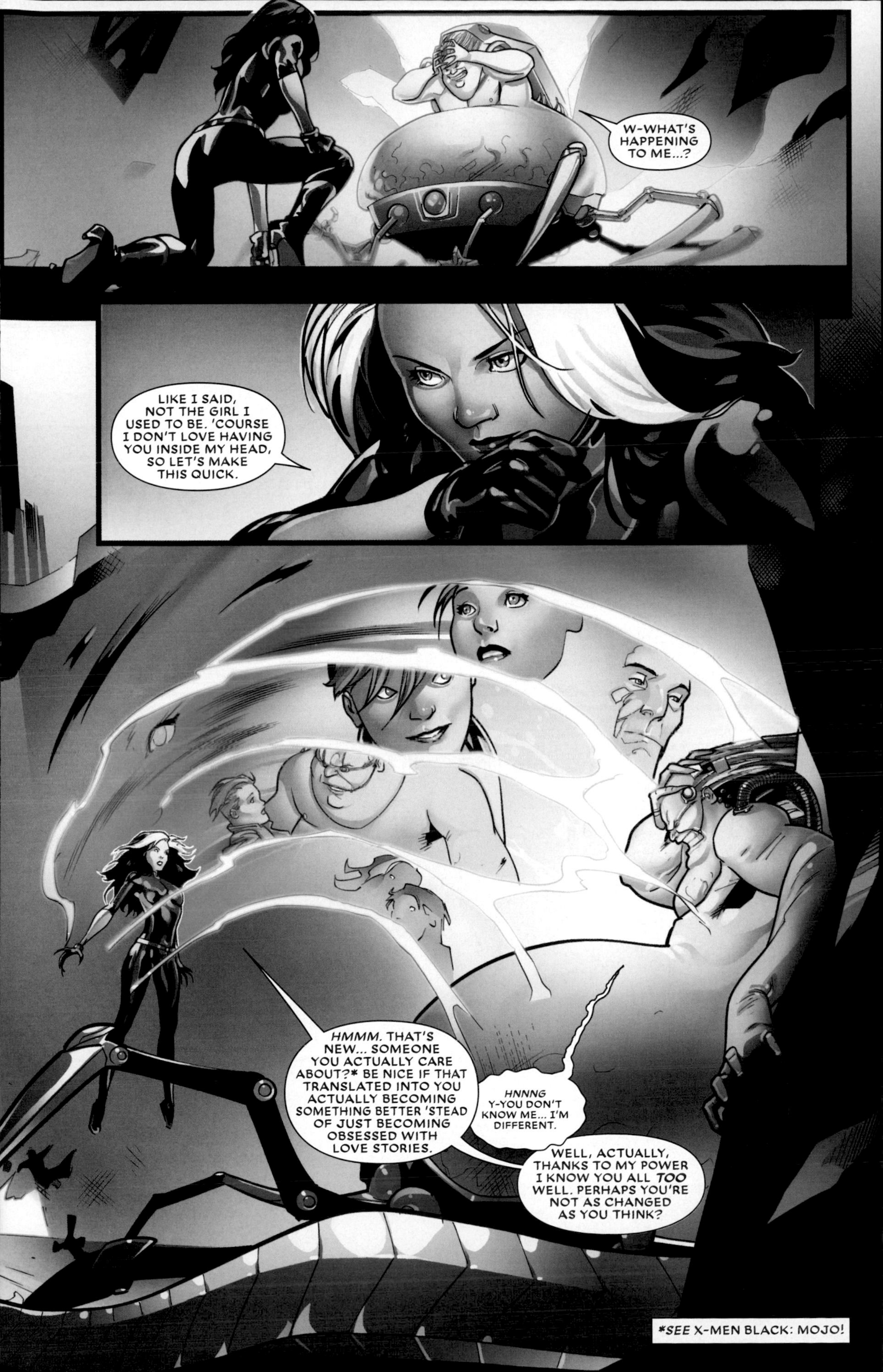
W-WHAT'S HAPPENING TO ME...?
LIKE I SAID, NOT THE GIRL I USED TO BE. 'COURSE I DON'T LOVE HAVING YOU INSIDE MY HEAD, SO LET'S MAKE THIS QUICK.
HMMM. THAT'S NEW... SOMEONE YOU ACTUALLY CARE ABOUT?* BE NICE IF THAT TRANSLATED INTO YOU ACTUALLY BECOMING SOMETHING BETTER 'STEAD OF JUST BECOMING OBSESSED WITH LOVE STORIES.
HNNNG Y-YOU DON'T KNOW ME... I'M DIFFERENT.
WELL, ACTUALLY, THANKS TO MY POWER I KNOW YOU ALL TOO WELL. PERHAPS YOU'RE NOT AS CHANGED AS YOU THINK?
*SEE X-MEN BLACK: MOJO!

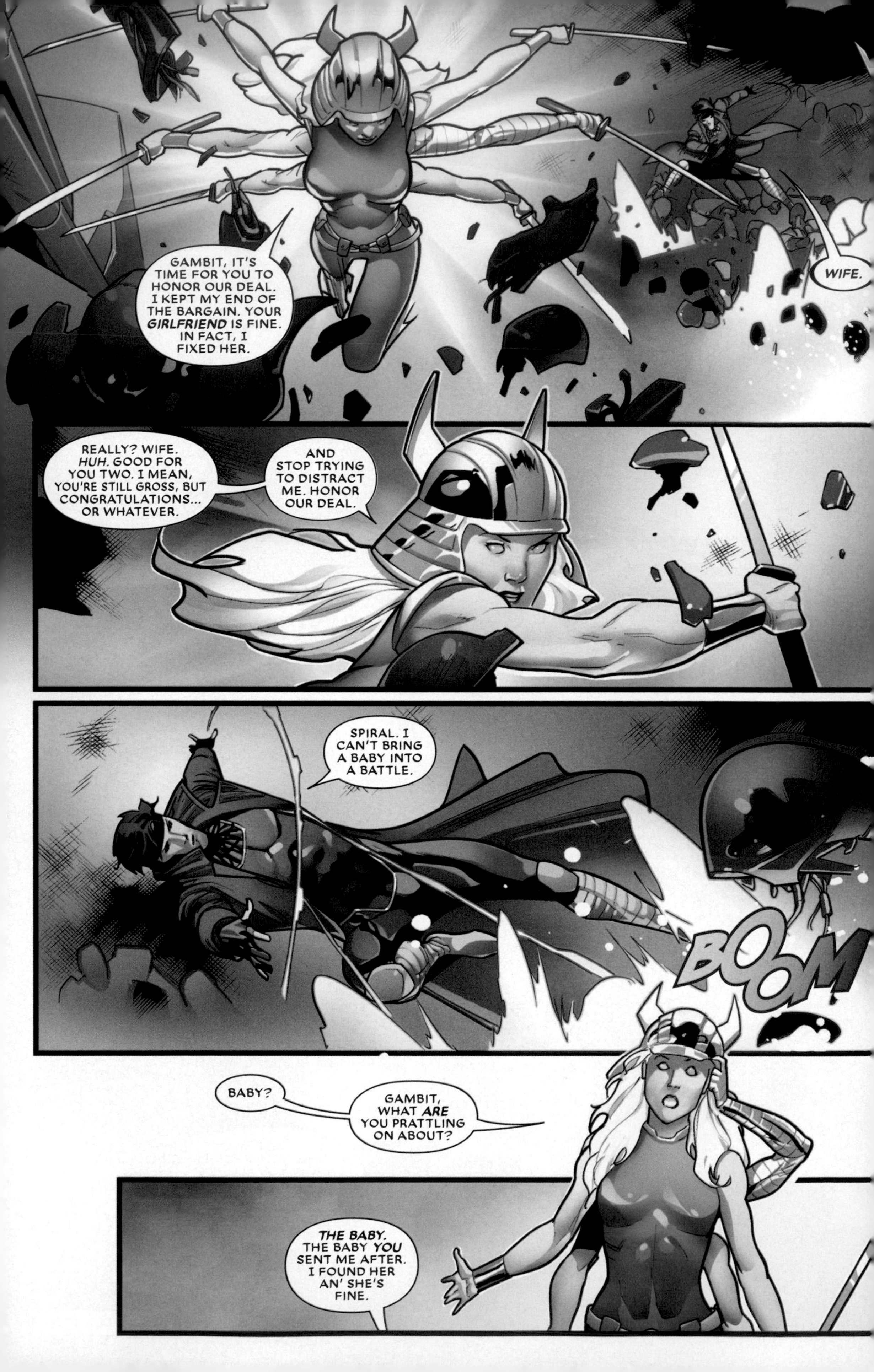
GAMBIT, IT'S TIME FOR YOU TO HONOR OUR DEAL. I KEPT MY END OF THE BARGAIN. YOUR GIRLFRIEND IS FINE. IN FACT, I FIXED HER.
WIFE.
REALLY? WIFE. HUH. GOOD FOR YOU TWO. I MEAN, YOU'RE STILL GROSS, BUT CONGRATULATIONS... OR WHATEVER.
AND STOP TRYING TO DISTRACT ME. HONOR OUR DEAL.
SPIRAL. I CAN'T BRING A BABY INTO A BATTLE.
BOOM
BABY?
GAMBIT, WHAT ARE YOU PRATTLING ON ABOUT?
THE BABY. THE BABY YOU SENT ME AFTER. I FOUND HER AN' SHE'S FINE.

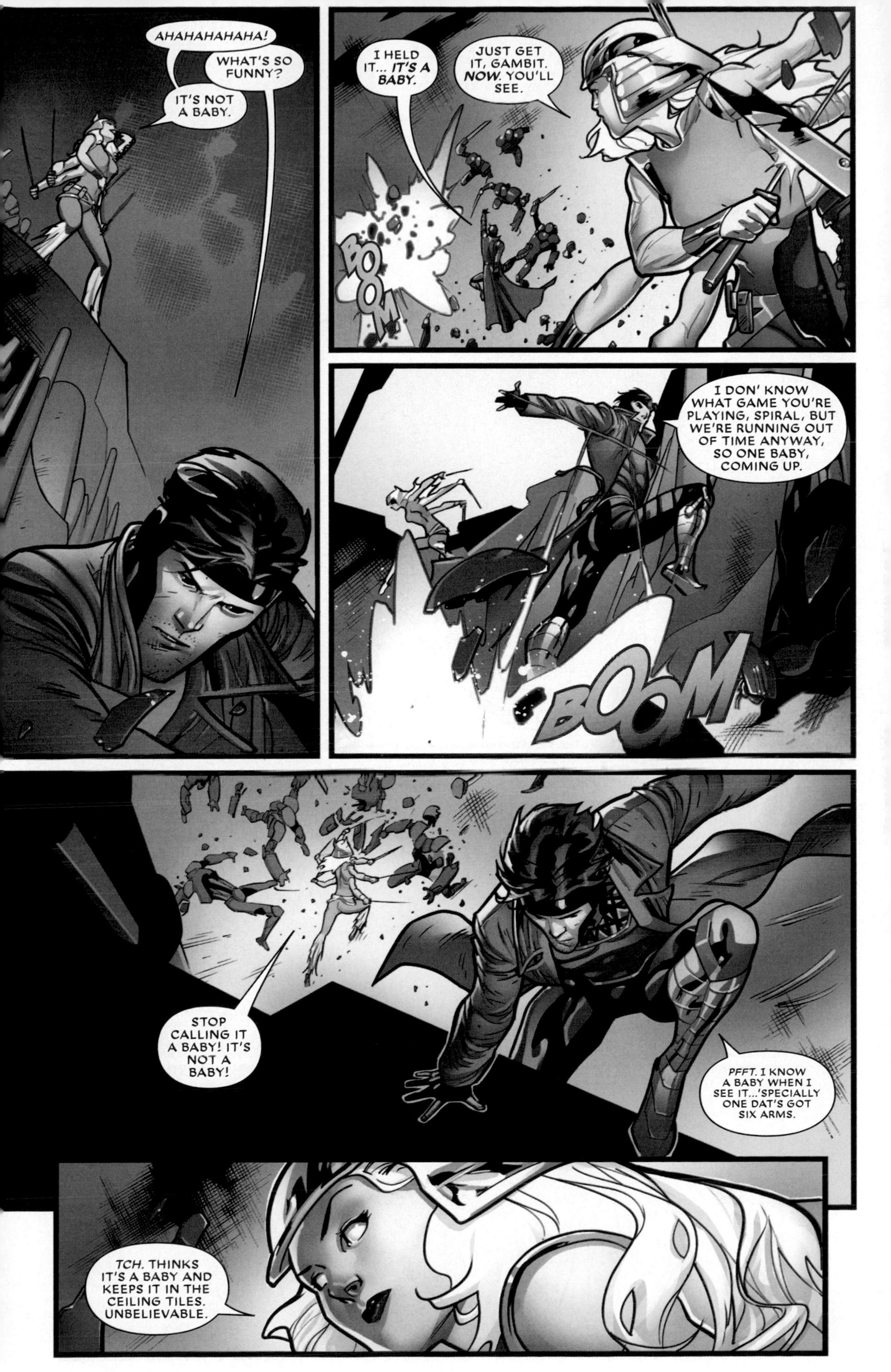
AHAHAHAHAHA!
WHAT'S SO FUNNY?
IT'S NOT A BABY.
I HELD IT... IT'S A BABY.
JUST GET IT, GAMBIT. NOW. YOU'LL SEE.
BOOM
I DON' KNOW WHAT GAME YOU'RE PLAYING, SPIRAL, BUT WE'RE RUNNING OUT OF TIME ANYWAY, SO ONE BABY, COMING UP.
BOOM
STOP CALLING IT A BABY! IT'S NOT A BABY!
PFFT. I KNOW A BABY WHEN I SEE IT...'SPECIALLY ONE DAT'S GOT SIX ARMS.
TCH. THINKS IT'S A BABY AND KEEPS IT IN THE CEILING TILES. UNBELIEVABLE.

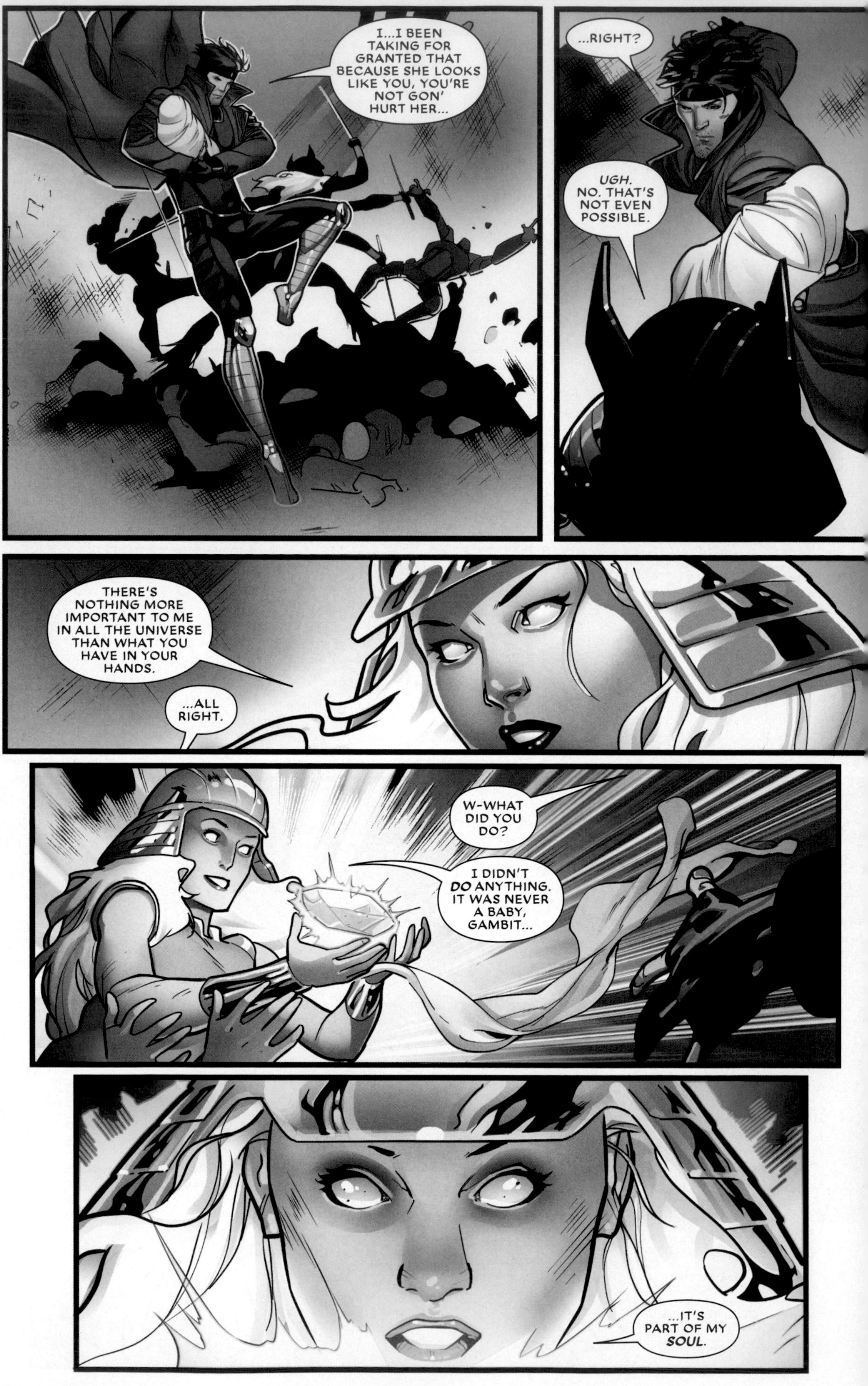
I...I BEEN TAKING FOR GRANTED THAT BECAUSE SHE LOOKS LIKE YOU, YOU'RE NOT GON' HURT HER...
...RIGHT?
UGH. NO. THAT'S NOT EVEN POSSIBLE.
THERE'S NOTHING MORE IMPORTANT TO ME IN ALL THE UNIVERSE THAN WHAT YOU HAVE IN YOUR HANDS.
...ALL RIGHT.
W-WHAT DID YOU DO?
I DIDN'T *DO* ANYTHING. IT WAS NEVER A BABY, GAMBIT...
...IT'S PART OF MY *SOUL*.

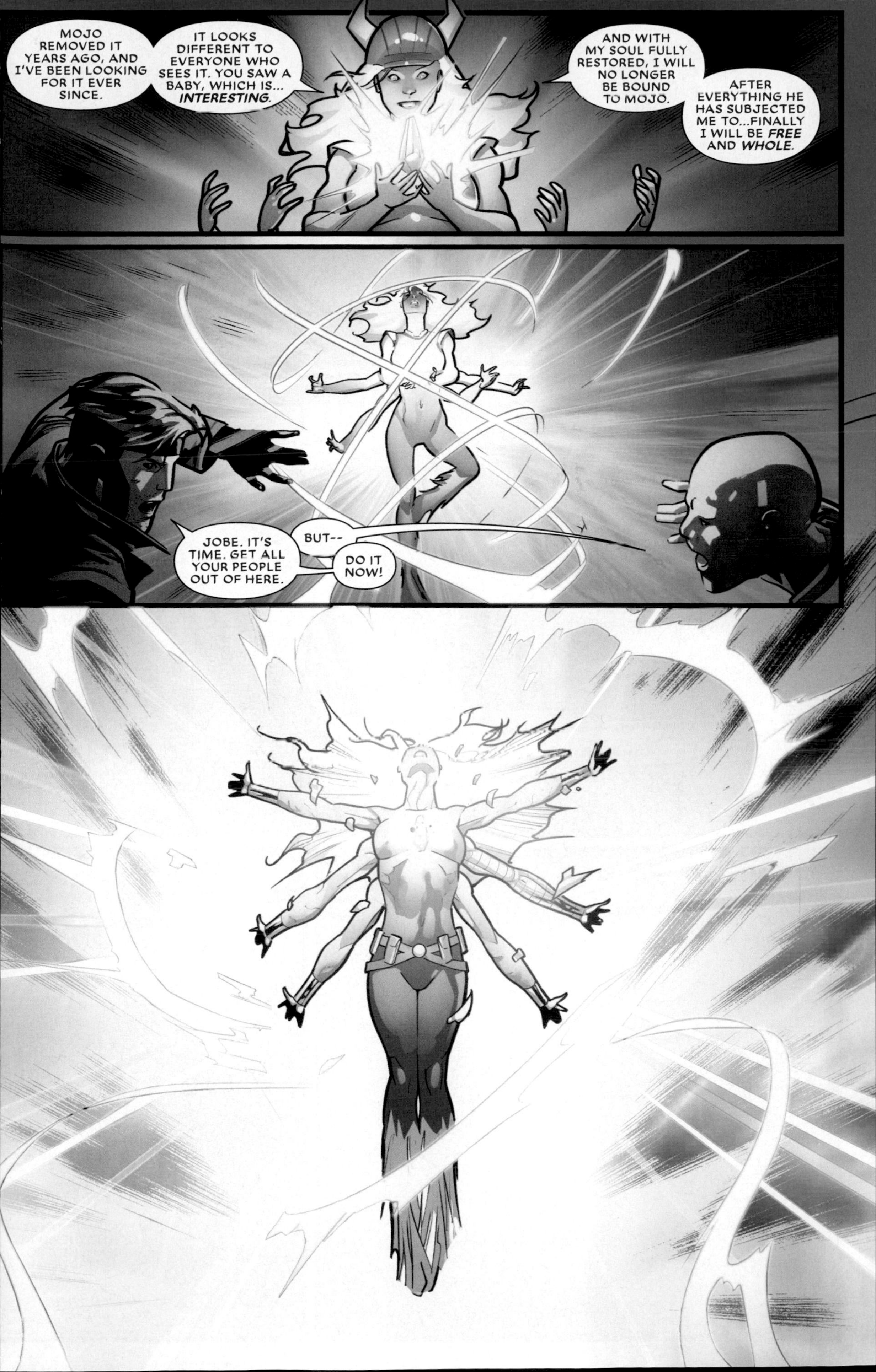
MOJO REMOVED IT YEARS AGO, AND I'VE BEEN LOOKING FOR IT EVER SINCE.
IT LOOKS DIFFERENT TO EVERYONE WHO SEES IT. YOU SAW A BABY, WHICH IS... INTERESTING.
AND WITH MY SOUL FULLY RESTORED, I WILL NO LONGER BE BOUND TO MOJO.
AFTER EVERYTHING HE HAS SUBJECTED ME TO...FINALLY I WILL BE FREE AND WHOLE.
JOBE. IT'S TIME. GET ALL YOUR PEOPLE OUT OF HERE.
BUT--
DO IT NOW!

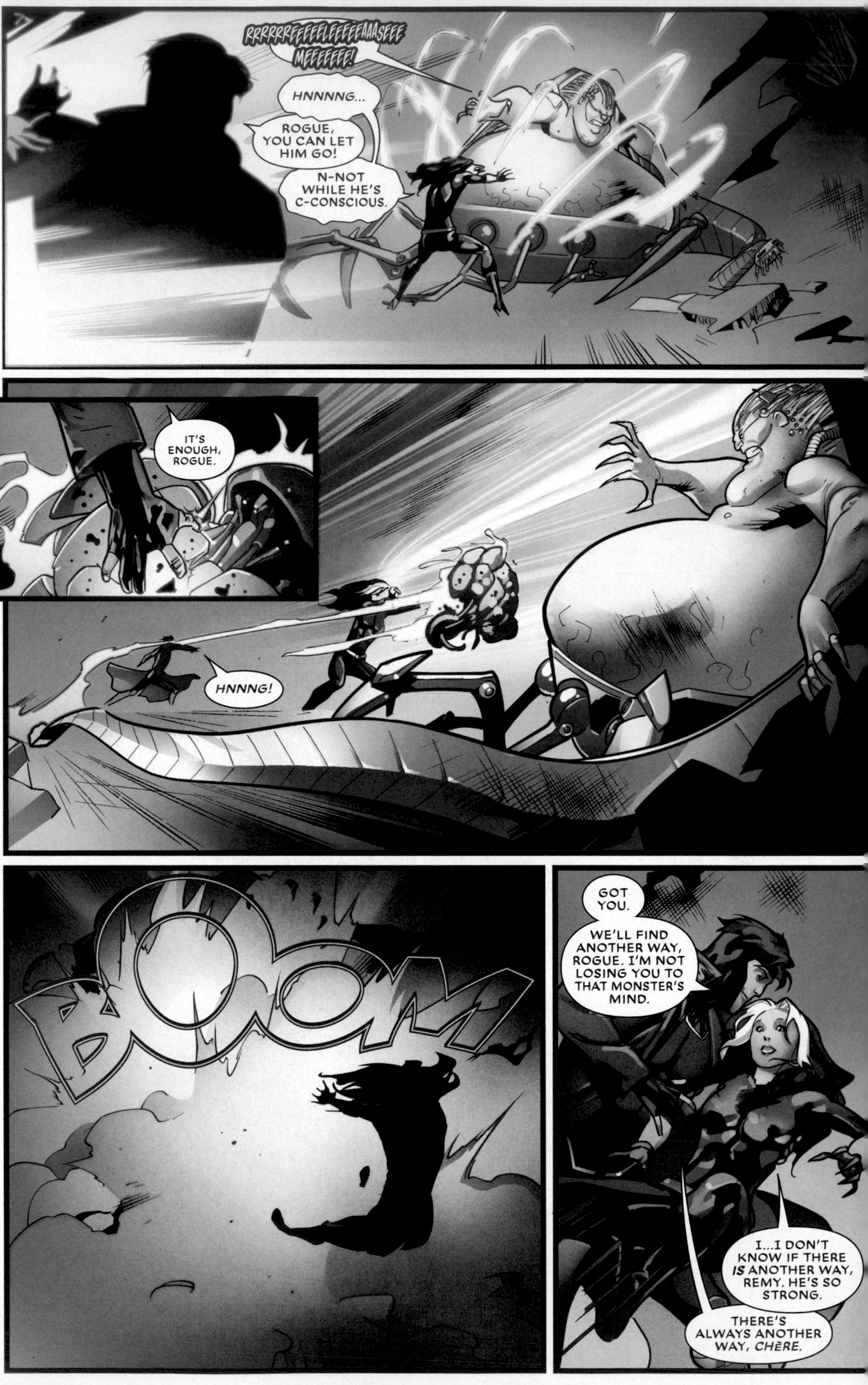
RRRRRREEEEELEEEEEAAASEEE MEEEEEEE!
HNNNNG...
ROGUE, YOU CAN LET HIM GO!
N-NOT WHILE HE'S C-CONSCIOUS.
IT'S ENOUGH, ROGUE.
HNNNG!
BOOM
GOT YOU.
WE'LL FIND ANOTHER WAY, ROGUE. I'M NOT LOSING YOU TO THAT MONSTER'S MIND.
I...I DON'T KNOW IF THERE IS ANOTHER WAY, REMY. HE'S SO STRONG.
THERE'S ALWAYS ANOTHER WAY, CHÈRE.

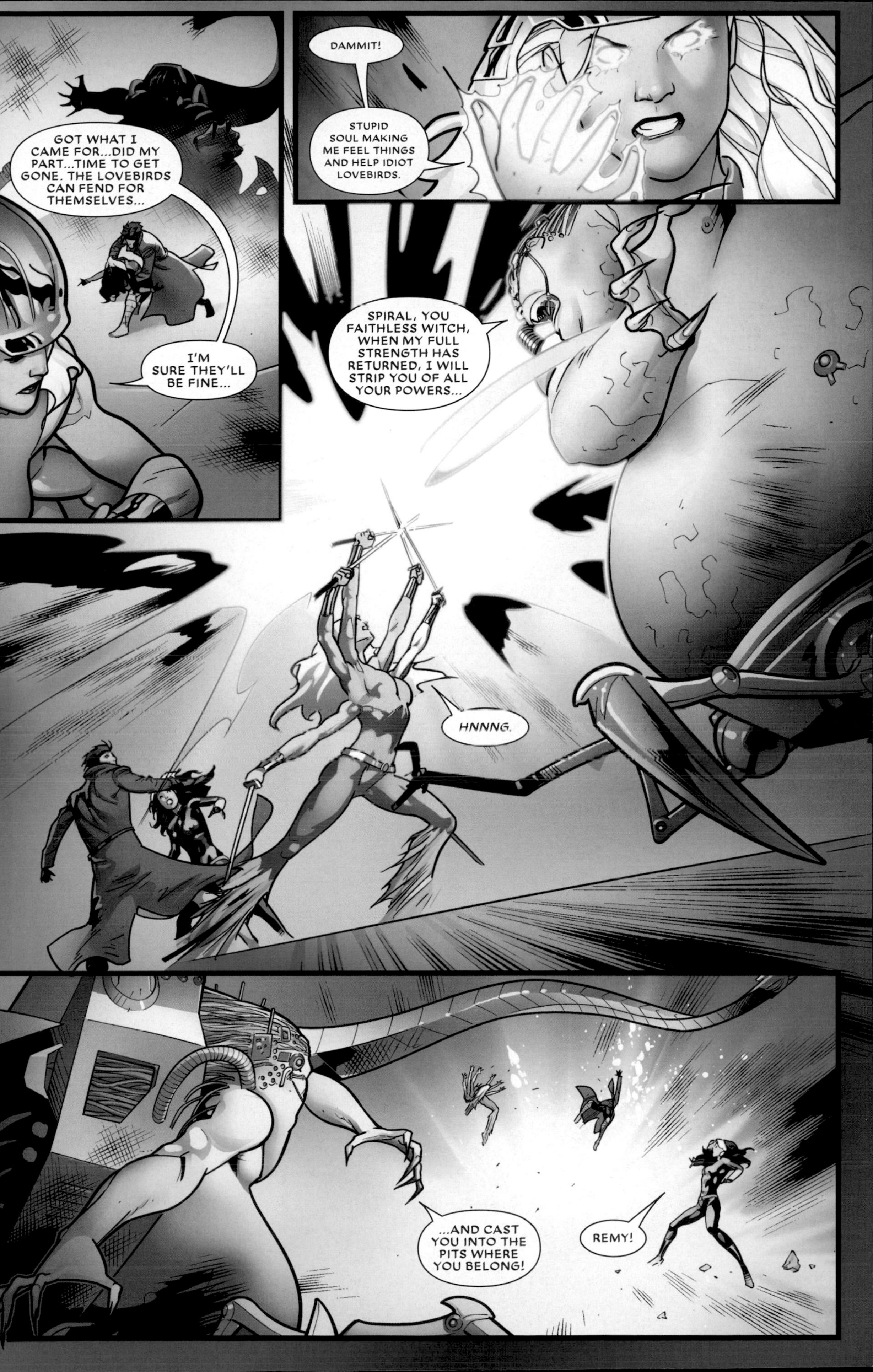
GOT WHAT I CAME FOR...DID MY PART...TIME TO GET GONE. THE LOVEBIRDS CAN FEND FOR THEMSELVES...
I'M SURE THEY'LL BE FINE...
DAMMIT!
STUPID SOUL MAKING ME FEEL THINGS AND HELP IDIOT LOVEBIRDS.
SPIRAL, YOU FAITHLESS WITCH, WHEN MY FULL STRENGTH HAS RETURNED, I WILL STRIP YOU OF ALL YOUR POWERS...
HNNNG.
...AND CAST YOU INTO THE PITS WHERE YOU BELONG!
REMY!

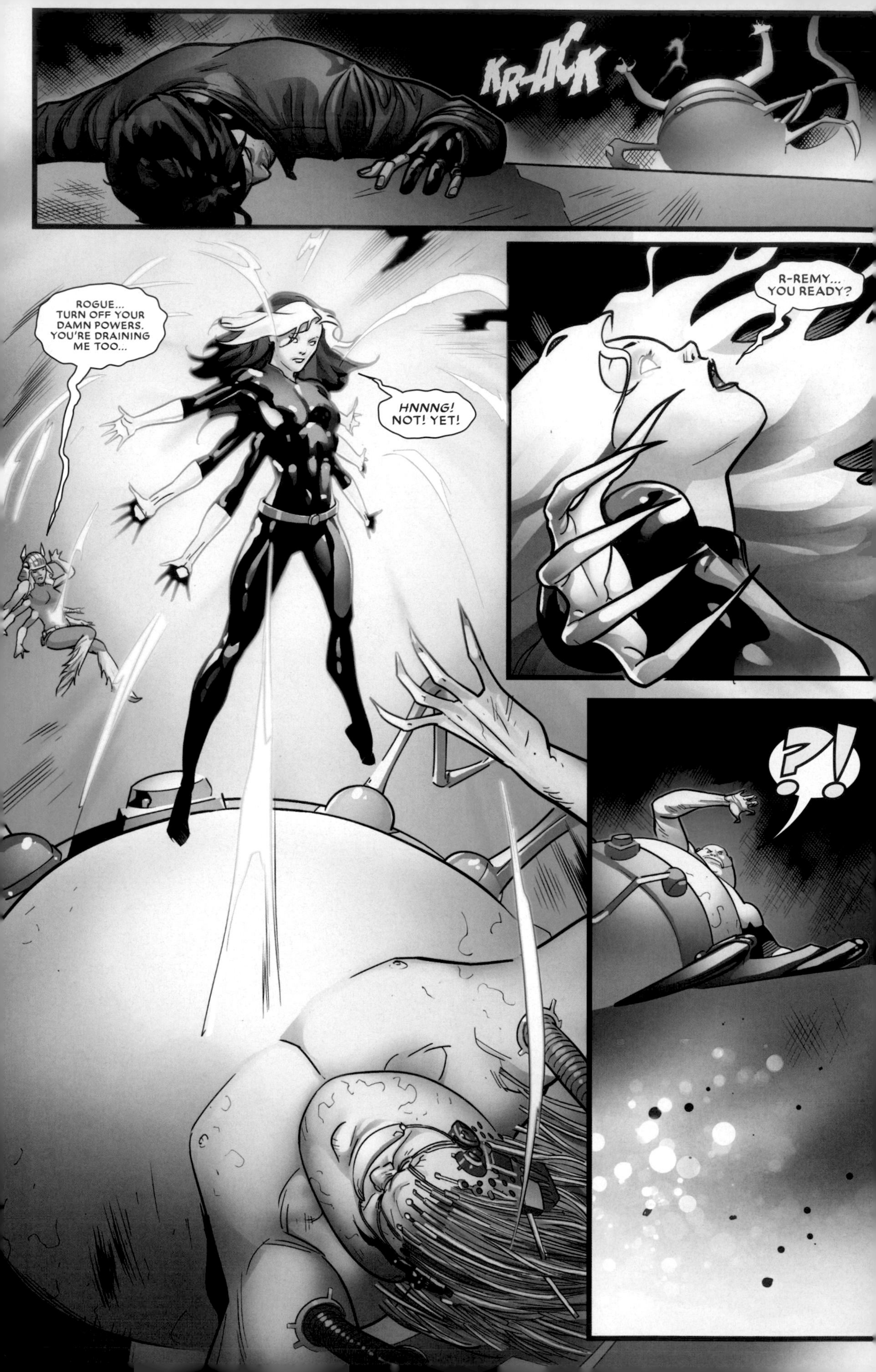
KR-ACK
ROGUE... TURN OFF YOUR DAMN POWERS. YOU'RE DRAINING ME TOO...
HNNNG! NOT! YET!
R-REMY... YOU READY?
?!

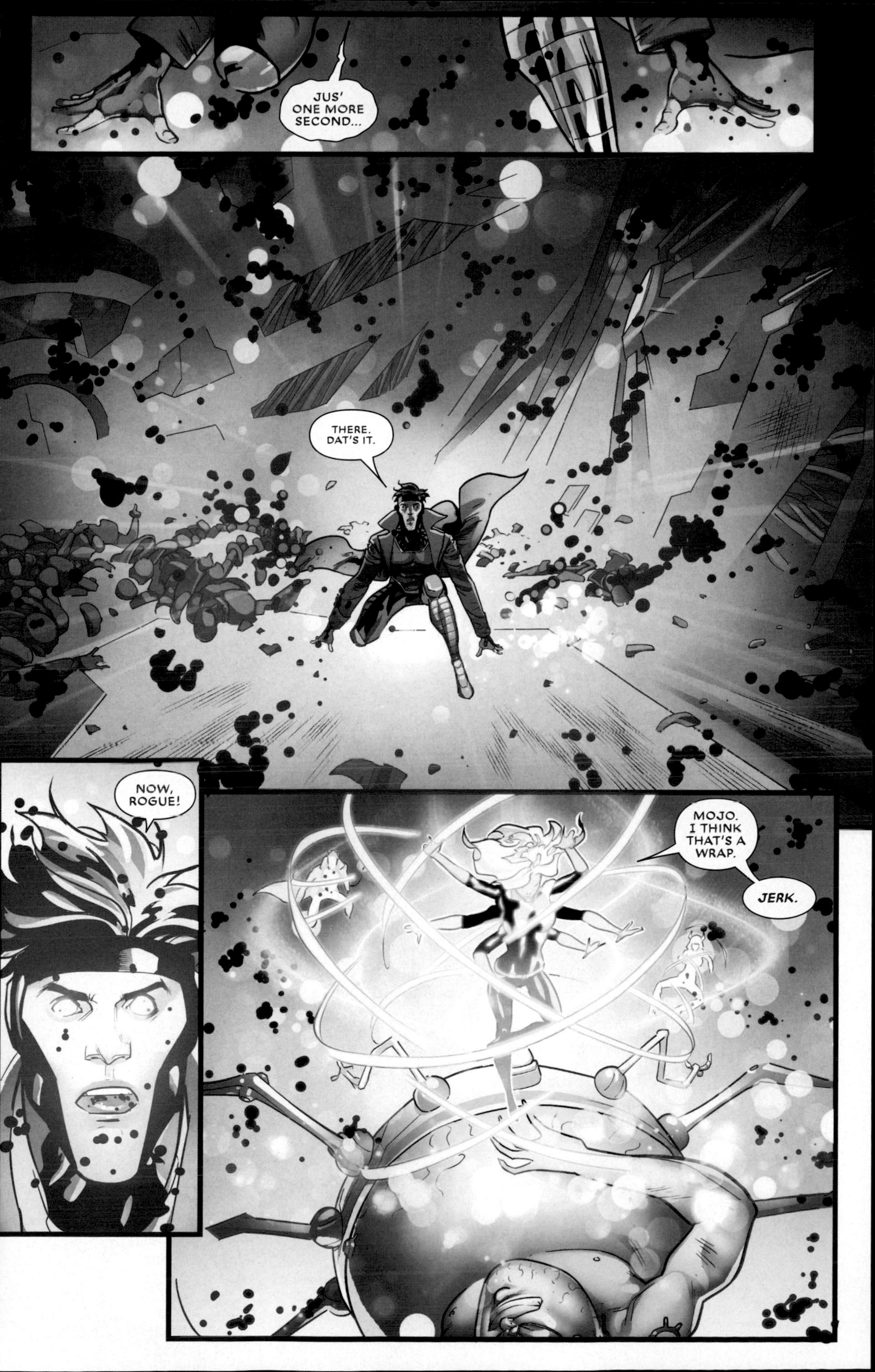

JUS' ONE MORE SECOND...
THERE. DAT'S IT.
NOW, ROGUE!
MOJO. I THINK THAT'S A WRAP.
JERK.

KA-BLOOM
LET NOBODY SAY YOU GUYS DON'T KNOW HOW TO PARTY.
ALTHOUGH, "JERK" IS THE BEST YOU COULD DO FOR A MEGALOMANIACAL TYRANT, ROGUE?
CUSSING AIN'T MY STRONG SUIT.
NO KIDDING.
DO YOU THINK WE ACTUALLY KILLED HIM?
I DOUBT IT. MOJO IS DISTURBINGLY HARD TO KILL.

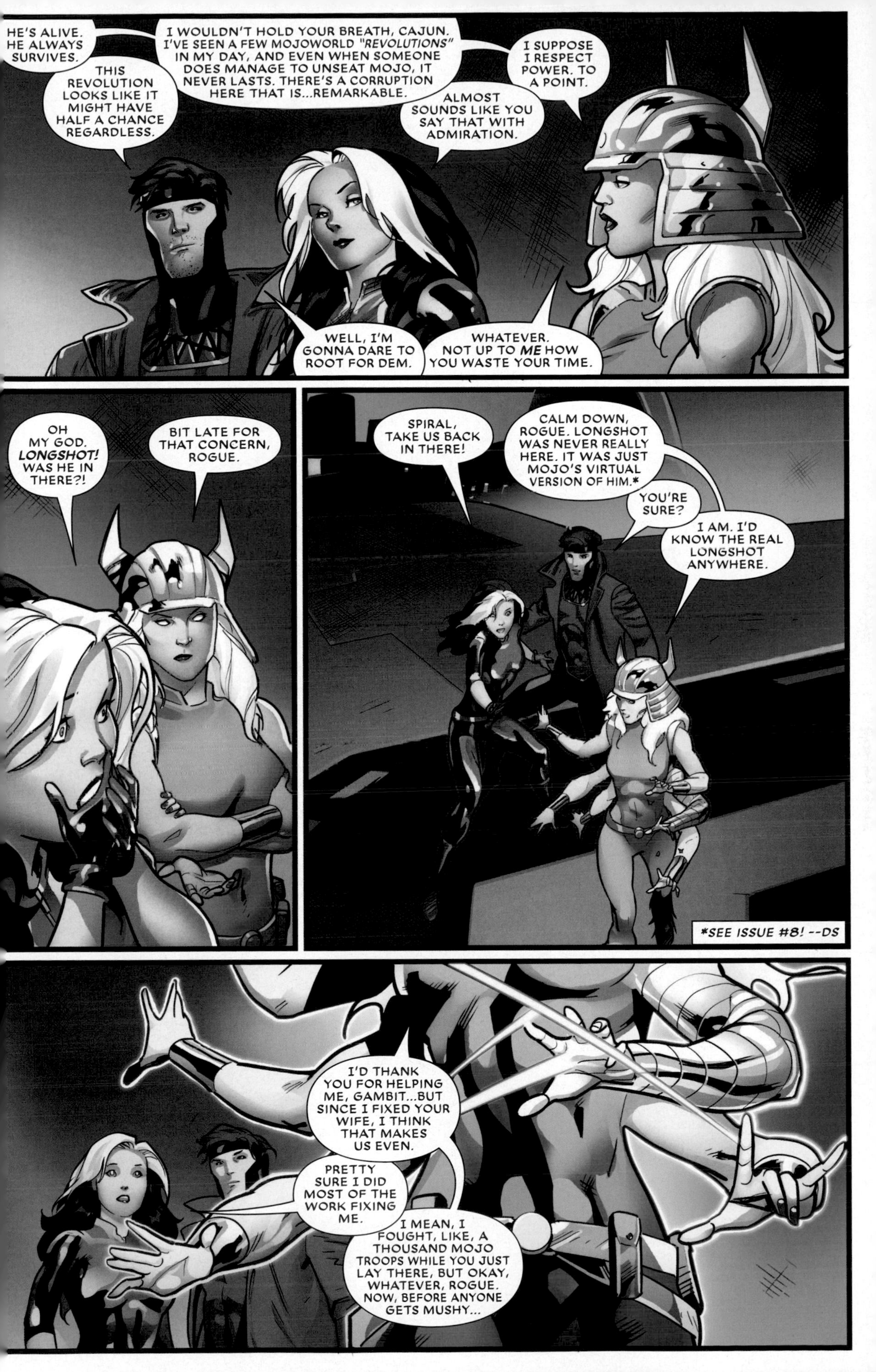
HE'S ALIVE. HE ALWAYS SURVIVES.
I WOULDN'T HOLD YOUR BREATH, CAJUN. I'VE SEEN A FEW MOJOWORLD "REVOLUTIONS" IN MY DAY, AND EVEN WHEN SOMEONE DOES MANAGE TO UNSEAT MOJO, IT NEVER LASTS. THERE'S A CORRUPTION HERE THAT IS...REMARKABLE.
THIS REVOLUTION LOOKS LIKE IT MIGHT HAVE HALF A CHANCE REGARDLESS.
I SUPPOSE I RESPECT POWER. TO A POINT.
ALMOST SOUNDS LIKE YOU SAY THAT WITH ADMIRATION.
WELL, I'M GONNA DARE TO ROOT FOR DEM.
WHATEVER. NOT UP TO ME HOW YOU WASTE YOUR TIME.
OH MY GOD. LONGSHOT! WAS HE IN THERE?!
BIT LATE FOR THAT CONCERN, ROGUE.
SPIRAL, TAKE US BACK IN THERE!
CALM DOWN, ROGUE. LONGSHOT WAS NEVER REALLY HERE. IT WAS JUST MOJO'S VIRTUAL VERSION OF HIM.*
YOU'RE SURE?
I AM. I'D KNOW THE REAL LONGSHOT ANYWHERE.
*SEE ISSUE #8! --DS
I'D THANK YOU FOR HELPING ME, GAMBIT...BUT SINCE I FIXED YOUR WIFE, I THINK THAT MAKES US EVEN.
PRETTY SURE I DID MOST OF THE WORK FIXING ME.
I MEAN, I FOUGHT, LIKE, A THOUSAND MOJO TROOPS WHILE YOU JUST LAY THERE, BUT OKAY, WHATEVER, ROGUE. NOW, BEFORE ANYONE GETS MUSHY...

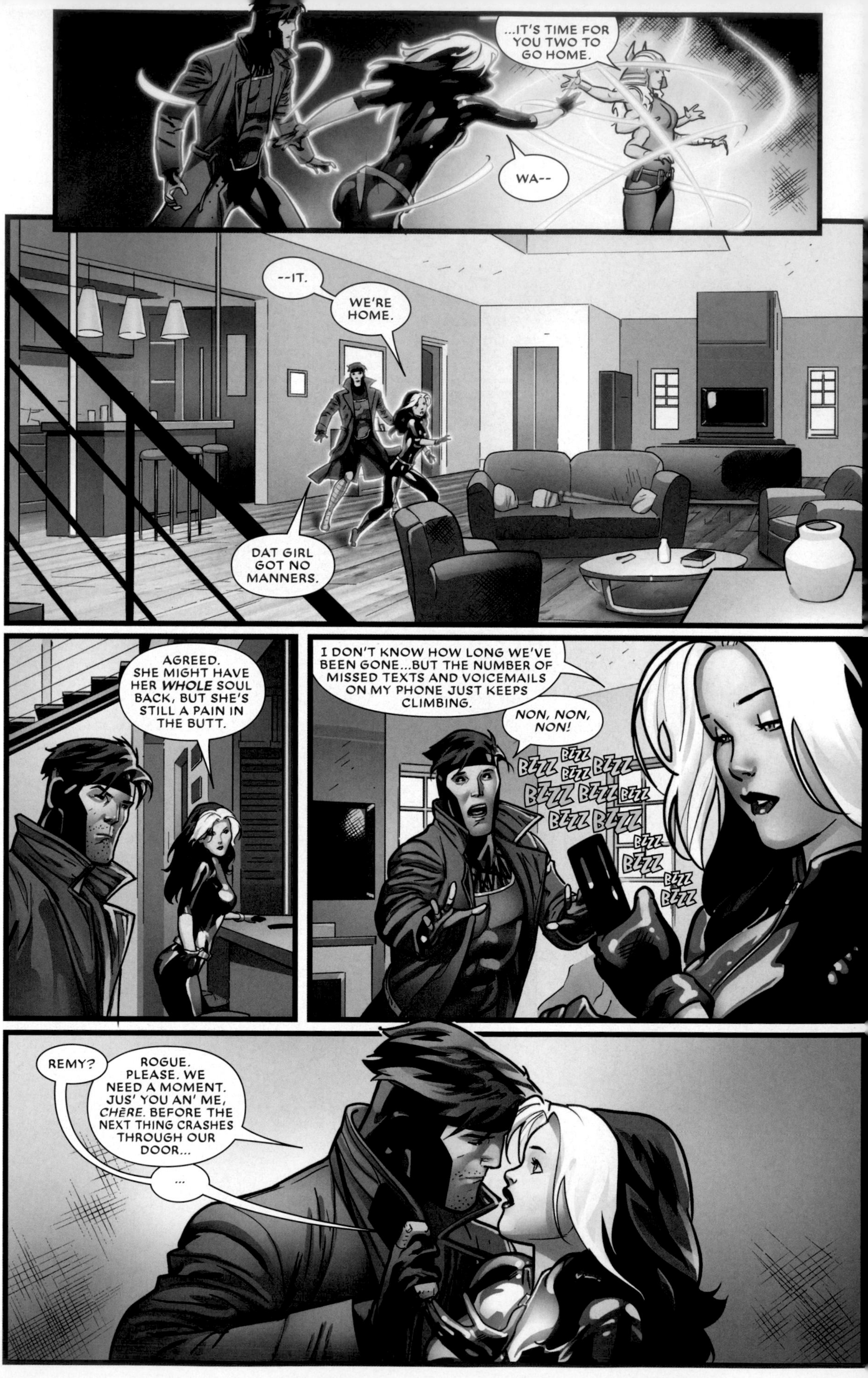
...IT'S TIME FOR YOU TWO TO GO HOME.
WA--
--IT.
WE'RE HOME.
DAT GIRL GOT NO MANNERS.
AGREED. SHE MIGHT HAVE HER *WHOLE* SOUL BACK, BUT SHE'S STILL A PAIN IN THE BUTT.
I DON'T KNOW HOW LONG WE'VE BEEN GONE...BUT THE NUMBER OF MISSED TEXTS AND VOICEMAILS ON MY PHONE JUST KEEPS CLIMBING.
NON, NON, NON!
BZZZ BZZZ BZZZ BZZZ BZZZ BZZZ BZZZ BZZZ BZZZ BZZZ BZZZ BZZZ BZZZ BZZZ
REMY?
ROGUE. PLEASE. WE NEED A MOMENT. JUS' YOU AN' ME, *CHÈRE*. BEFORE THE NEXT THING CRASHES THROUGH OUR DOOR...
...

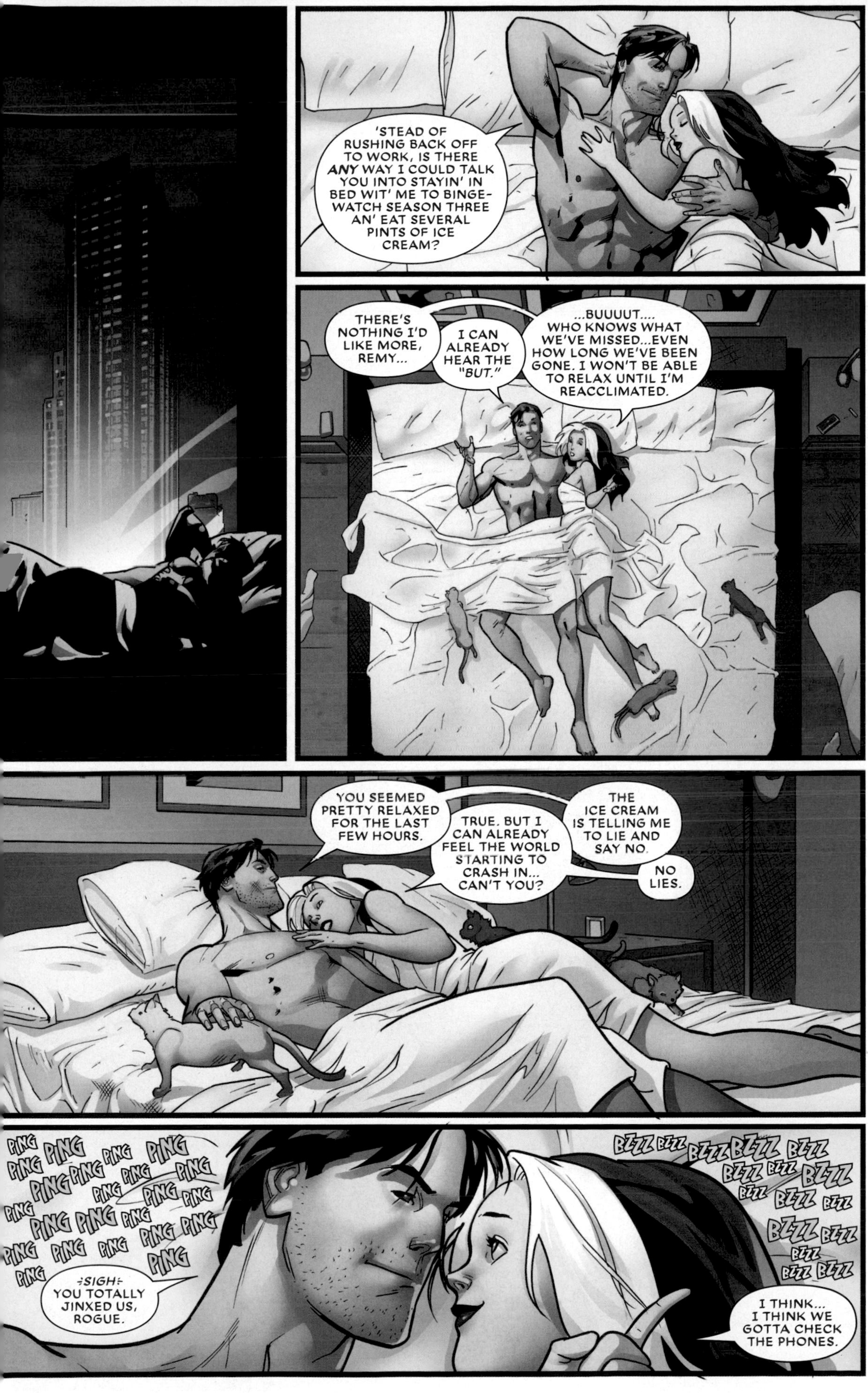
'STEAD OF RUSHING BACK OFF TO WORK, IS THERE ANY WAY I COULD TALK YOU INTO STAYIN' IN BED WIT' ME TO BINGE-WATCH SEASON THREE AN' EAT SEVERAL PINTS OF ICE CREAM?
THERE'S NOTHING I'D LIKE MORE, REMY...
I CAN ALREADY HEAR THE "BUT."
...BUUUUT.... WHO KNOWS WHAT WE'VE MISSED...EVEN HOW LONG WE'VE BEEN GONE. I WON'T BE ABLE TO RELAX UNTIL I'M REACCLIMATED.
YOU SEEMED PRETTY RELAXED FOR THE LAST FEW HOURS.
TRUE. BUT I CAN ALREADY FEEL THE WORLD STARTING TO CRASH IN... CAN'T YOU?
THE ICE CREAM IS TELLING ME TO LIE AND SAY NO.
NO LIES.
PING PING PING PING PING PING PING PING PING PING PING PING PING PING PING PING PING PING PING PING PING PING PING PING
BZZZ BZZZ BZZZ BZZZ BZZZ BZZZ BZZZ BZZZ BZZZ BZZZ BZZZ BZZZ BZZZ BZZZ BZZZ BZZZ
SIGH
YOU TOTALLY JINXED US, ROGUE.
I THINK... I THINK WE GOTTA CHECK THE PHONES.

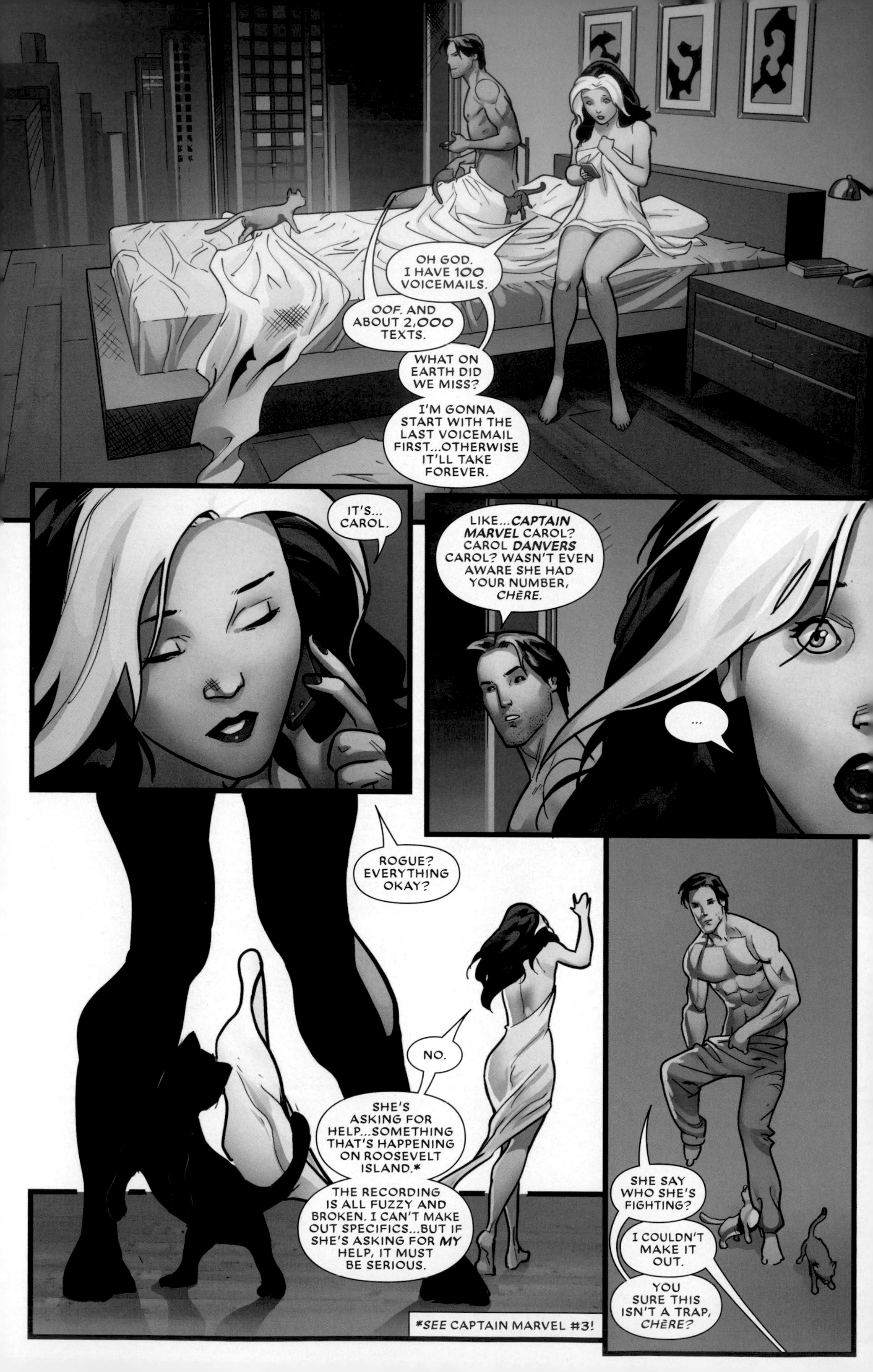

OH GOD. I HAVE 100 VOICEMAILS.
OOF. AND ABOUT 2,000 TEXTS.
WHAT ON EARTH DID WE MISS?
I'M GONNA START WITH THE LAST VOICEMAIL FIRST...OTHERWISE IT'LL TAKE FOREVER.
IT'S... CAROL.
LIKE...CAPTAIN MARVEL CAROL? CAROL DANVERS CAROL? WASN'T EVEN AWARE SHE HAD YOUR NUMBER, CHÈRE.
...
ROGUE? EVERYTHING OKAY?
NO.
SHE'S ASKING FOR HELP...SOMETHING THAT'S HAPPENING ON ROOSEVELT ISLAND.*
THE RECORDING IS ALL FUZZY AND BROKEN. I CAN'T MAKE OUT SPECIFICS...BUT IF SHE'S ASKING FOR MY HELP, IT MUST BE SERIOUS.
*SEE CAPTAIN MARVEL #3!
SHE SAY WHO SHE'S FIGHTING?
I COULDN'T MAKE IT OUT.
YOU SURE THIS ISN'T A TRAP, CHÈRE?

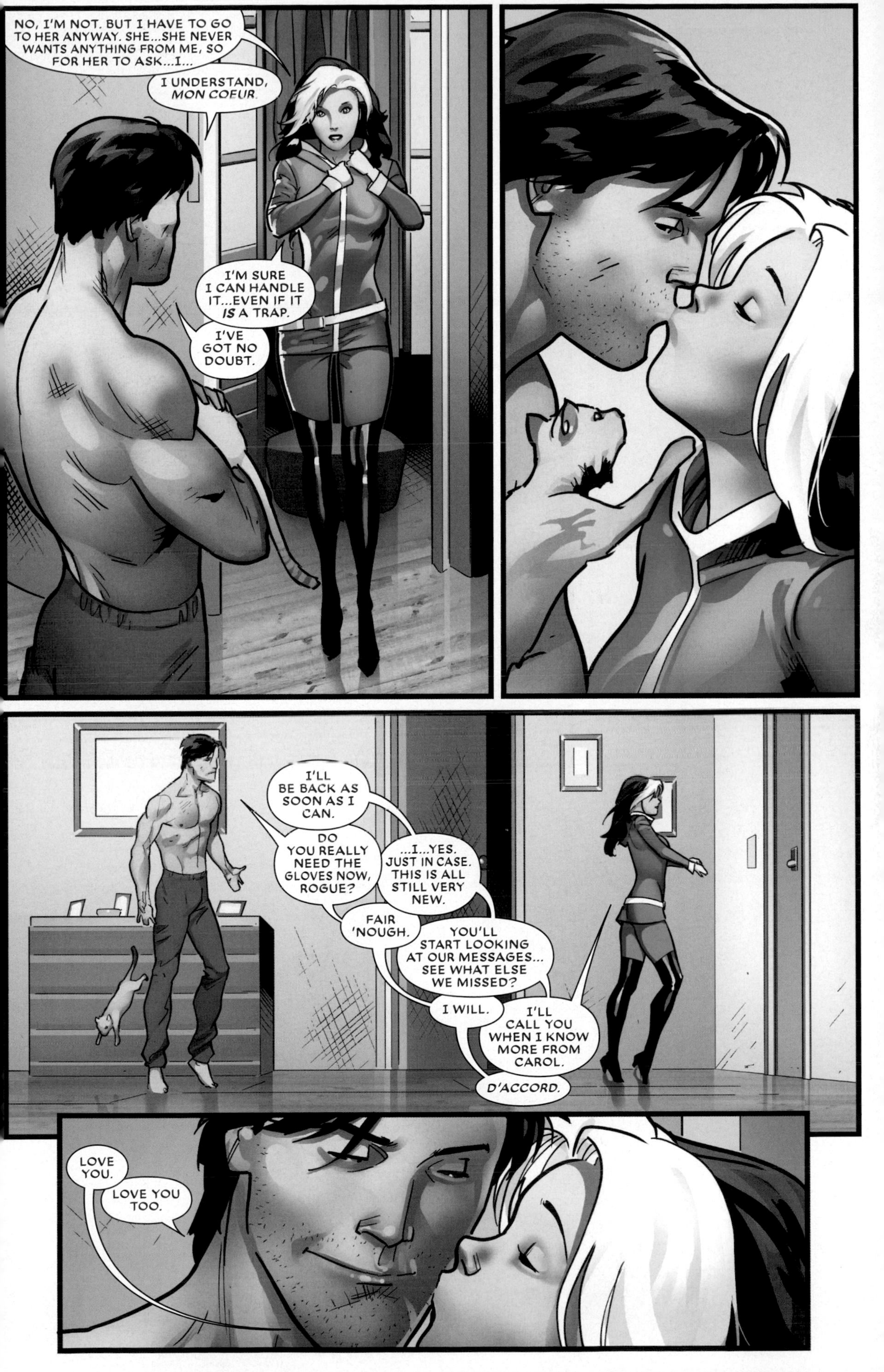
NO, I'M NOT. BUT I HAVE TO GO TO HER ANYWAY. SHE...SHE NEVER WANTS ANYTHING FROM ME, SO FOR HER TO ASK...I...
I UNDERSTAND, *MON COEUR.*
I'M SURE I CAN HANDLE IT...EVEN IF IT *IS* A TRAP.
I'VE GOT NO DOUBT.
I'LL BE BACK AS SOON AS I CAN.
DO YOU REALLY NEED THE GLOVES NOW, ROGUE?
...I...YES. JUST IN CASE. THIS IS ALL STILL VERY NEW.
FAIR 'NOUGH.
YOU'LL START LOOKING AT OUR MESSAGES... SEE WHAT ELSE WE MISSED?
I WILL.
I'LL CALL YOU WHEN I KNOW MORE FROM CAROL.
D'ACCORD.
LOVE YOU.
LOVE YOU TOO.

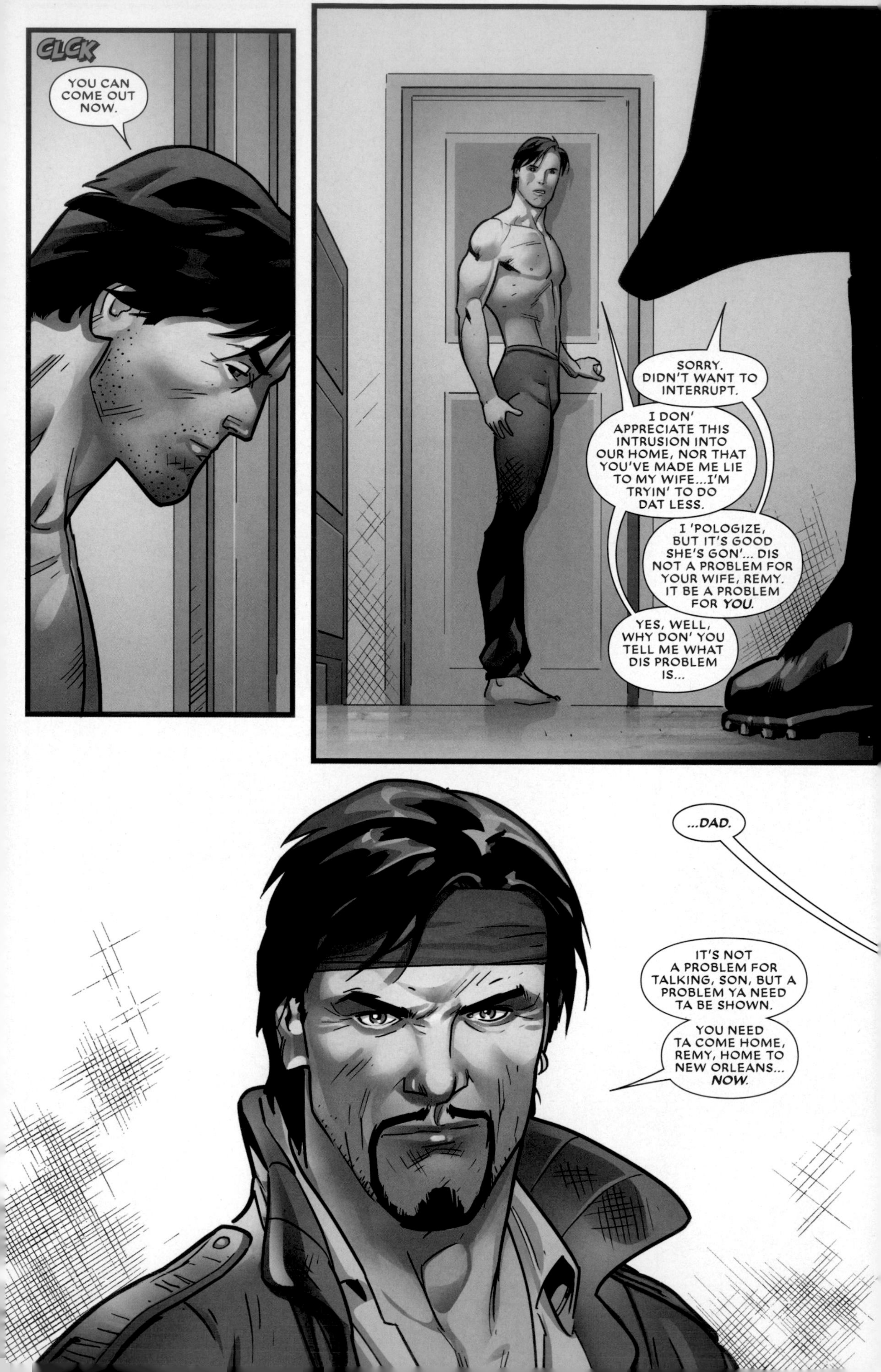
CLCK
YOU CAN COME OUT NOW.
SORRY. DIDN'T WANT TO INTERRUPT.
I DON' APPRECIATE THIS INTRUSION INTO OUR HOME, NOR THAT YOU'VE MADE ME LIE TO MY WIFE...I'M TRYIN' TO DO DAT LESS.
I 'POLOGIZE, BUT IT'S GOOD SHE'S GON'... DIS NOT A PROBLEM FOR YOUR WIFE, REMY. IT BE A PROBLEM FOR *YOU*.
YES, WELL, WHY DON' YOU TELL ME WHAT DIS PROBLEM IS...
...DAD.
IT'S NOT A PROBLEM FOR TALKING, SON, BUT A PROBLEM YA NEED TA BE SHOWN.
YOU NEED TA COME HOME, REMY, HOME TO NEW ORLEANS... *NOW*.

11

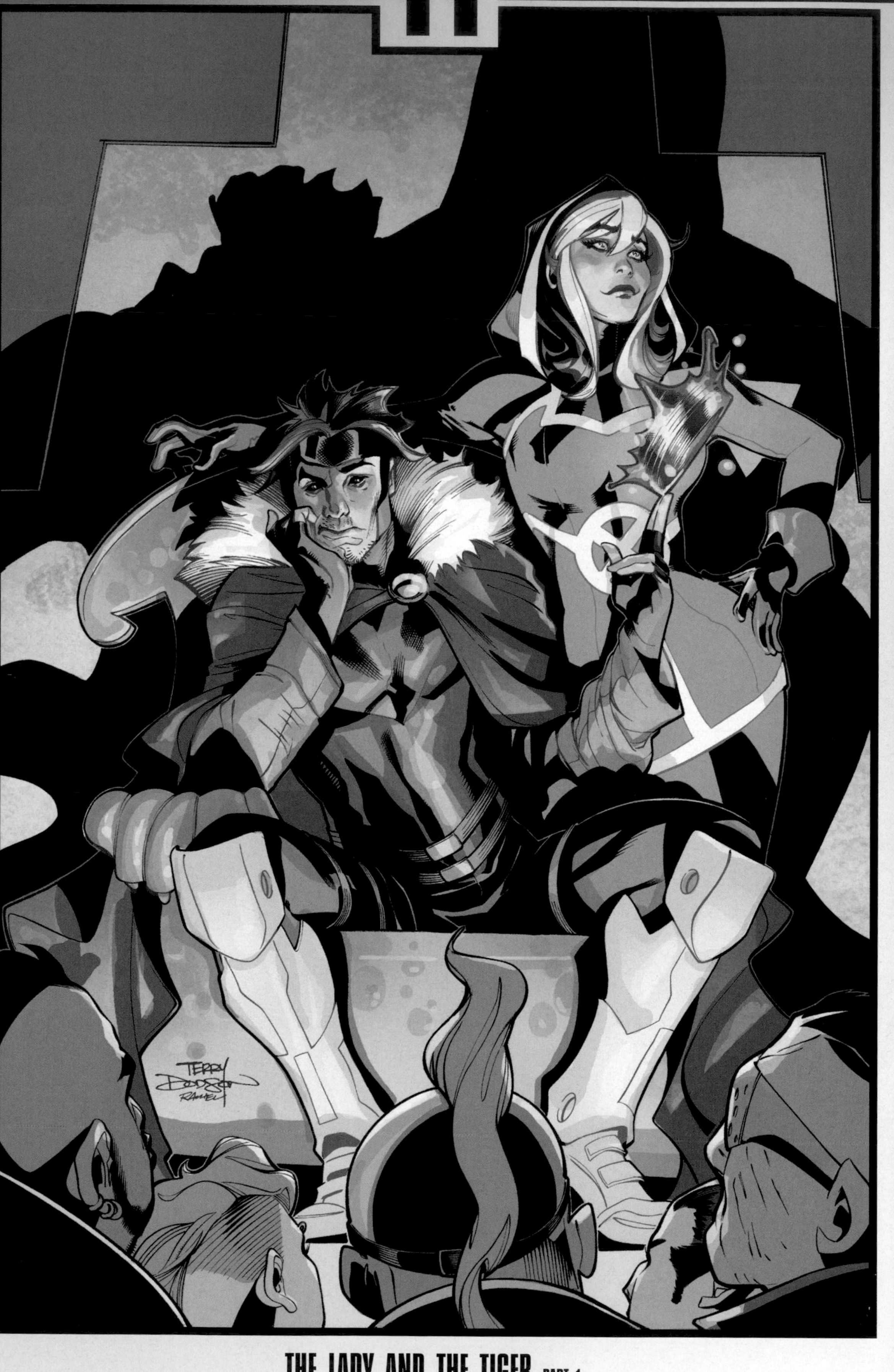

THE LADY AND THE TIGER PART 1

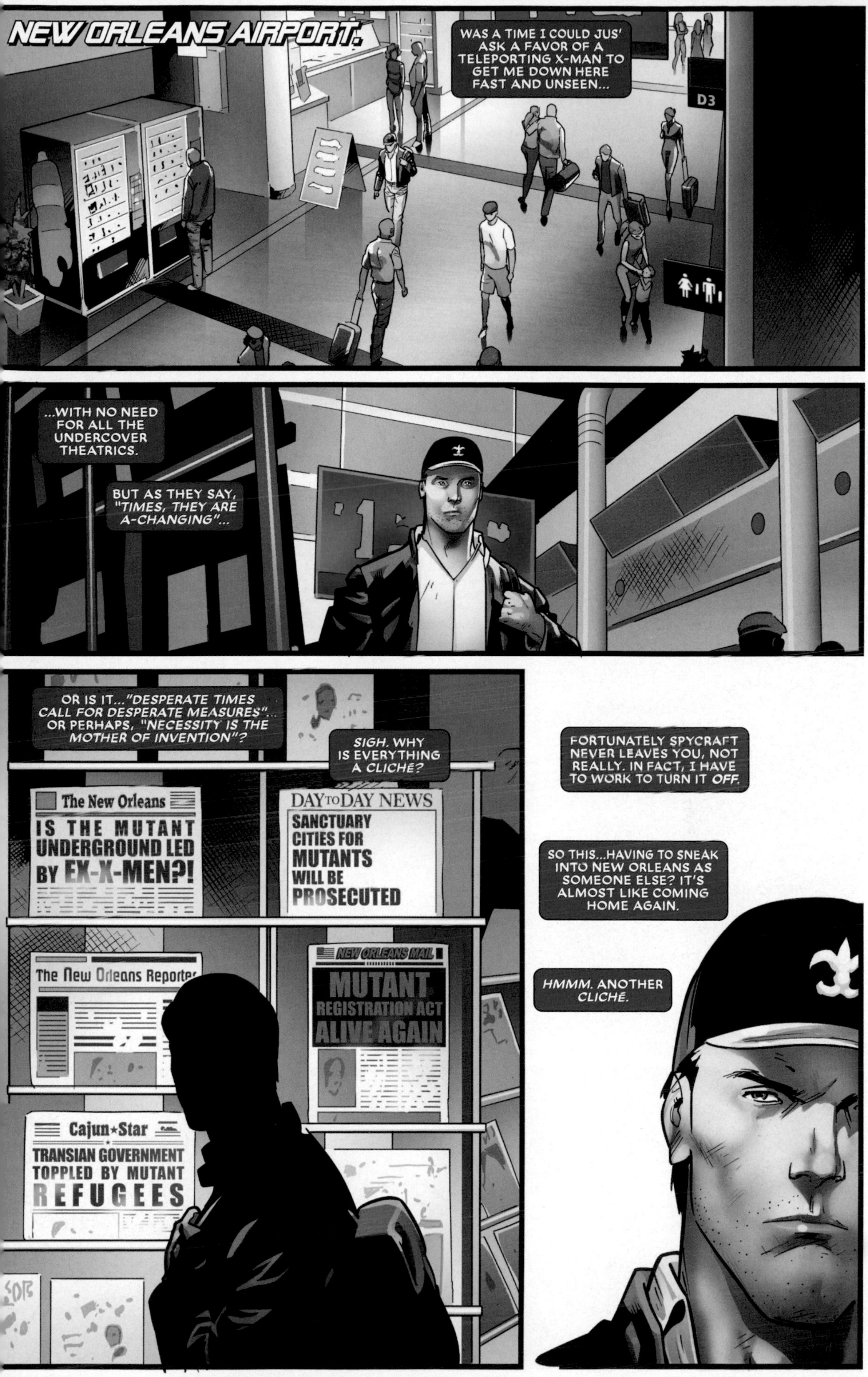
NEW ORLEANS AIRPORT.
WAS A TIME I COULD JUS' ASK A FAVOR OF A TELEPORTING X-MAN TO GET ME DOWN HERE FAST AND UNSEEN...
D3
...WITH NO NEED FOR ALL THE UNDERCOVER THEATRICS.
BUT AS THEY SAY, "TIMES, THEY ARE A-CHANGING"...
OR IS IT..."DESPERATE TIMES CALL FOR DESPERATE MEASURES"... OR PERHAPS, "NECESSITY IS THE MOTHER OF INVENTION"?
SIGH. WHY IS EVERYTHING A CLICHÉ?
The New Orleans
IS THE MUTANT UNDERGROUND LED BY EX-X-MEN?!
DAY TO DAY NEWS
SANCTUARY CITIES FOR MUTANTS WILL BE PROSECUTED
The New Orleans Reporter
NEW ORLEANS MAIL
MUTANT REGISTRATION ACT ALIVE AGAIN
Cajun★Star
TRANSIAN GOVERNMENT TOPPLED BY MUTANT REFUGEES
FORTUNATELY SPYCRAFT NEVER LEAVES YOU, NOT REALLY. IN FACT, I HAVE TO WORK TO TURN IT OFF.
SO THIS...HAVING TO SNEAK INTO NEW ORLEANS AS SOMEONE ELSE? IT'S ALMOST LIKE COMING HOME AGAIN.
HMMM. ANOTHER CLICHÉ.

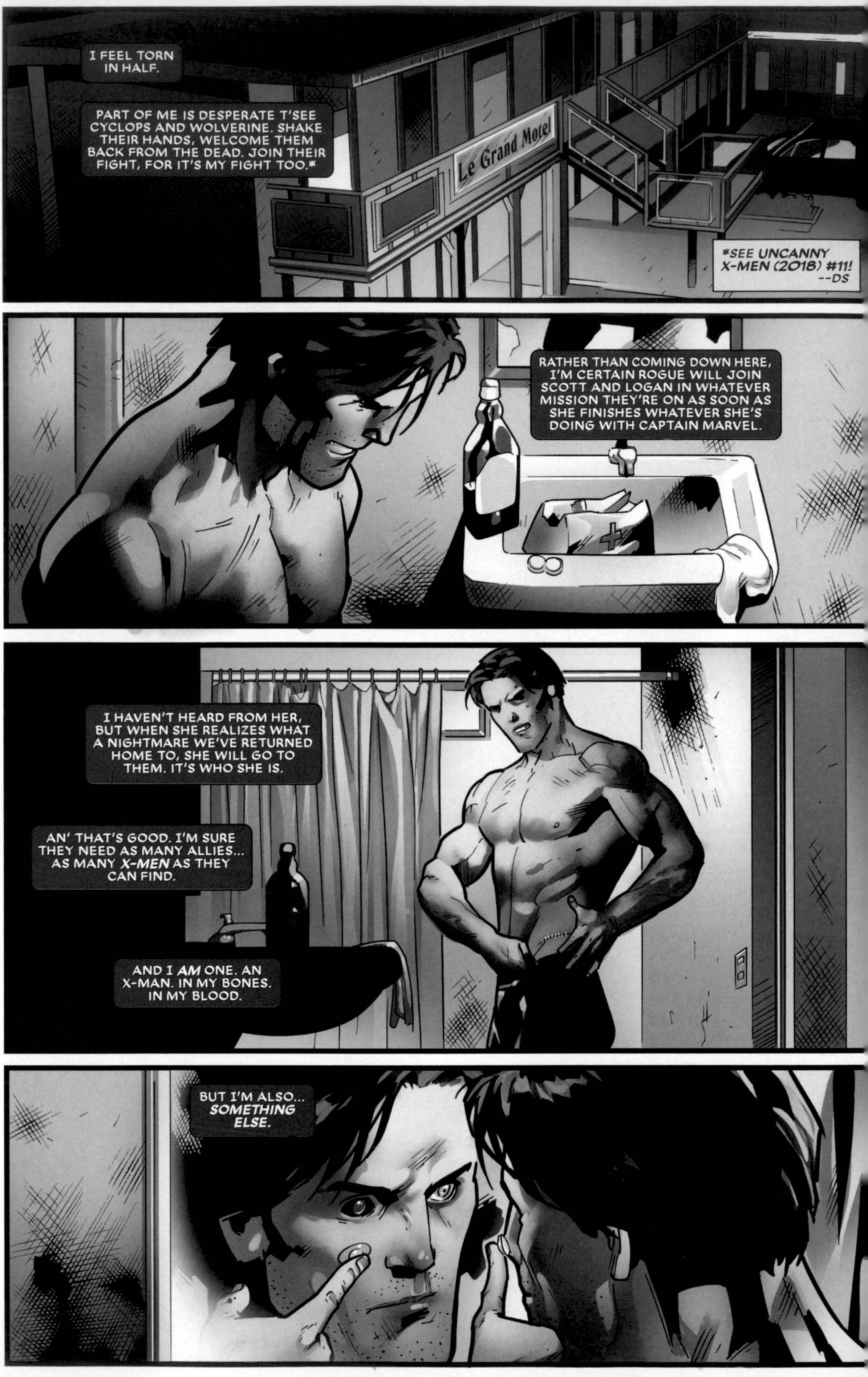
I FEEL TORN IN HALF.
PART OF ME IS DESPERATE T'SEE CYCLOPS AND WOLVERINE. SHAKE THEIR HANDS, WELCOME THEM BACK FROM THE DEAD. JOIN THEIR FIGHT, FOR IT'S MY FIGHT TOO.*
Le Grand Motel
*SEE UNCANNY X-MEN (2018) #11! --DS
RATHER THAN COMING DOWN HERE, I'M CERTAIN ROGUE WILL JOIN SCOTT AND LOGAN IN WHATEVER MISSION THEY'RE ON AS SOON AS SHE FINISHES WHATEVER SHE'S DOING WITH CAPTAIN MARVEL.
I HAVEN'T HEARD FROM HER, BUT WHEN SHE REALIZES WHAT A NIGHTMARE WE'VE RETURNED HOME TO, SHE WILL GO TO THEM. IT'S WHO SHE IS.
AN' THAT'S GOOD. I'M SURE THEY NEED AS MANY ALLIES... AS MANY *X-MEN* AS THEY CAN FIND.
AND I *AM* ONE. AN X-MAN. IN MY BONES. IN MY BLOOD.
BUT I'M ALSO... ***SOMETHING ELSE.***

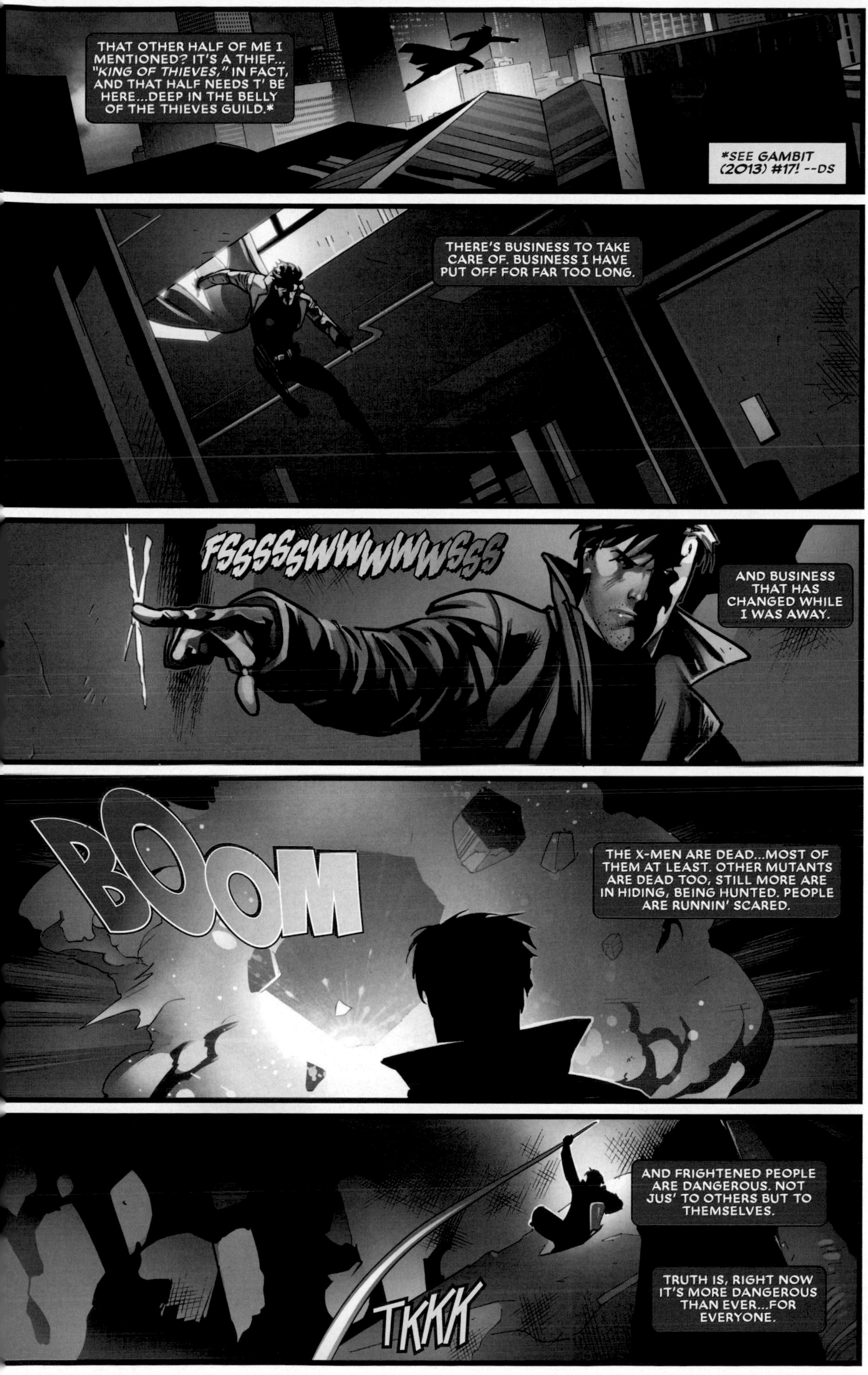
THAT OTHER HALF OF ME I MENTIONED? IT'S A THIEF... "KING OF THIEVES," IN FACT, AND THAT HALF NEEDS T' BE HERE...DEEP IN THE BELLY OF THE THIEVES GUILD.*
*SEE GAMBIT (2013) #17! --DS
THERE'S BUSINESS TO TAKE CARE OF. BUSINESS I HAVE PUT OFF FOR FAR TOO LONG.
FSSSSSWWWWWWSSS
AND BUSINESS THAT HAS CHANGED WHILE I WAS AWAY.
BOOM
THE X-MEN ARE DEAD...MOST OF THEM AT LEAST. OTHER MUTANTS ARE DEAD TOO, STILL MORE ARE IN HIDING, BEING HUNTED. PEOPLE ARE RUNNIN' SCARED.
AND FRIGHTENED PEOPLE ARE DANGEROUS. NOT JUS' TO OTHERS BUT TO THEMSELVES.
TRUTH IS, RIGHT NOW IT'S MORE DANGEROUS THAN EVER...FOR EVERYONE.
TKKK

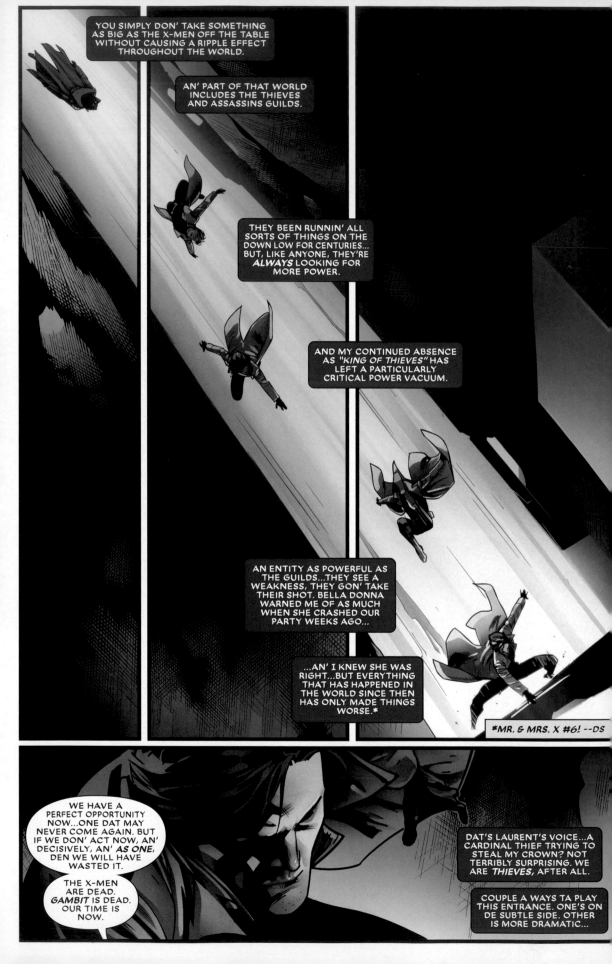

YOU SIMPLY DON' TAKE SOMETHING AS BIG AS THE X-MEN OFF THE TABLE WITHOUT CAUSING A RIPPLE EFFECT THROUGHOUT THE WORLD.

AN' PART OF THAT WORLD INCLUDES THE THIEVES AND ASSASSINS GUILDS.

THEY BEEN RUNNIN' ALL SORTS OF THINGS ON THE DOWN LOW FOR CENTURIES... BUT, LIKE ANYONE, THEY'RE *ALWAYS* LOOKING FOR MORE POWER.

AND MY CONTINUED ABSENCE AS *"KING OF THIEVES"* HAS LEFT A PARTICULARLY CRITICAL POWER VACUUM.

AN ENTITY AS POWERFUL AS THE GUILDS...THEY SEE A WEAKNESS, THEY GON' TAKE THEIR SHOT. BELLA DONNA WARNED ME OF AS MUCH WHEN SHE CRASHED OUR PARTY WEEKS AGO...

...AN' I KNEW SHE WAS RIGHT...BUT EVERYTHING THAT HAS HAPPENED IN THE WORLD SINCE THEN HAS ONLY MADE THINGS WORSE.*

*MR. & MRS. X #6! --DS

WE HAVE A PERFECT OPPORTUNITY NOW...ONE DAT MAY NEVER COME AGAIN. BUT IF WE DON' ACT NOW, AN' DECISIVELY, AN' *AS ONE*, DEN WE WILL HAVE WASTED IT.

THE X-MEN ARE DEAD. *GAMBIT* IS DEAD. OUR TIME IS NOW.

DAT'S LAURENT'S VOICE...A CARDINAL THIEF TRYING TO STEAL MY CROWN? NOT TERRIBLY SURPRISING. WE ARE *THIEVES*, AFTER ALL.

COUPLE A WAYS TA PLAY THIS ENTRANCE. ONE'S ON DE SUBTLE SIDE. OTHER IS MORE DRAMATIC...

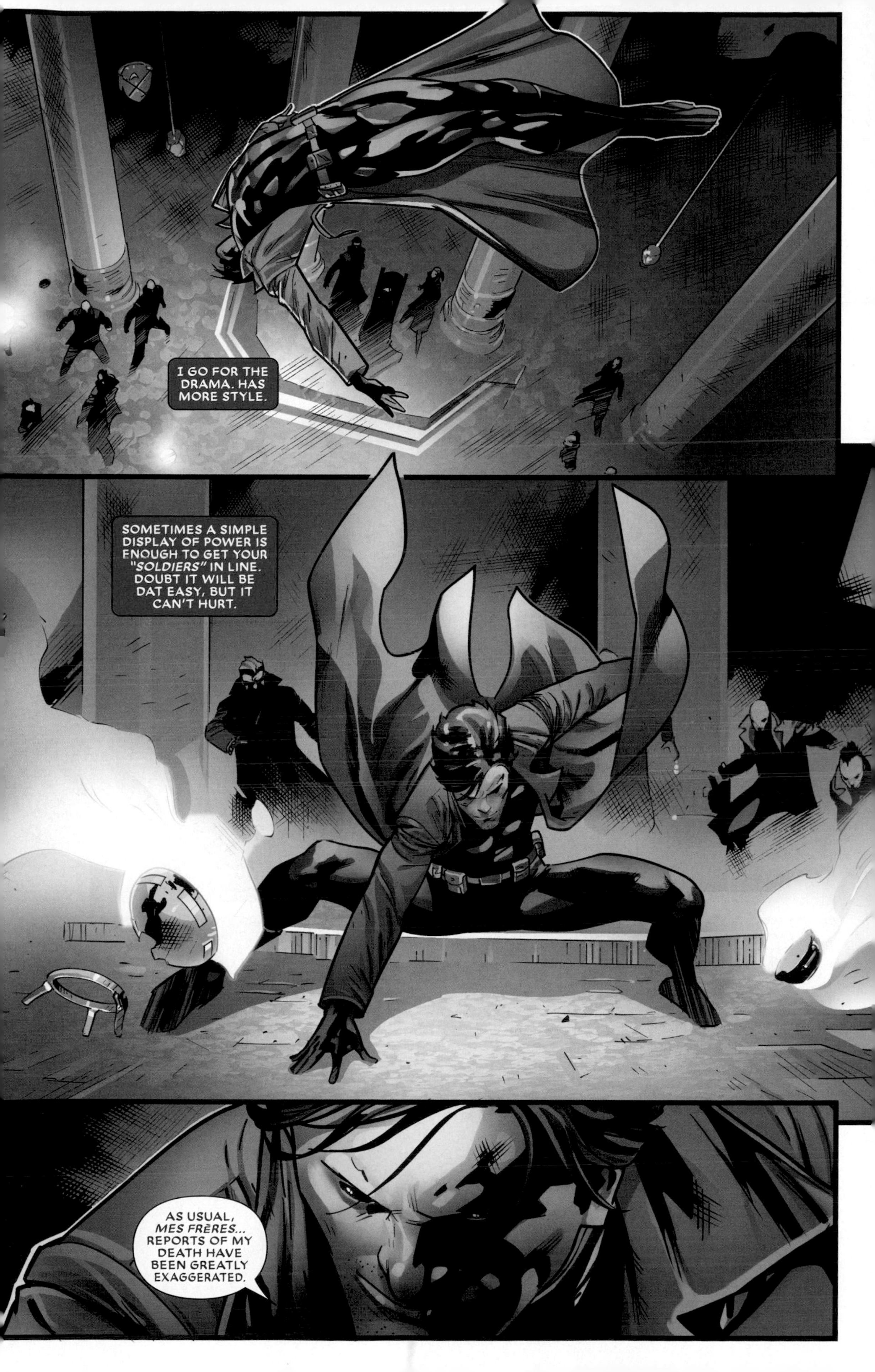

I GO FOR THE DRAMA. HAS MORE STYLE.
SOMETIMES A SIMPLE DISPLAY OF POWER IS ENOUGH TO GET YOUR "SOLDIERS" IN LINE. DOUBT IT WILL BE DAT EASY, BUT IT CAN'T HURT.
AS USUAL, MES FRÈRES... REPORTS OF MY DEATH HAVE BEEN GREATLY EXAGGERATED.

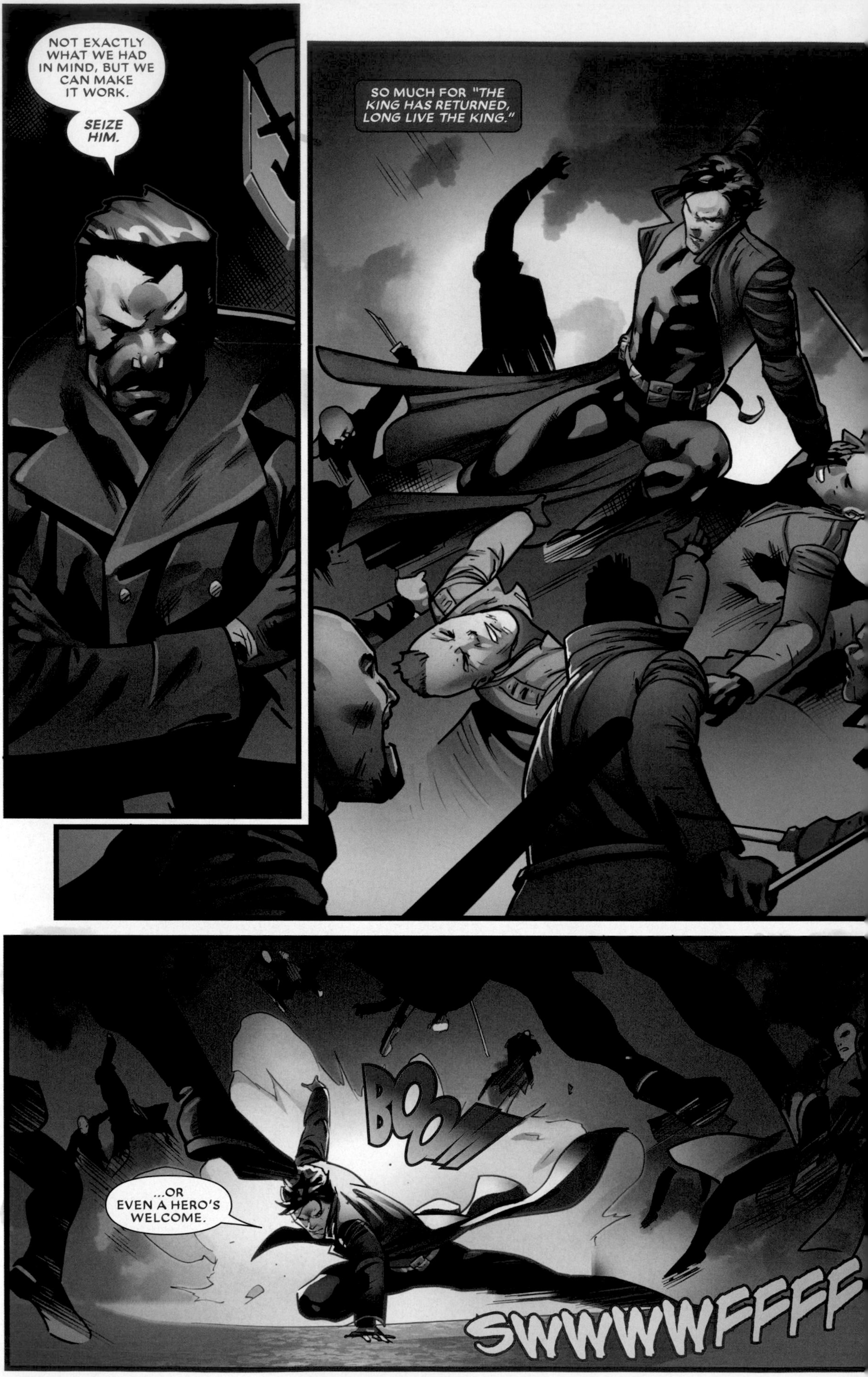

NOT EXACTLY WHAT WE HAD IN MIND, BUT WE CAN MAKE IT WORK.
SEIZE HIM.
SO MUCH FOR "THE KING HAS RETURNED, LONG LIVE THE KING."
BOOM
...OR EVEN A HERO'S WELCOME.
SWWWWFFFF

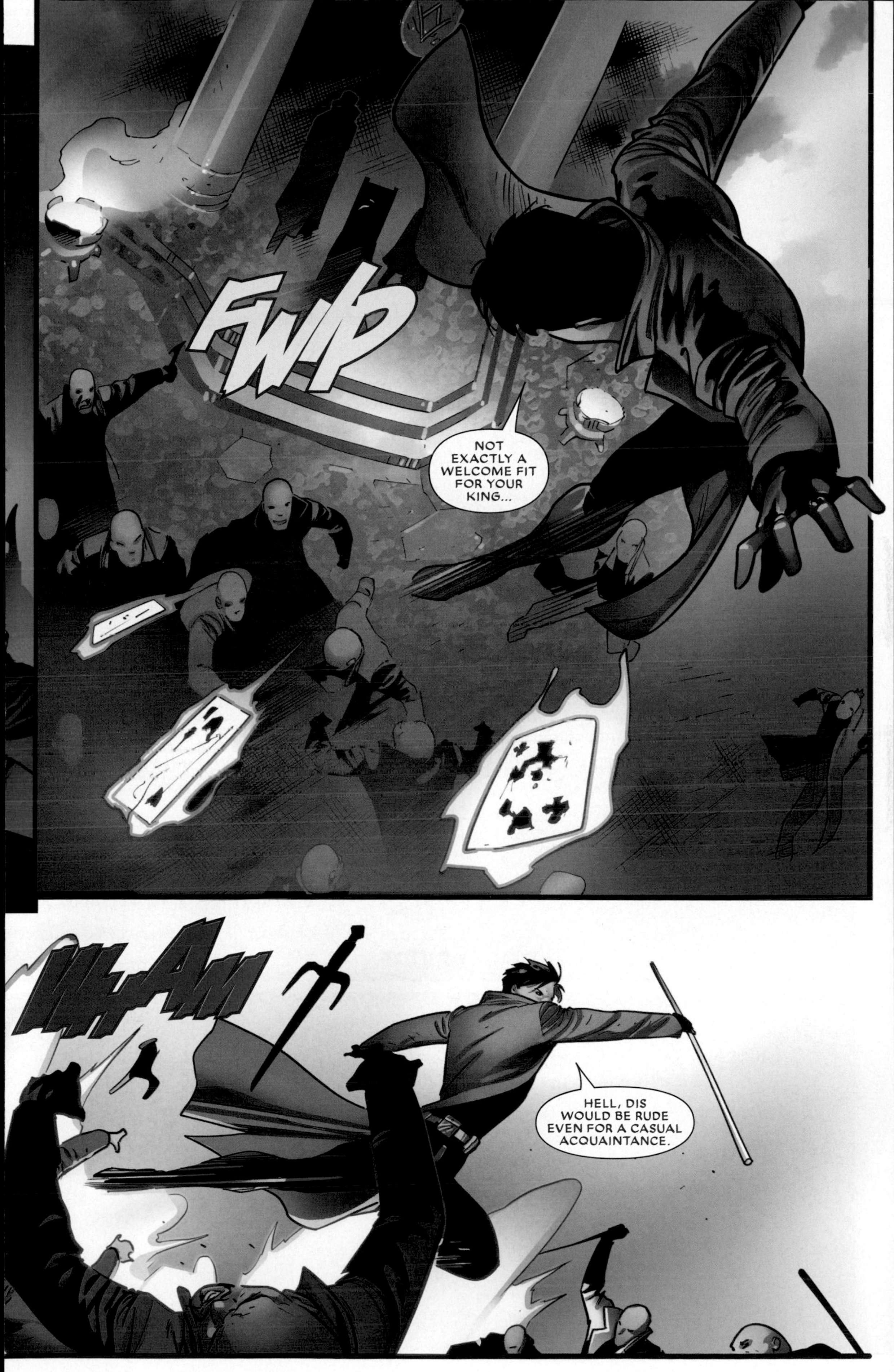
FWIP
NOT EXACTLY A WELCOME FIT FOR YOUR KING...
WHAM
HELL, DIS WOULD BE RUDE EVEN FOR A CASUAL ACQUAINTANCE.

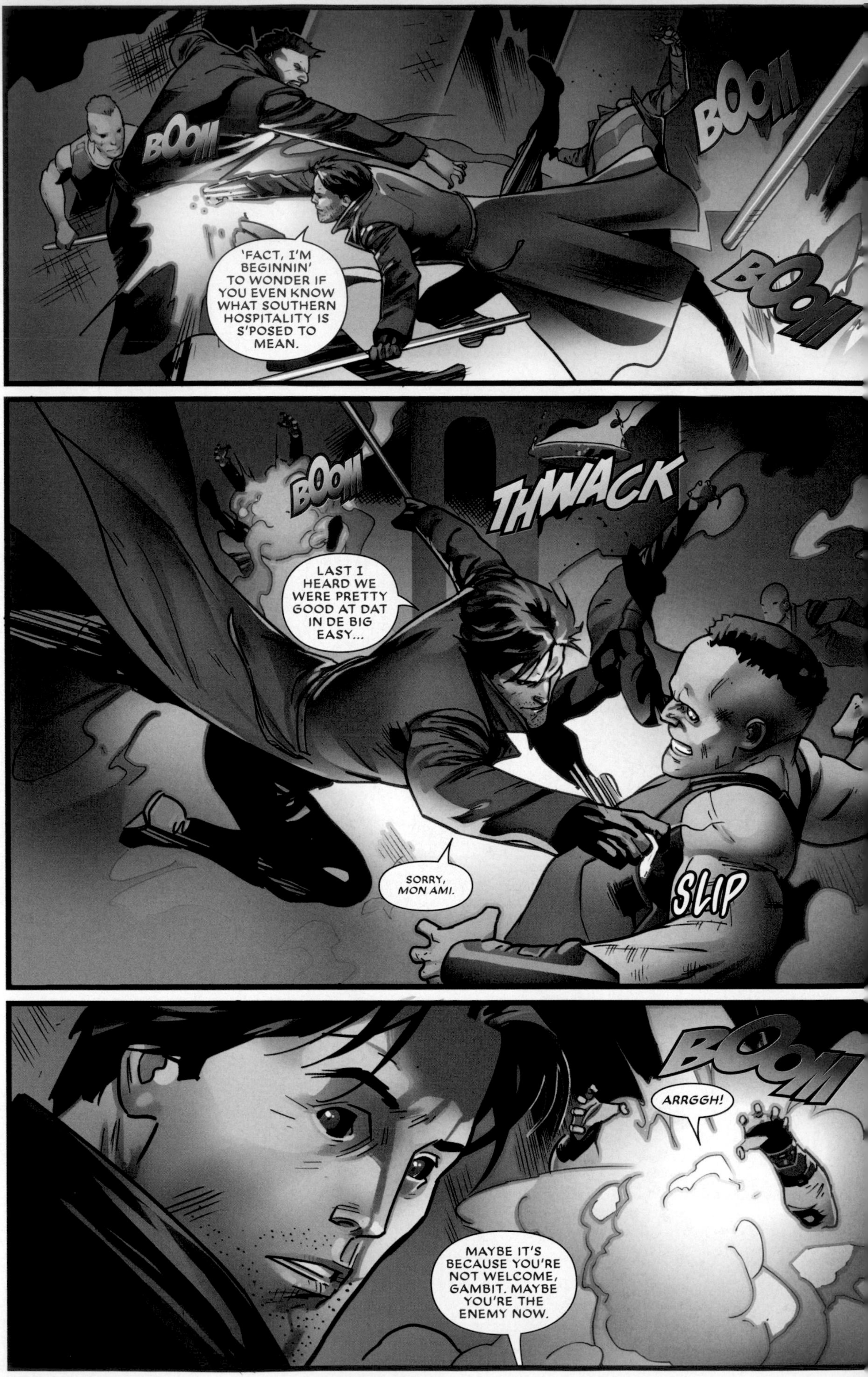
BOOM
BOOM
'FACT, I'M BEGINNIN' TO WONDER IF YOU EVEN KNOW WHAT SOUTHERN HOSPITALITY IS S'POSED TO MEAN.
BOOM
BOOM
THWACK
LAST I HEARD WE WERE PRETTY GOOD AT DAT IN DE BIG EASY...
SORRY, MON AMI.
SLIP
BOOM
ARRGGH!
MAYBE IT'S BECAUSE YOU'RE NOT WELCOME, GAMBIT. MAYBE YOU'RE THE ENEMY NOW.

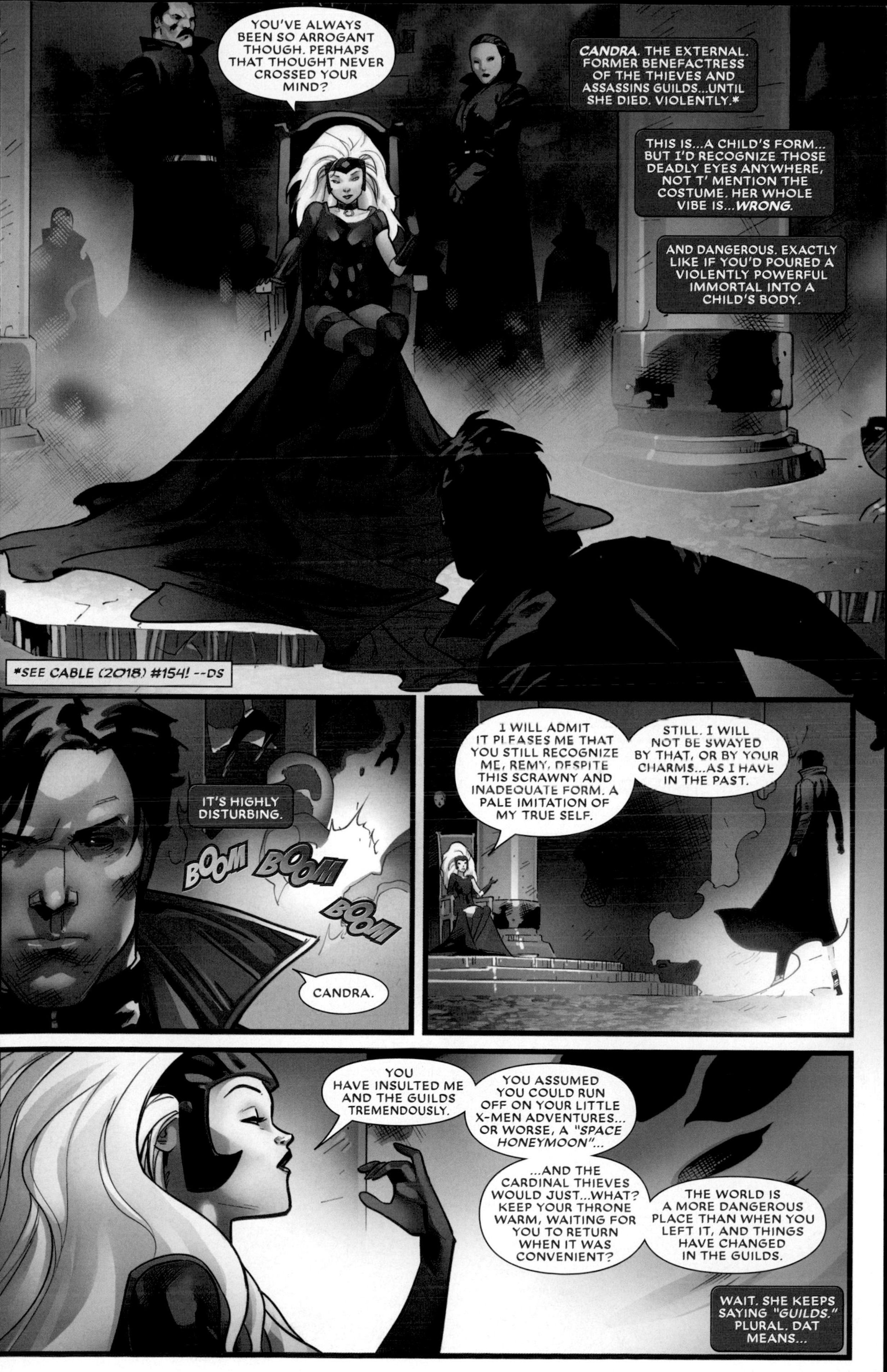
YOU'VE ALWAYS BEEN SO ARROGANT THOUGH. PERHAPS THAT THOUGHT NEVER CROSSED YOUR MIND?
CANDRA. THE EXTERNAL. FORMER BENEFACTRESS OF THE THIEVES AND ASSASSINS GUILDS...UNTIL SHE DIED. VIOLENTLY.*
THIS IS...A CHILD'S FORM... BUT I'D RECOGNIZE THOSE DEADLY EYES ANYWHERE, NOT T' MENTION THE COSTUME. HER WHOLE VIBE IS...WRONG.
AND DANGEROUS. EXACTLY LIKE IF YOU'D POURED A VIOLENTLY POWERFUL IMMORTAL INTO A CHILD'S BODY.
*SEE CABLE (2018) #154! --DS
IT'S HIGHLY DISTURBING.
BOOM BOOM BOOM
CANDRA.
I WILL ADMIT IT PLEASES ME THAT YOU STILL RECOGNIZE ME, REMY, DESPITE THIS SCRAWNY AND INADEQUATE FORM. A PALE IMITATION OF MY TRUE SELF.
STILL. I WILL NOT BE SWAYED BY THAT, OR BY YOUR CHARMS...AS I HAVE IN THE PAST.
YOU HAVE INSULTED ME AND THE GUILDS TREMENDOUSLY.
YOU ASSUMED YOU COULD RUN OFF ON YOUR LITTLE X-MEN ADVENTURES... OR WORSE, A "SPACE HONEYMOON"...
...AND THE CARDINAL THIEVES WOULD JUST...WHAT? KEEP YOUR THRONE WARM, WAITING FOR YOU TO RETURN WHEN IT WAS CONVENIENT?
THE WORLD IS A MORE DANGEROUS PLACE THAN WHEN YOU LEFT IT, AND THINGS HAVE CHANGED IN THE GUILDS.
WAIT. SHE KEEPS SAYING "GUILDS." PLURAL. DAT MEANS...

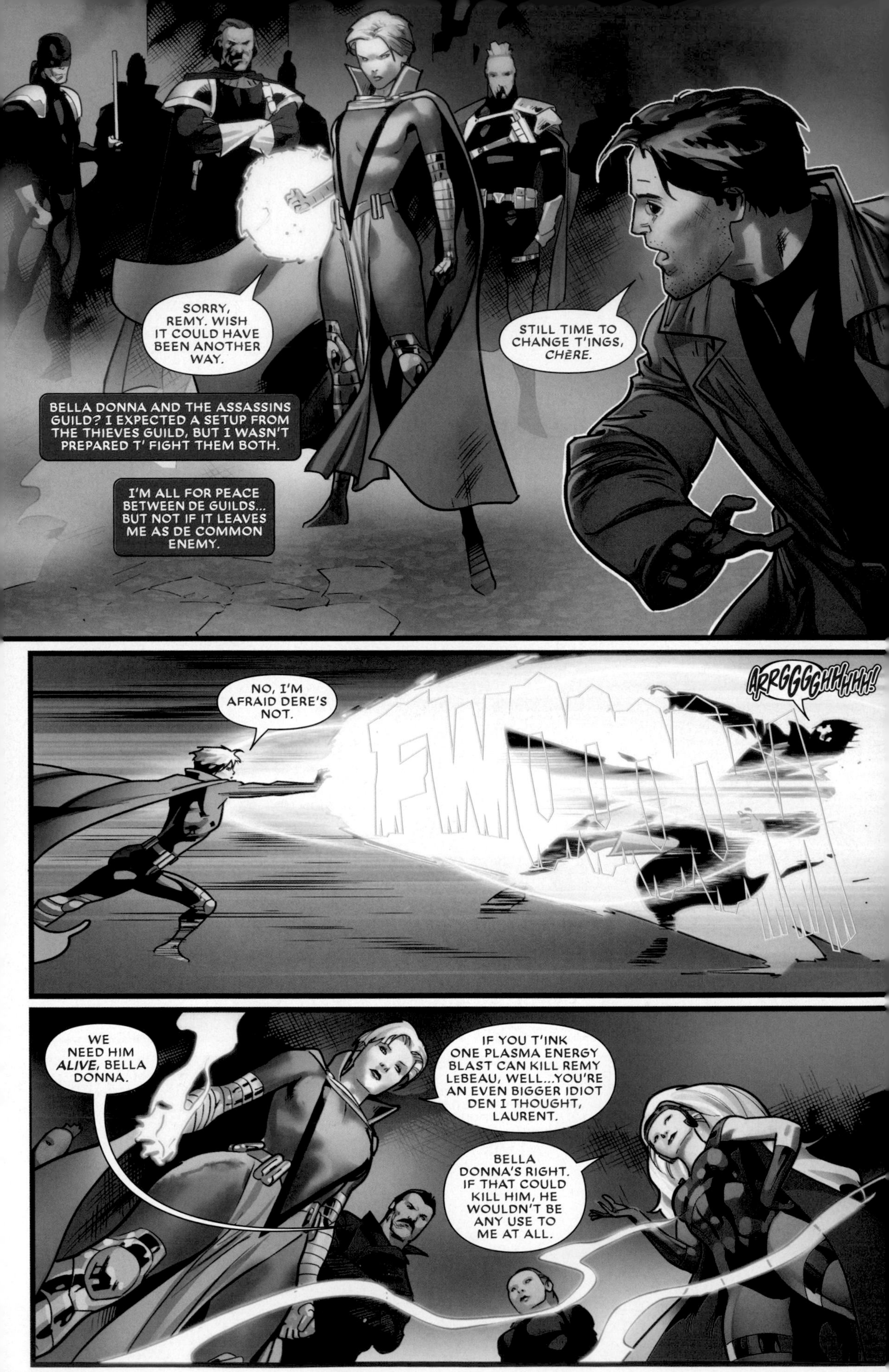

SORRY, REMY. WISH IT COULD HAVE BEEN ANOTHER WAY.
STILL TIME TO CHANGE T'INGS, *CHÈRE.*
BELLA DONNA AND THE ASSASSINS GUILD? I EXPECTED A SETUP FROM THE THIEVES GUILD, BUT I WASN'T PREPARED T' FIGHT THEM BOTH.
I'M ALL FOR PEACE BETWEEN DE GUILDS... BUT NOT IF IT LEAVES ME AS DE COMMON ENEMY.
NO, I'M AFRAID DERE'S NOT.
FWOOOM
ARRGGGGHHHHH!
WE NEED HIM *ALIVE*, BELLA DONNA.
IF YOU T'INK ONE PLASMA ENERGY BLAST CAN KILL REMY LEBEAU, WELL...YOU'RE AN EVEN BIGGER IDIOT DEN I THOUGHT, LAURENT.
BELLA DONNA'S RIGHT. IF THAT COULD KILL HIM, HE WOULDN'T BE ANY USE TO ME AT ALL.

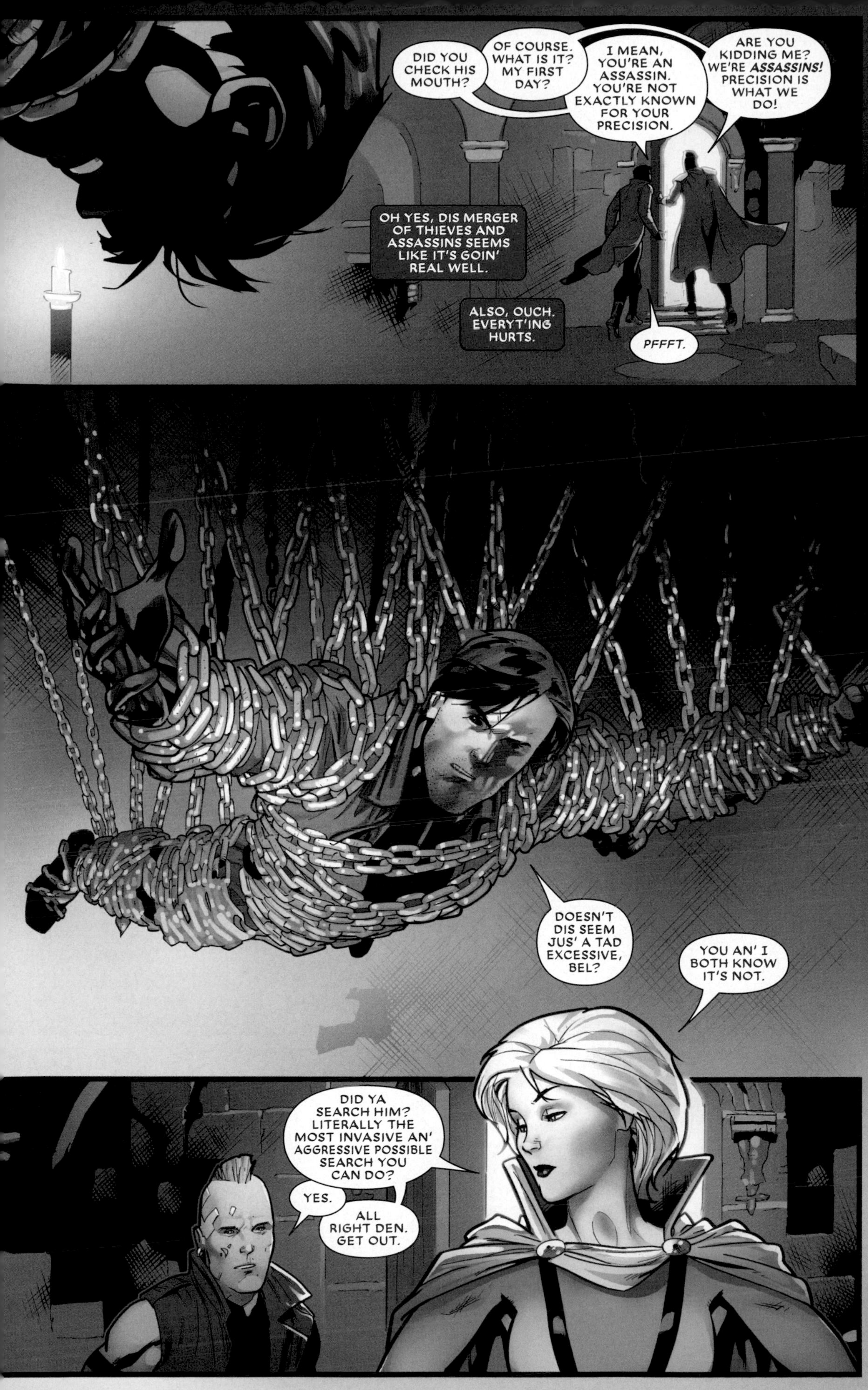
DID YOU CHECK HIS MOUTH?
OF COURSE. WHAT IS IT? MY FIRST DAY?
I MEAN, YOU'RE AN ASSASSIN. YOU'RE NOT EXACTLY KNOWN FOR YOUR PRECISION.
ARE YOU KIDDING ME? WE'RE ASSASSINS! PRECISION IS WHAT WE DO!
OH YES, DIS MERGER OF THIEVES AND ASSASSINS SEEMS LIKE IT'S GOIN' REAL WELL.
ALSO, OUCH. EVERYT'ING HURTS.
PFFFT.
DOESN'T DIS SEEM JUS' A TAD EXCESSIVE, BEL?
YOU AN' I BOTH KNOW IT'S NOT.
DID YA SEARCH HIM? LITERALLY THE MOST INVASIVE AN' AGGRESSIVE POSSIBLE SEARCH YOU CAN DO?
YES.
ALL RIGHT DEN. GET OUT.

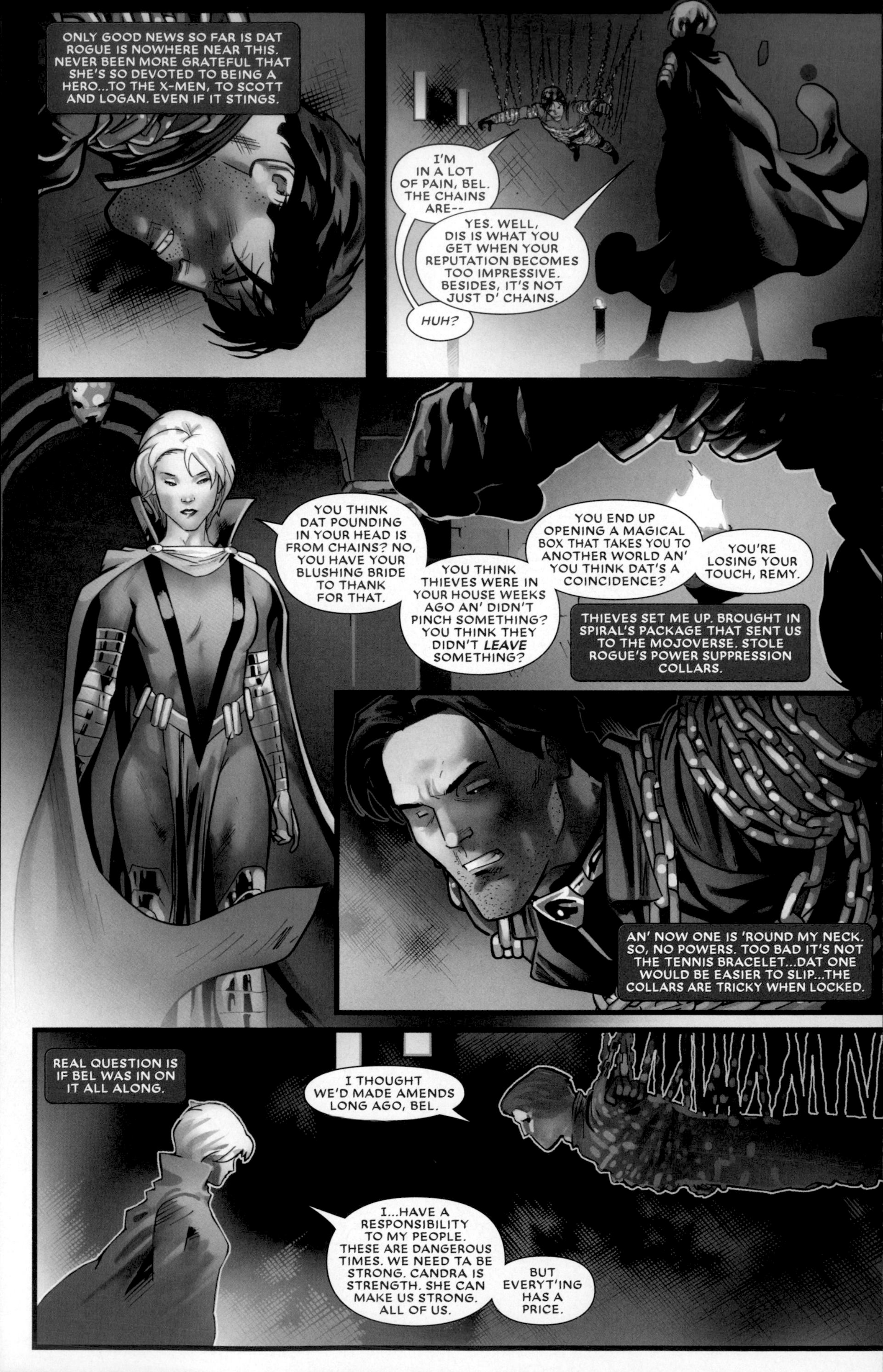
ONLY GOOD NEWS SO FAR IS DAT ROGUE IS NOWHERE NEAR THIS. NEVER BEEN MORE GRATEFUL THAT SHE'S SO DEVOTED TO BEING A HERO...TO THE X-MEN, TO SCOTT AND LOGAN. EVEN IF IT STINGS.
I'M IN A LOT OF PAIN, BEL. THE CHAINS ARE--
YES. WELL, DIS IS WHAT YOU GET WHEN YOUR REPUTATION BECOMES TOO IMPRESSIVE. BESIDES, IT'S NOT JUST D' CHAINS.
HUH?
YOU THINK DAT POUNDING IN YOUR HEAD IS FROM CHAINS? NO, YOU HAVE YOUR BLUSHING BRIDE TO THANK FOR THAT.
YOU THINK THIEVES WERE IN YOUR HOUSE WEEKS AGO AN' DIDN'T PINCH SOMETHING? YOU THINK THEY DIDN'T *LEAVE* SOMETHING?
YOU END UP OPENING A MAGICAL BOX THAT TAKES YOU TO ANOTHER WORLD AN' YOU THINK DAT'S A COINCIDENCE?
YOU'RE LOSING YOUR TOUCH, REMY.
THIEVES SET ME UP. BROUGHT IN SPIRAL'S PACKAGE THAT SENT US TO THE MOJOVERSE. STOLE ROGUE'S POWER SUPPRESSION COLLARS.
AN' NOW ONE IS 'ROUND MY NECK. SO, NO POWERS. TOO BAD IT'S NOT THE TENNIS BRACELET...DAT ONE WOULD BE EASIER TO SLIP...THE COLLARS ARE TRICKY WHEN LOCKED.
REAL QUESTION IS IF BEL WAS IN ON IT ALL ALONG.
I THOUGHT WE'D MADE AMENDS LONG AGO, BEL.
I...HAVE A RESPONSIBILITY TO MY PEOPLE. THESE ARE DANGEROUS TIMES. WE NEED TA BE STRONG. CANDRA IS STRENGTH. SHE CAN MAKE US STRONG. ALL OF US.
BUT EVERYT'ING HAS A PRICE.

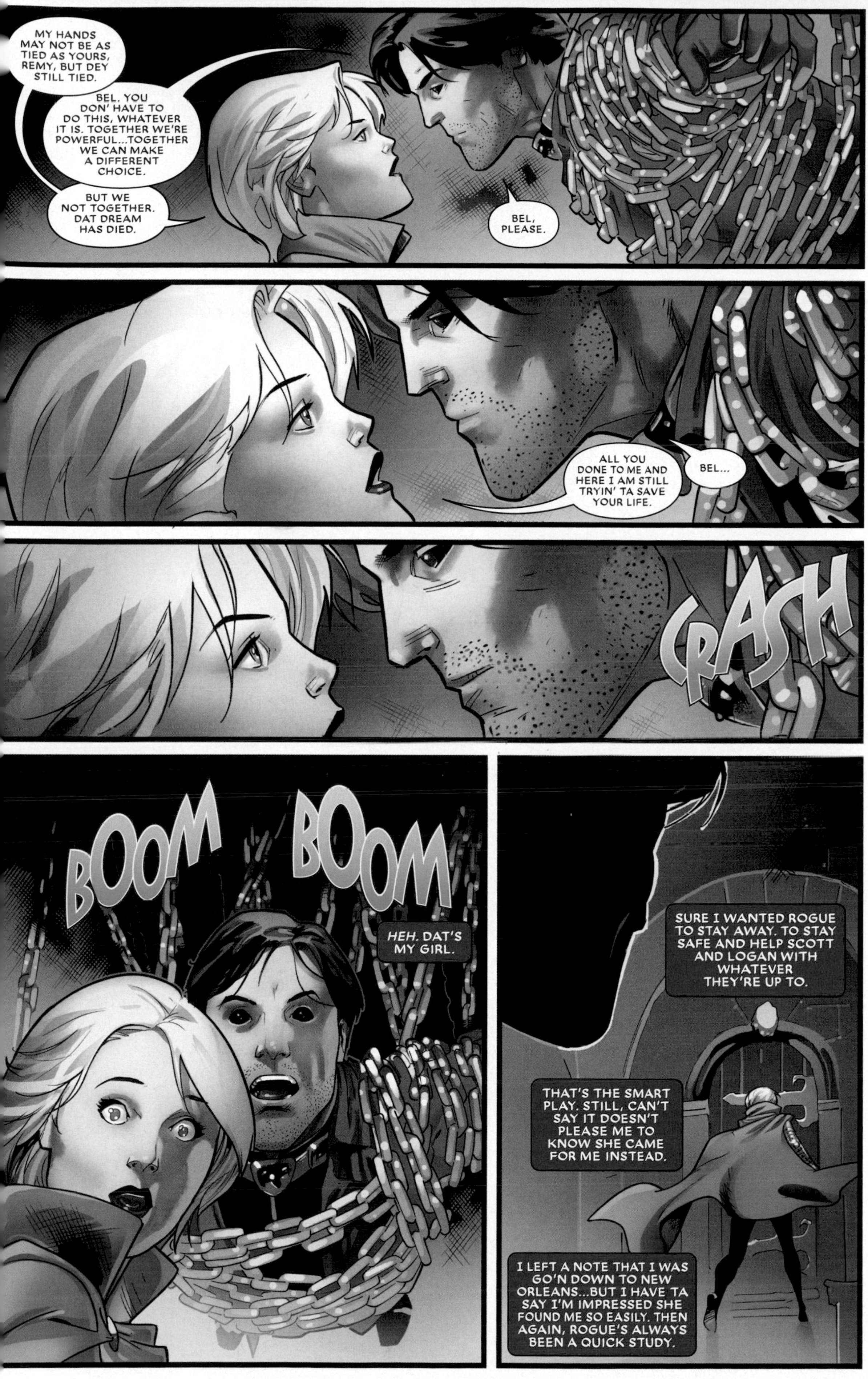
MY HANDS MAY NOT BE AS TIED AS YOURS, REMY, BUT DEY STILL TIED.
BEL, YOU DON' HAVE TO DO THIS, WHATEVER IT IS. TOGETHER WE'RE POWERFUL...TOGETHER WE CAN MAKE A DIFFERENT CHOICE.
BUT WE NOT TOGETHER. DAT DREAM HAS DIED.
BEL, PLEASE.
BEL...
ALL YOU DONE TO ME AND HERE I AM STILL TRYIN' TA SAVE YOUR LIFE.
CRASH
BOOM
BOOM
HEH. DAT'S MY GIRL.
SURE I WANTED ROGUE TO STAY AWAY. TO STAY SAFE AND HELP SCOTT AND LOGAN WITH WHATEVER THEY'RE UP TO.
THAT'S THE SMART PLAY. STILL, CAN'T SAY IT DOESN'T PLEASE ME TO KNOW SHE CAME FOR ME INSTEAD.
I LEFT A NOTE THAT I WAS GO'N DOWN TO NEW ORLEANS...BUT I HAVE TA SAY I'M IMPRESSED SHE FOUND ME SO EASILY. THEN AGAIN, ROGUE'S ALWAYS BEEN A QUICK STUDY.

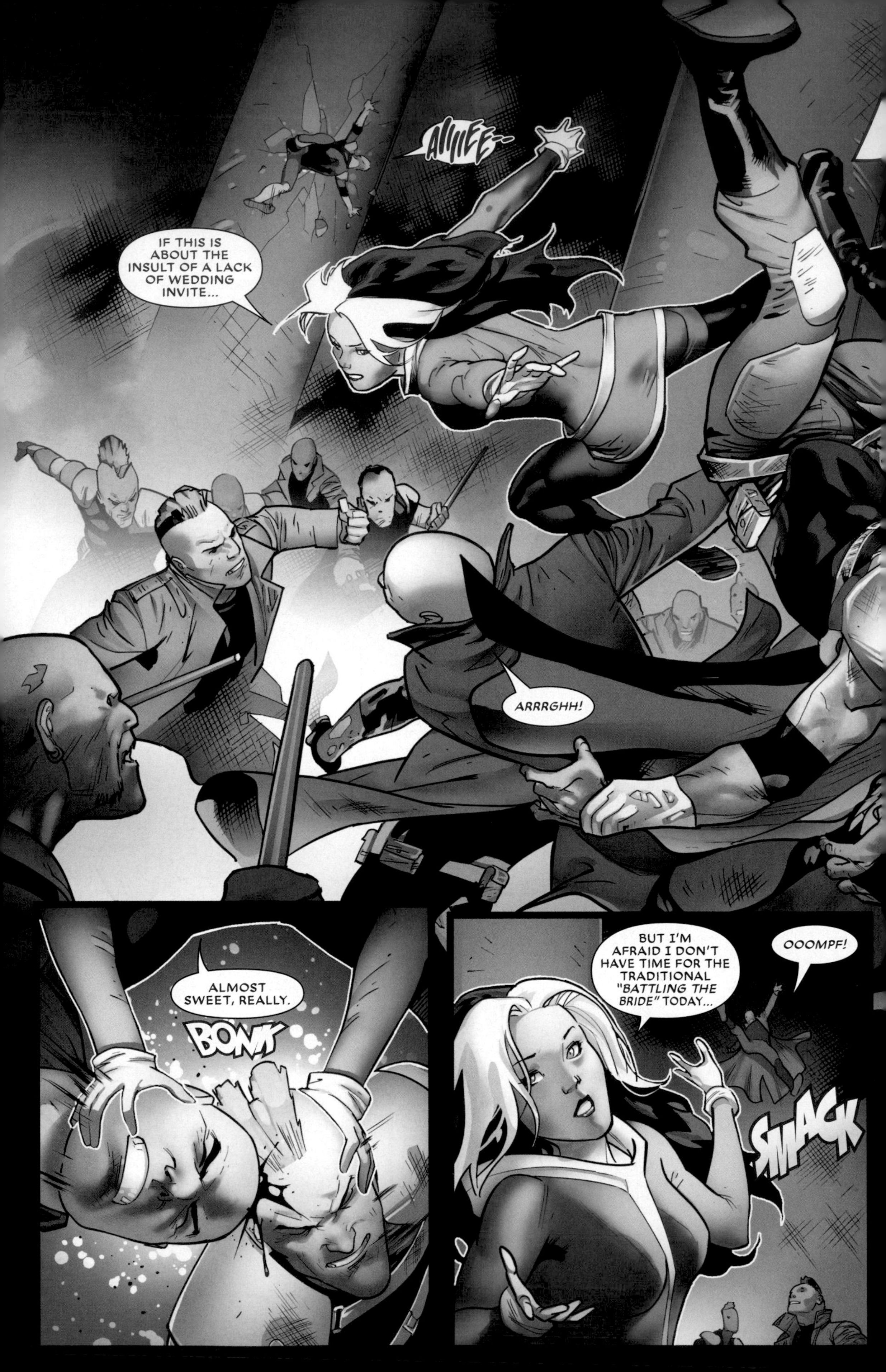
AIIIEE--
IF THIS IS ABOUT THE INSULT OF A LACK OF WEDDING INVITE...
ARRRGHH!
ALMOST SWEET, REALLY.
BONK
BUT I'M AFRAID I DON'T HAVE TIME FOR THE TRADITIONAL "BATTLING THE BRIDE" TODAY...
OOOMPF!
SMACK

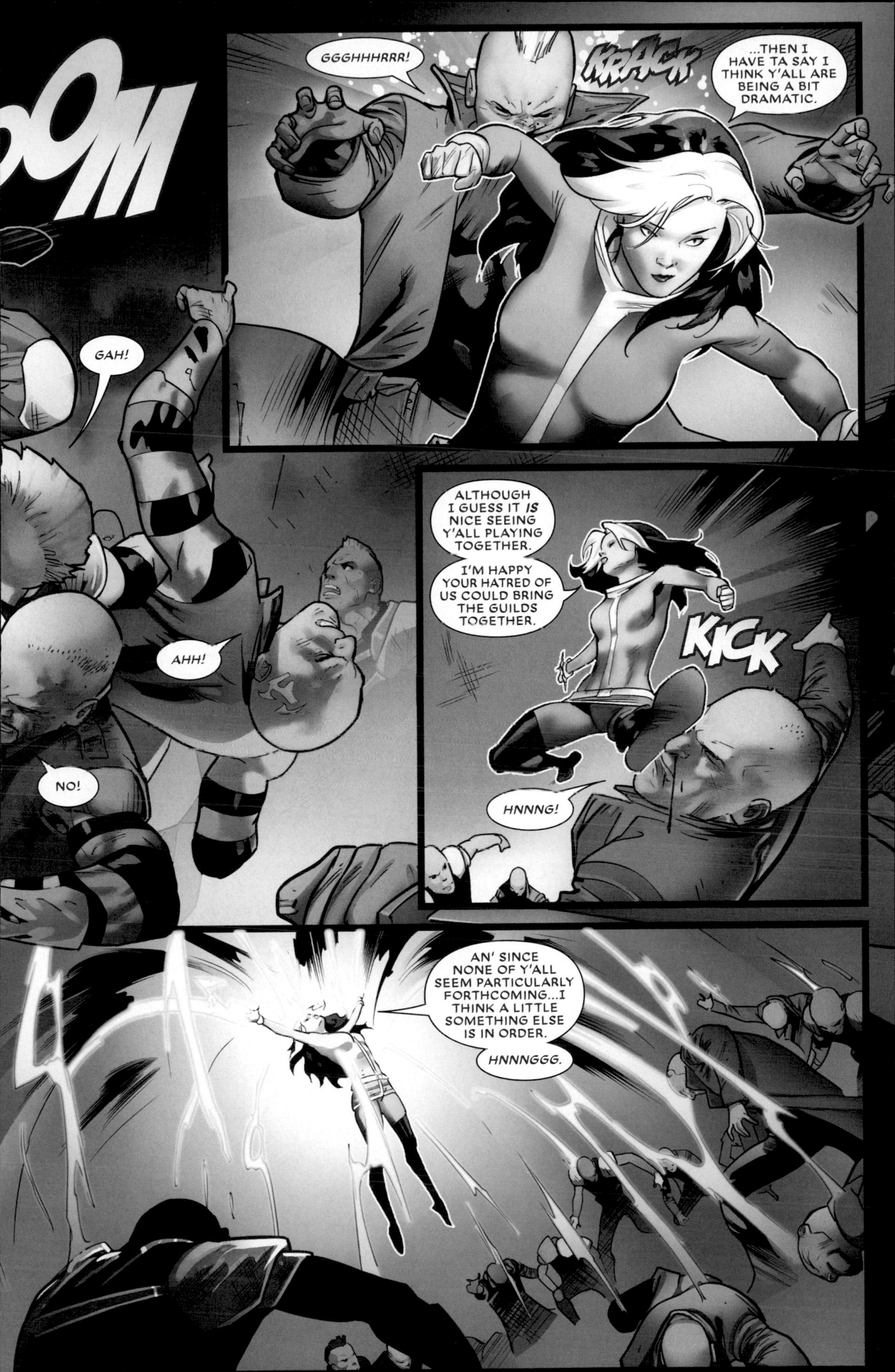
OOM
GGGHHHRRR!
KRACK
...THEN I HAVE TA SAY I THINK Y'ALL ARE BEING A BIT DRAMATIC.
GAH!
AHH!
NO!
ALTHOUGH I GUESS IT IS NICE SEEING Y'ALL PLAYING TOGETHER.
I'M HAPPY YOUR HATRED OF US COULD BRING THE GUILDS TOGETHER.
KICK
HNNNG!
AN' SINCE NONE OF Y'ALL SEEM PARTICULARLY FORTHCOMING...I THINK A LITTLE SOMETHING ELSE IS IN ORDER.
HNNNGGG.

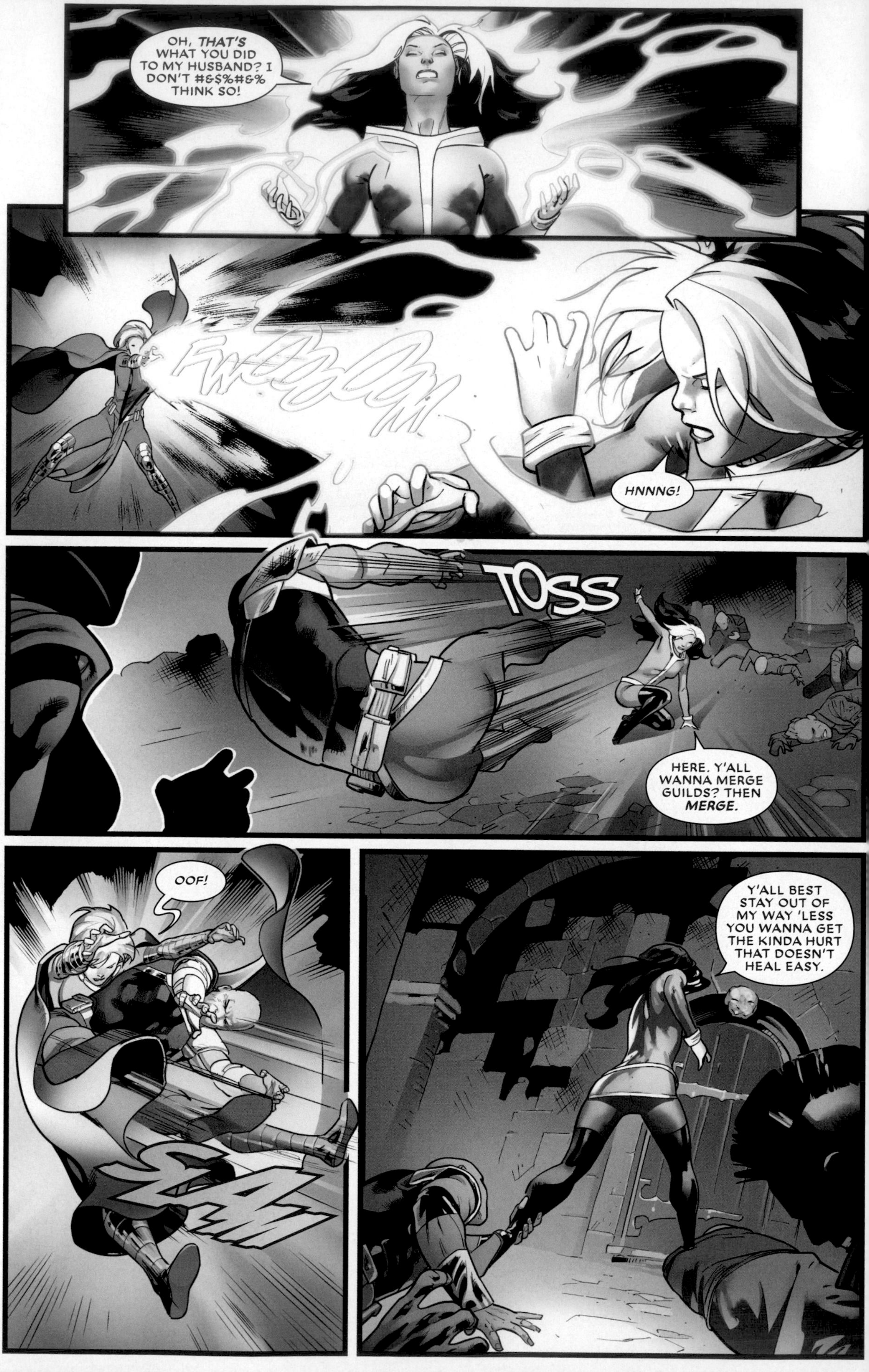
OH, THAT'S WHAT YOU DID TO MY HUSBAND? I DON'T #&$%#&% THINK SO!
FWOOOOM
HNNNG!
TOSS
HERE. Y'ALL WANNA MERGE GUILDS? THEN MERGE.
OOF!
SAM
Y'ALL BEST STAY OUT OF MY WAY 'LESS YOU WANNA GET THE KINDA HURT THAT DOESN'T HEAL EASY.

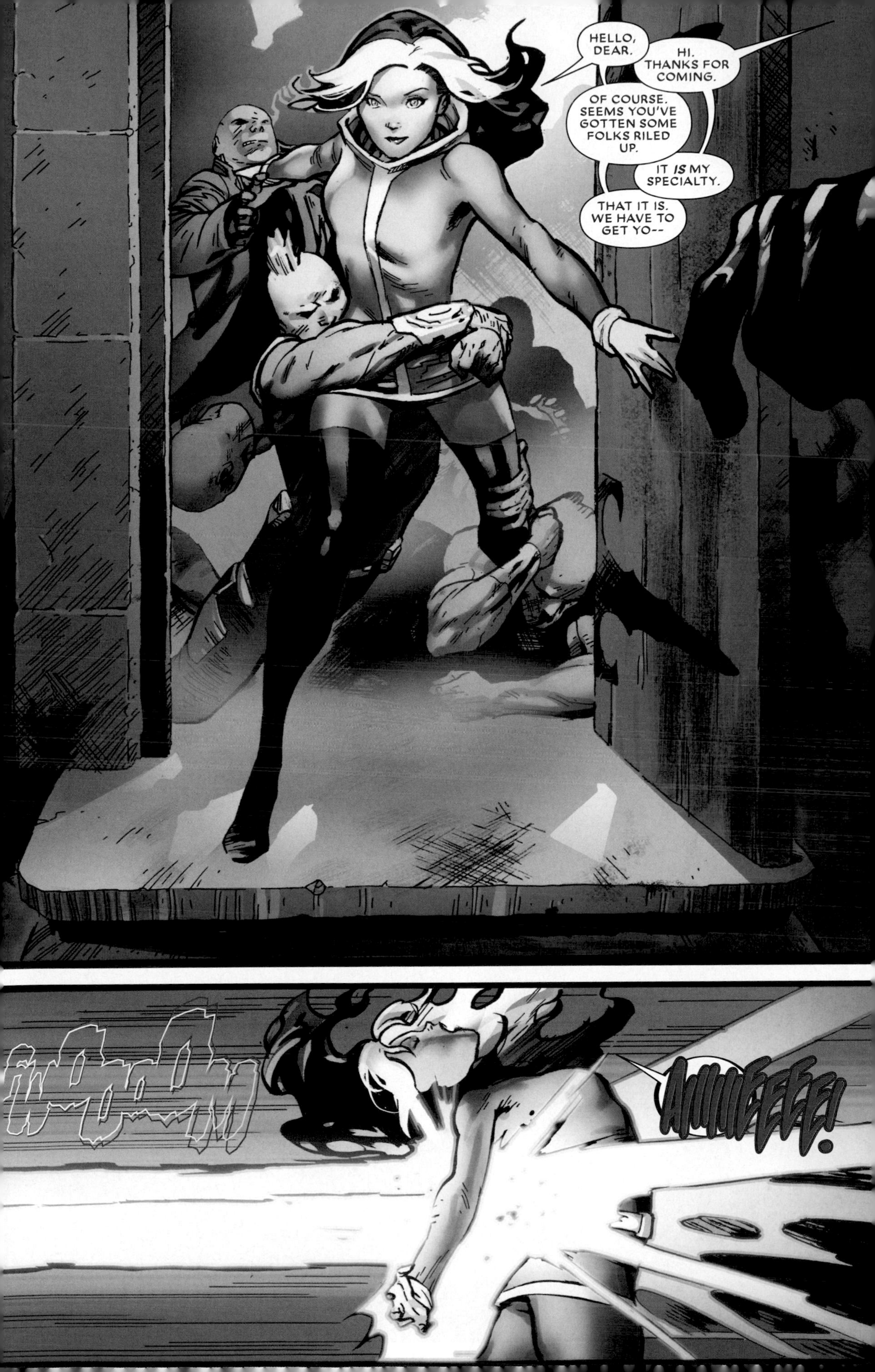
HELLO, DEAR.
HI. THANKS FOR COMING.
OF COURSE. SEEMS YOU'VE GOTTEN SOME FOLKS RILED UP.
IT *IS* MY SPECIALTY.
THAT IT IS. WE HAVE TO GET YO--
AIIIIEEEE!

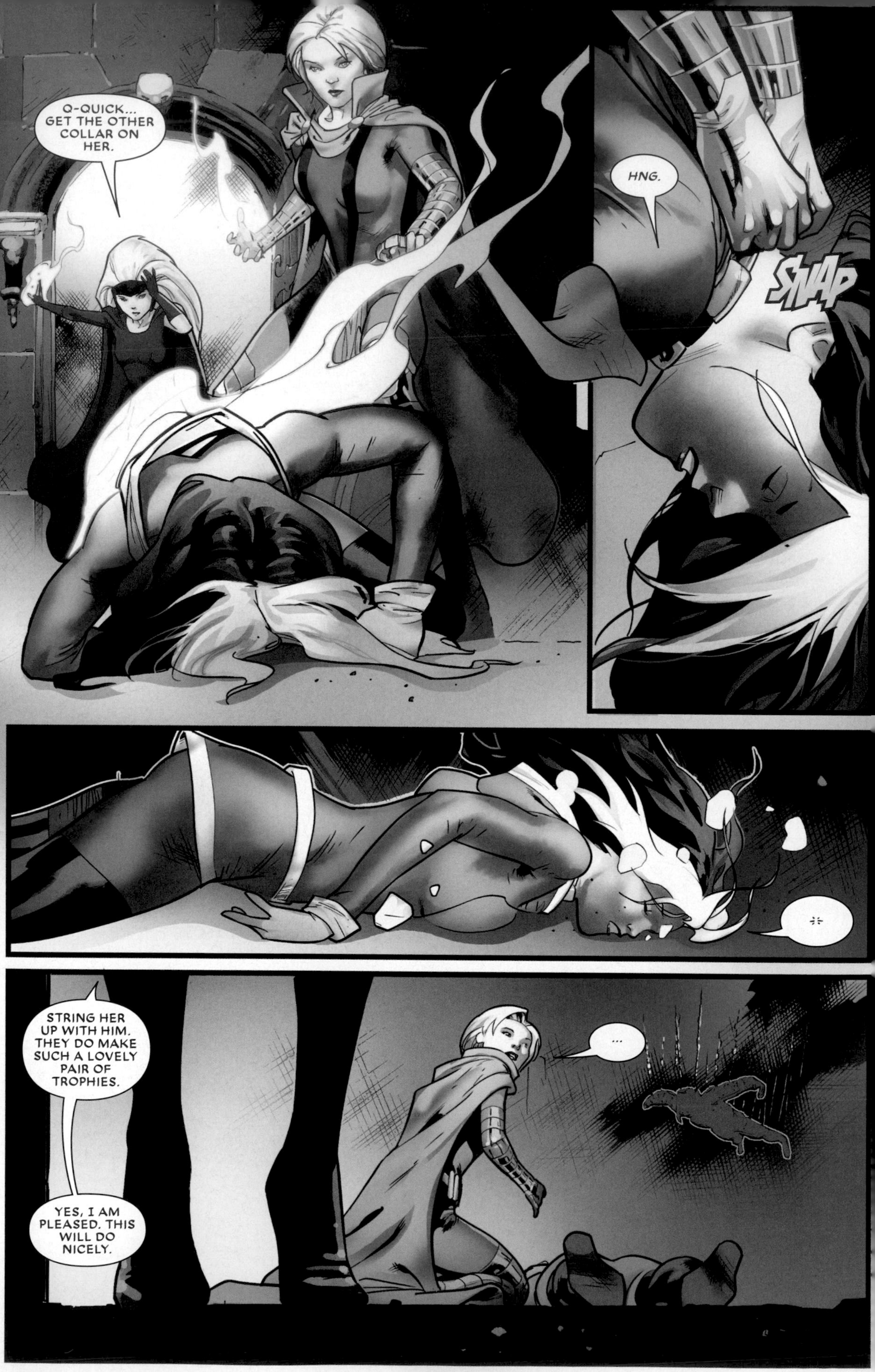

Q-QUICK... GET THE OTHER COLLAR ON HER.
HNG.
SNAP
...
STRING HER UP WITH HIM. THEY DO MAKE SUCH A LOVELY PAIR OF TROPHIES.
YES, I AM PLEASED. THIS WILL DO NICELY.

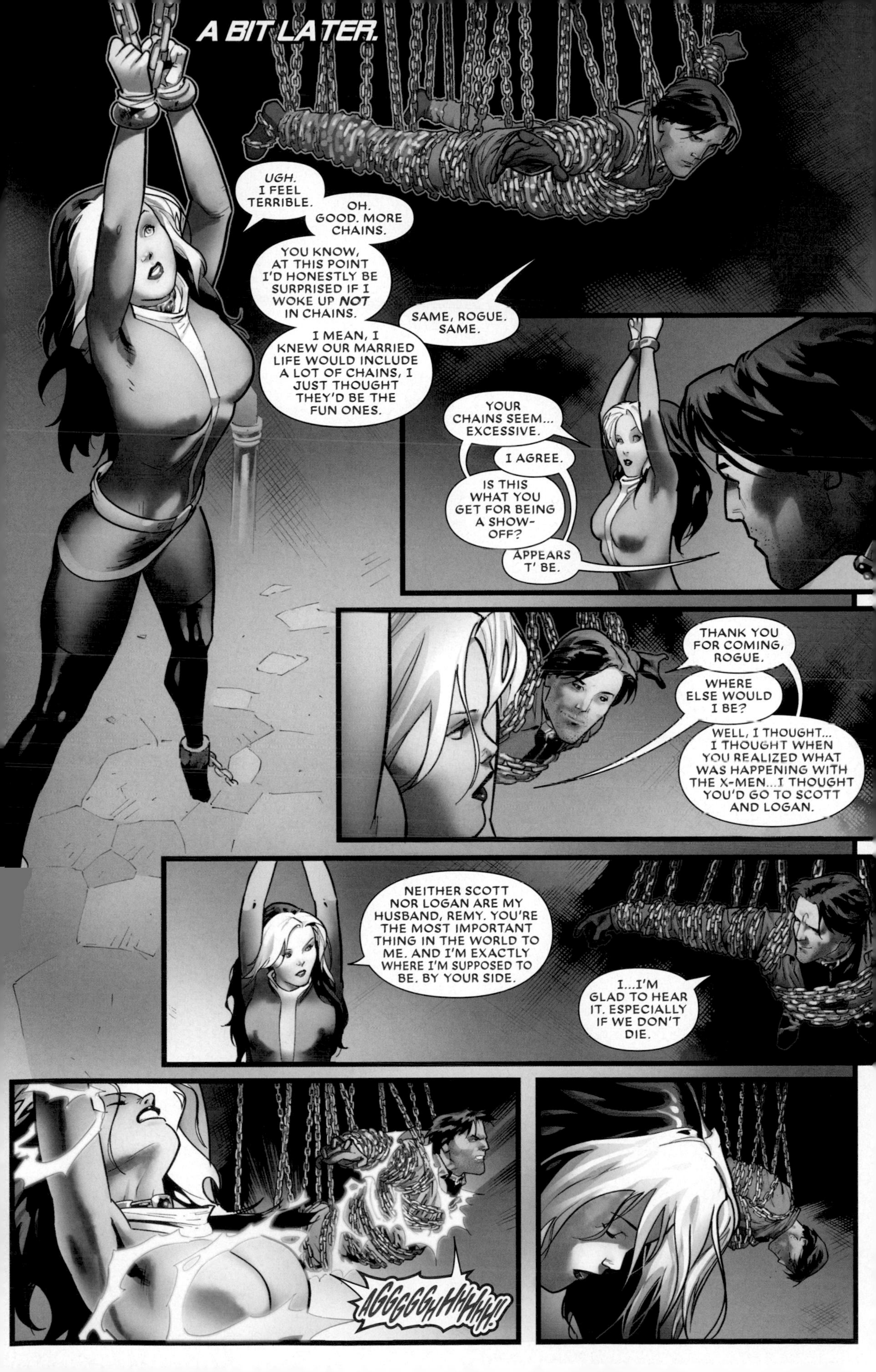
A BIT LATER.
UGH. I FEEL TERRIBLE.
OH. GOOD. MORE CHAINS.
YOU KNOW, AT THIS POINT I'D HONESTLY BE SURPRISED IF I WOKE UP NOT IN CHAINS.
SAME, ROGUE. SAME.
I MEAN, I KNEW OUR MARRIED LIFE WOULD INCLUDE A LOT OF CHAINS, I JUST THOUGHT THEY'D BE THE FUN ONES.
YOUR CHAINS SEEM... EXCESSIVE.
I AGREE.
IS THIS WHAT YOU GET FOR BEING A SHOW-OFF?
APPEARS T' BE.
THANK YOU FOR COMING, ROGUE.
WHERE ELSE WOULD I BE?
WELL, I THOUGHT... I THOUGHT WHEN YOU REALIZED WHAT WAS HAPPENING WITH THE X-MEN... I THOUGHT YOU'D GO TO SCOTT AND LOGAN.
NEITHER SCOTT NOR LOGAN ARE MY HUSBAND, REMY. YOU'RE THE MOST IMPORTANT THING IN THE WORLD TO ME. AND I'M EXACTLY WHERE I'M SUPPOSED TO BE. BY YOUR SIDE.
I...I'M GLAD TO HEAR IT. ESPECIALLY IF WE DON'T DIE.
AGGGGGHHHHH!!

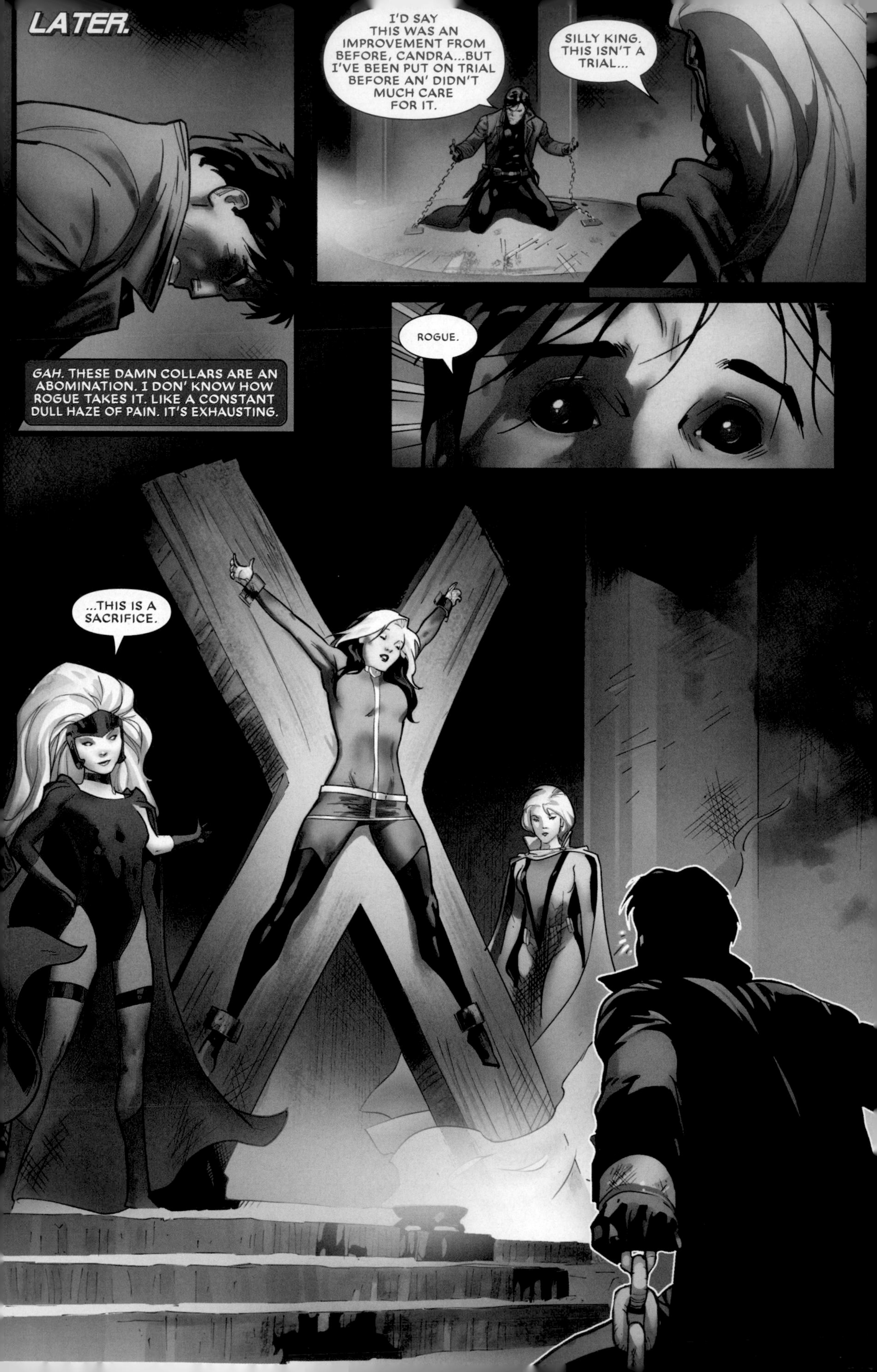
LATER.
GAH. THESE DAMN COLLARS ARE AN ABOMINATION. I DON' KNOW HOW ROGUE TAKES IT. LIKE A CONSTANT DULL HAZE OF PAIN. IT'S EXHAUSTING.
I'D SAY THIS WAS AN IMPROVEMENT FROM BEFORE, CANDRA...BUT I'VE BEEN PUT ON TRIAL BEFORE AN' DIDN'T MUCH CARE FOR IT.
SILLY KING. THIS ISN'T A TRIAL...
ROGUE.
...THIS IS A SACRIFICE.

12

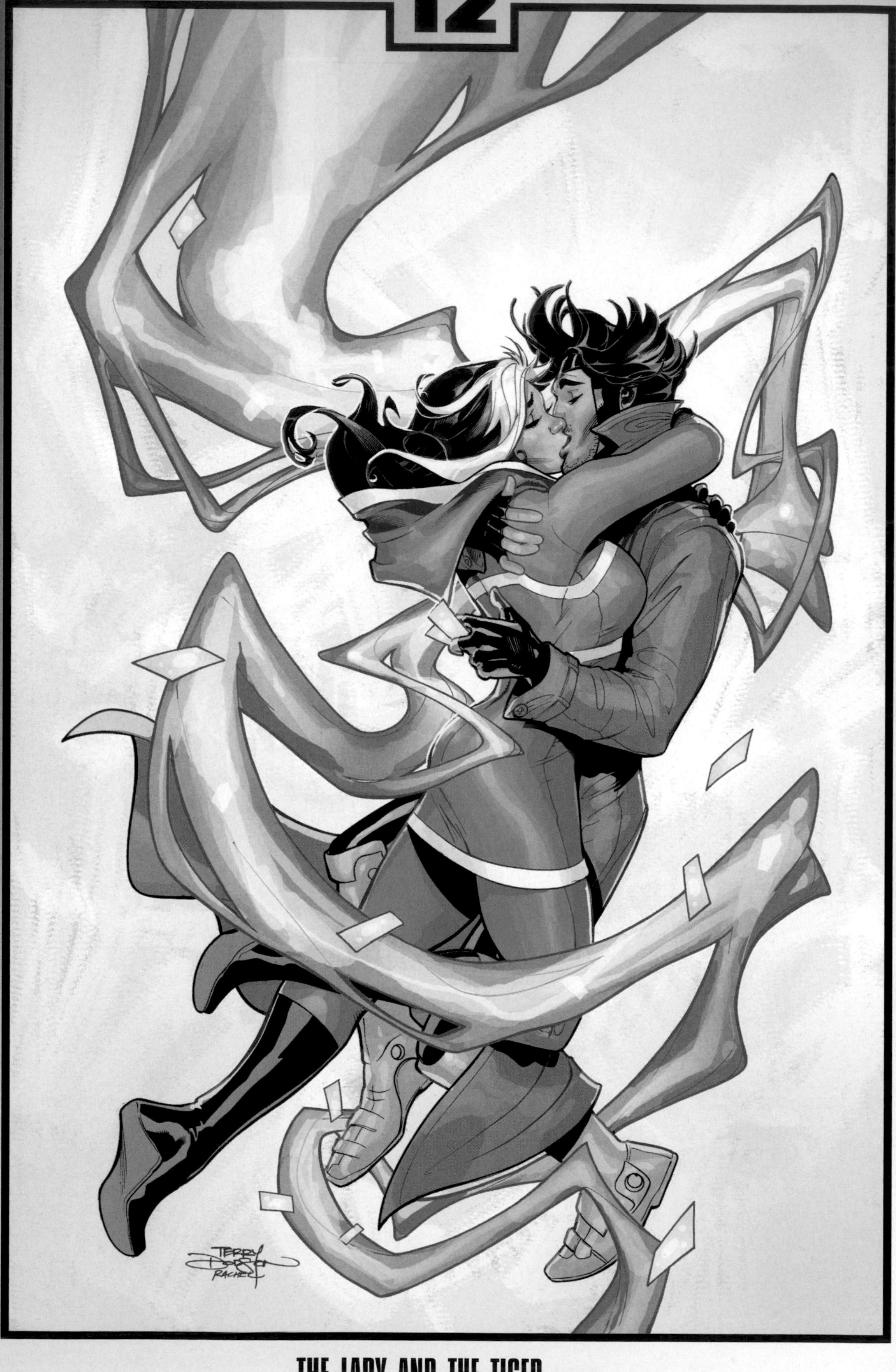

THE LADY AND THE TIGER PART 2

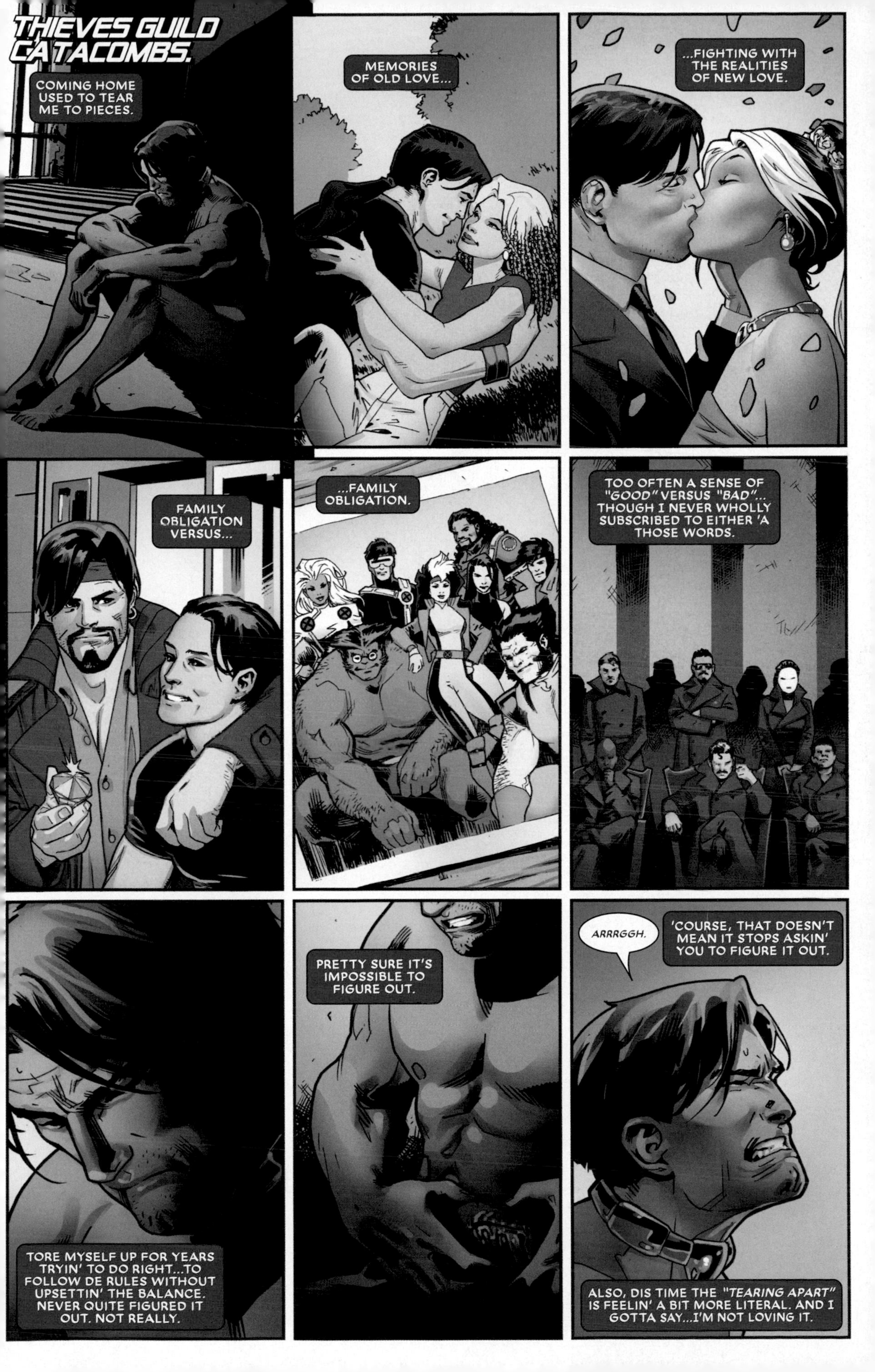
THIEVES GUILD CATACOMBS.
COMING HOME USED TO TEAR ME TO PIECES.
MEMORIES OF OLD LOVE...
...FIGHTING WITH THE REALITIES OF NEW LOVE.
FAMILY OBLIGATION VERSUS...
...FAMILY OBLIGATION.
TOO OFTEN A SENSE OF "GOOD" VERSUS "BAD"... THOUGH I NEVER WHOLLY SUBSCRIBED TO EITHER 'A THOSE WORDS.
TORE MYSELF UP FOR YEARS TRYIN' TO DO RIGHT...TO FOLLOW DE RULES WITHOUT UPSETTIN' THE BALANCE. NEVER QUITE FIGURED IT OUT. NOT REALLY.
PRETTY SURE IT'S IMPOSSIBLE TO FIGURE OUT.
ARRRGGH.
'COURSE, THAT DOESN'T MEAN IT STOPS ASKIN' YOU TO FIGURE IT OUT.
ALSO, DIS TIME THE "TEARING APART" IS FEELIN' A BIT MORE LITERAL. AND I GOTTA SAY...I'M NOT LOVING IT.

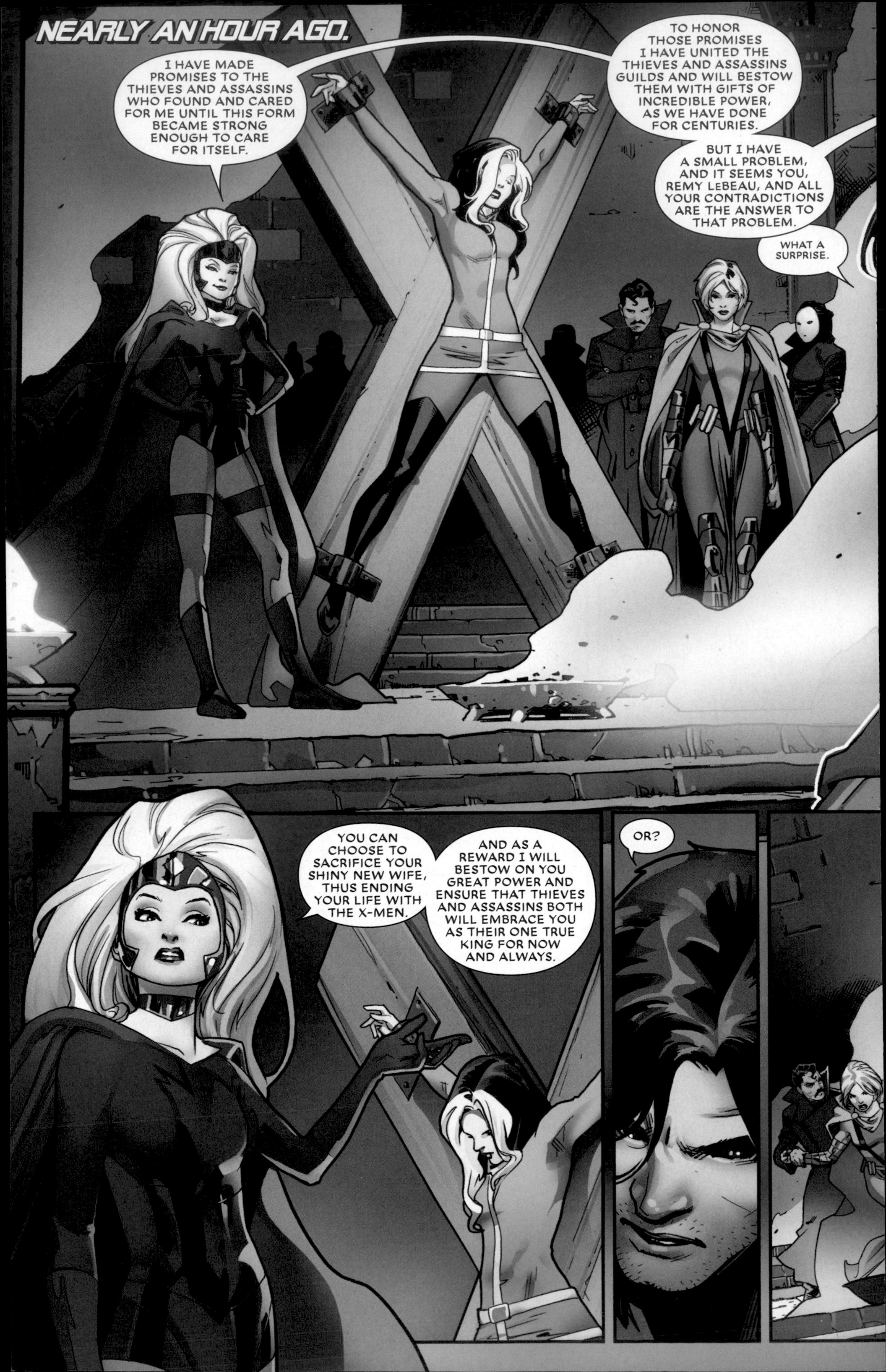
NEARLY AN HOUR AGO.
I HAVE MADE PROMISES TO THE THIEVES AND ASSASSINS WHO FOUND AND CARED FOR ME UNTIL THIS FORM BECAME STRONG ENOUGH TO CARE FOR ITSELF.
TO HONOR THOSE PROMISES I HAVE UNITED THE THIEVES AND ASSASSINS GUILDS AND WILL BESTOW THEM WITH GIFTS OF INCREDIBLE POWER, AS WE HAVE DONE FOR CENTURIES.
BUT I HAVE A SMALL PROBLEM, AND IT SEEMS YOU, REMY LEBEAU, AND ALL YOUR CONTRADICTIONS ARE THE ANSWER TO THAT PROBLEM.
WHAT A SURPRISE.
YOU CAN CHOOSE TO SACRIFICE YOUR SHINY NEW WIFE, THUS ENDING YOUR LIFE WITH THE X-MEN.
AND AS A REWARD I WILL BESTOW ON YOU GREAT POWER AND ENSURE THAT THIEVES AND ASSASSINS BOTH WILL EMBRACE YOU AS THEIR ONE TRUE KING FOR NOW AND ALWAYS.
OR?

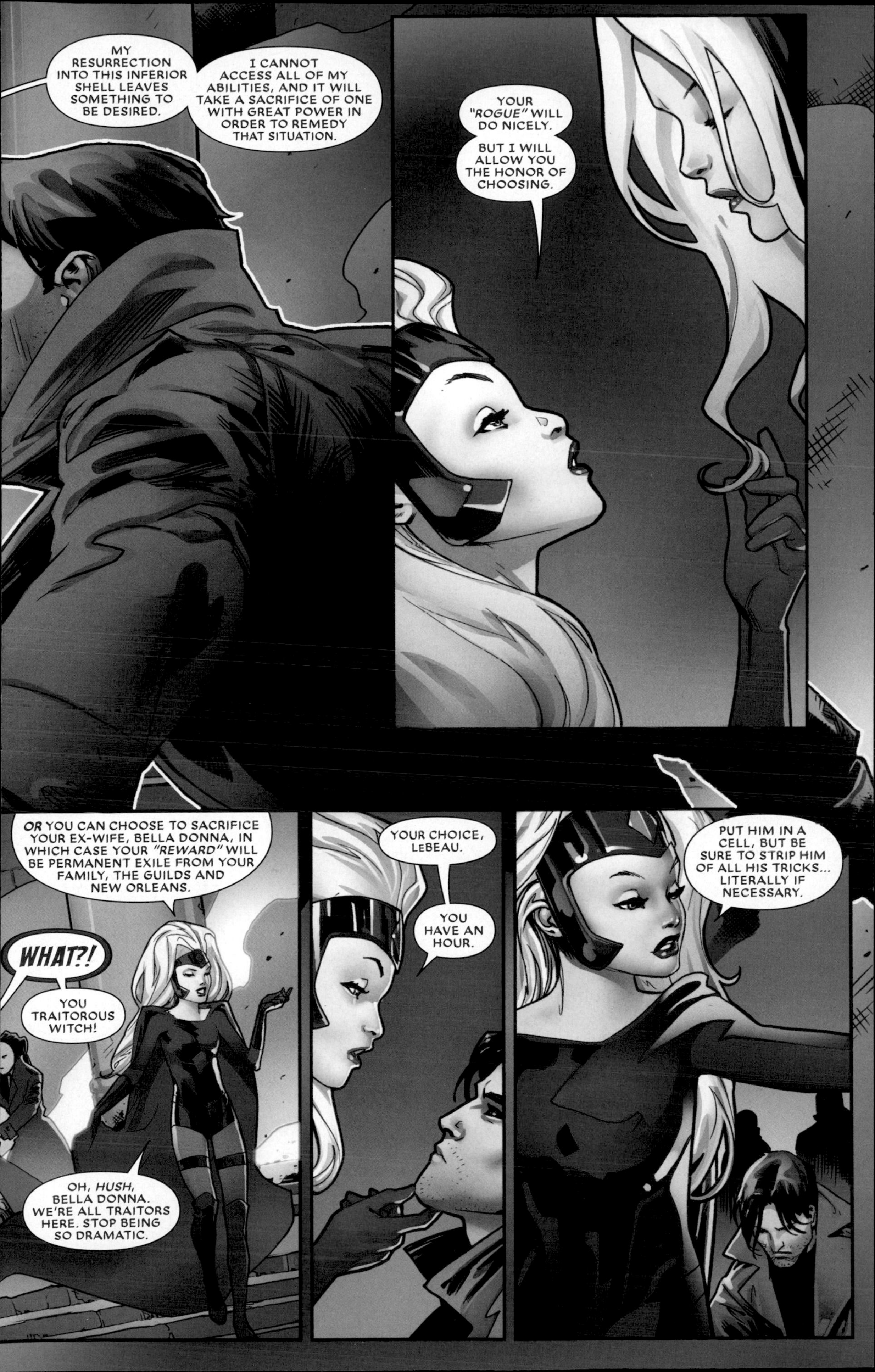
MY RESURRECTION INTO THIS INFERIOR SHELL LEAVES SOMETHING TO BE DESIRED.
I CANNOT ACCESS ALL OF MY ABILITIES, AND IT WILL TAKE A SACRIFICE OF ONE WITH GREAT POWER IN ORDER TO REMEDY THAT SITUATION.
YOUR "ROGUE" WILL DO NICELY.
BUT I WILL ALLOW YOU THE HONOR OF CHOOSING.
OR YOU CAN CHOOSE TO SACRIFICE YOUR EX-WIFE, BELLA DONNA, IN WHICH CASE YOUR "REWARD" WILL BE PERMANENT EXILE FROM YOUR FAMILY, THE GUILDS AND NEW ORLEANS.
WHAT?!
YOU TRAITOROUS WITCH!
OH, HUSH, BELLA DONNA. WE'RE ALL TRAITORS HERE. STOP BEING SO DRAMATIC.
YOUR CHOICE, LeBEAU.
YOU HAVE AN HOUR.
PUT HIM IN A CELL, BUT BE SURE TO STRIP HIM OF ALL HIS TRICKS... LITERALLY IF NECESSARY.

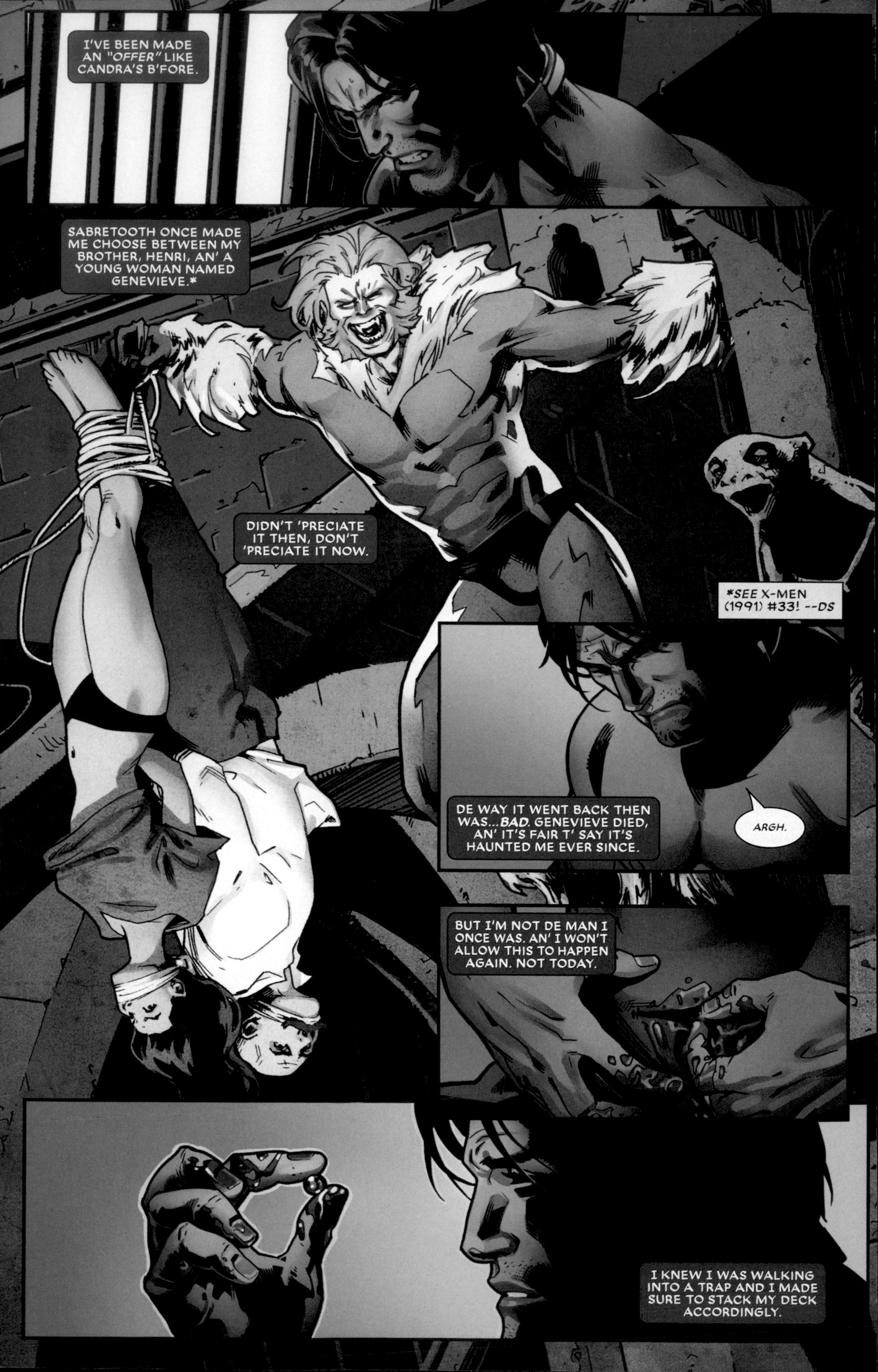
I'VE BEEN MADE AN "OFFER" LIKE CANDRA'S B'FORE.
SABRETOOTH ONCE MADE ME CHOOSE BETWEEN MY BROTHER, HENRI, AN' A YOUNG WOMAN NAMED GENEVIEVE.*
DIDN'T 'PRECIATE IT THEN, DON'T 'PRECIATE IT NOW.
*SEE X-MEN (1991) #33! --DS
DE WAY IT WENT BACK THEN WAS...BAD. GENEVIEVE DIED, AN' IT'S FAIR T' SAY IT'S HAUNTED ME EVER SINCE.
ARGH.
BUT I'M NOT DE MAN I ONCE WAS. AN' I WON'T ALLOW THIS TO HAPPEN AGAIN. NOT TODAY.
I KNEW I WAS WALKING INTO A TRAP AND I MADE SURE TO STACK MY DECK ACCORDINGLY.

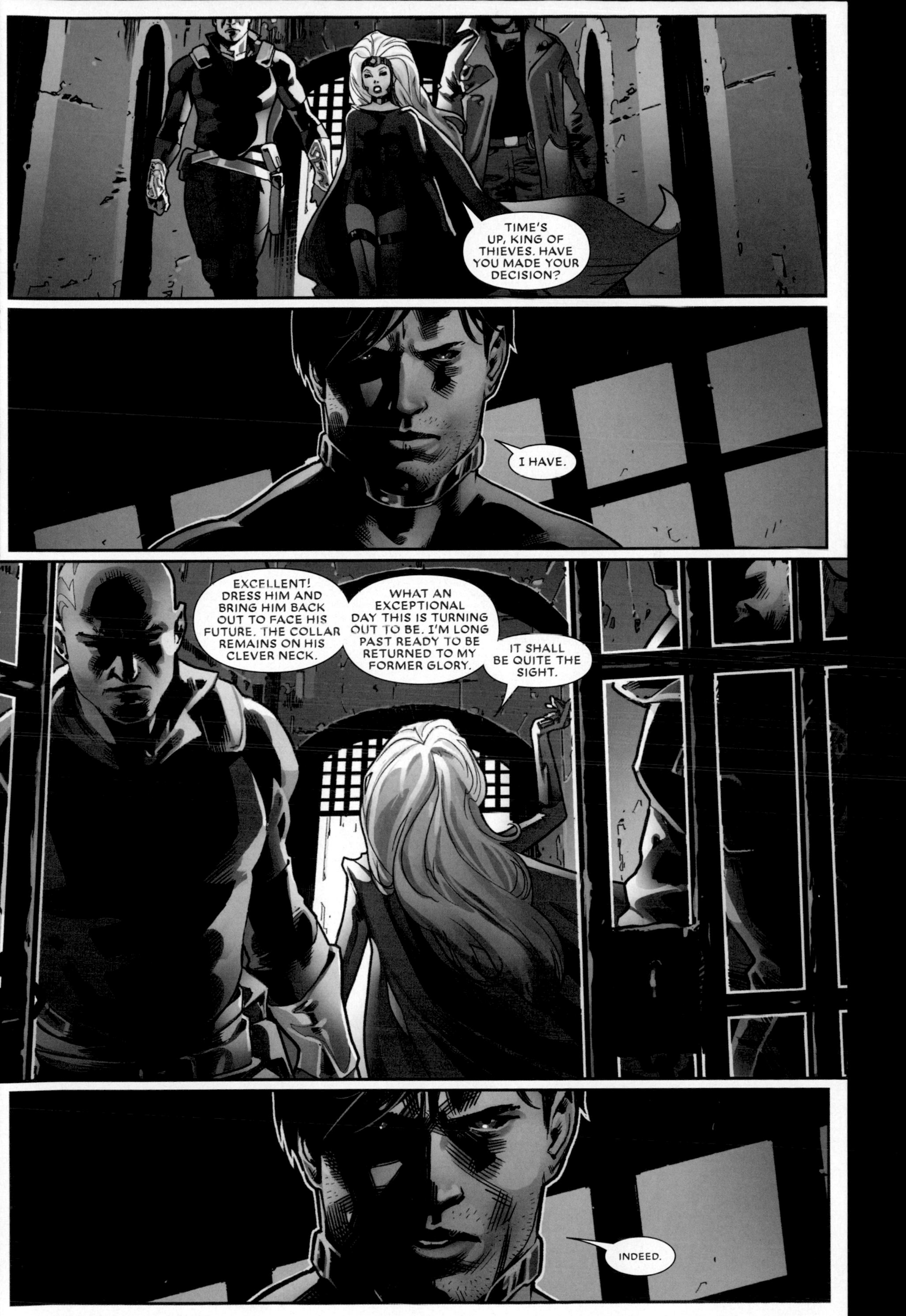
TIME'S UP, KING OF THIEVES. HAVE YOU MADE YOUR DECISION?
I HAVE.
EXCELLENT! DRESS HIM AND BRING HIM BACK OUT TO FACE HIS FUTURE. THE COLLAR REMAINS ON HIS CLEVER NECK.
WHAT AN EXCEPTIONAL DAY THIS IS TURNING OUT TO BE. I'M LONG PAST READY TO BE RETURNED TO MY FORMER GLORY.
IT SHALL BE QUITE THE SIGHT.
INDEED.

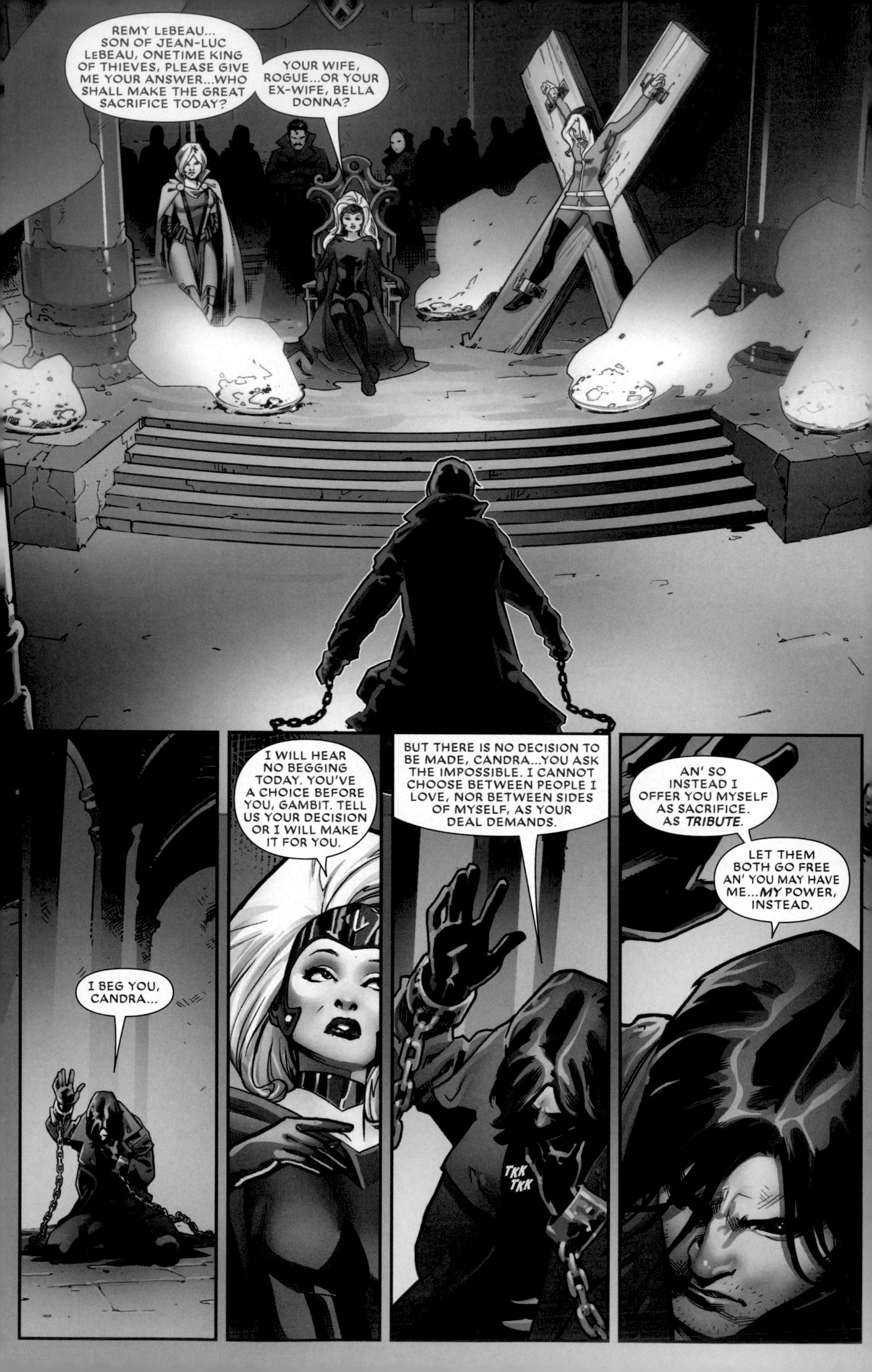
REMY LeBEAU... SON OF JEAN-LUC LeBEAU, ONETIME KING OF THIEVES, PLEASE GIVE ME YOUR ANSWER...WHO SHALL MAKE THE GREAT SACRIFICE TODAY?
YOUR WIFE, ROGUE...OR YOUR EX-WIFE, BELLA DONNA?
I BEG YOU, CANDRA...
I WILL HEAR NO BEGGING TODAY. YOU'VE A CHOICE BEFORE YOU, GAMBIT. TELL US YOUR DECISION OR I WILL MAKE IT FOR YOU.
BUT THERE IS NO DECISION TO BE MADE, CANDRA...YOU ASK THE IMPOSSIBLE. I CANNOT CHOOSE BETWEEN PEOPLE I LOVE, NOR BETWEEN SIDES OF MYSELF, AS YOUR DEAL DEMANDS.
TKK TKK
AN' SO INSTEAD I OFFER YOU MYSELF AS SACRIFICE. AS *TRIBUTE*.
LET THEM BOTH GO FREE AN' YOU MAY HAVE ME...*MY* POWER, INSTEAD.

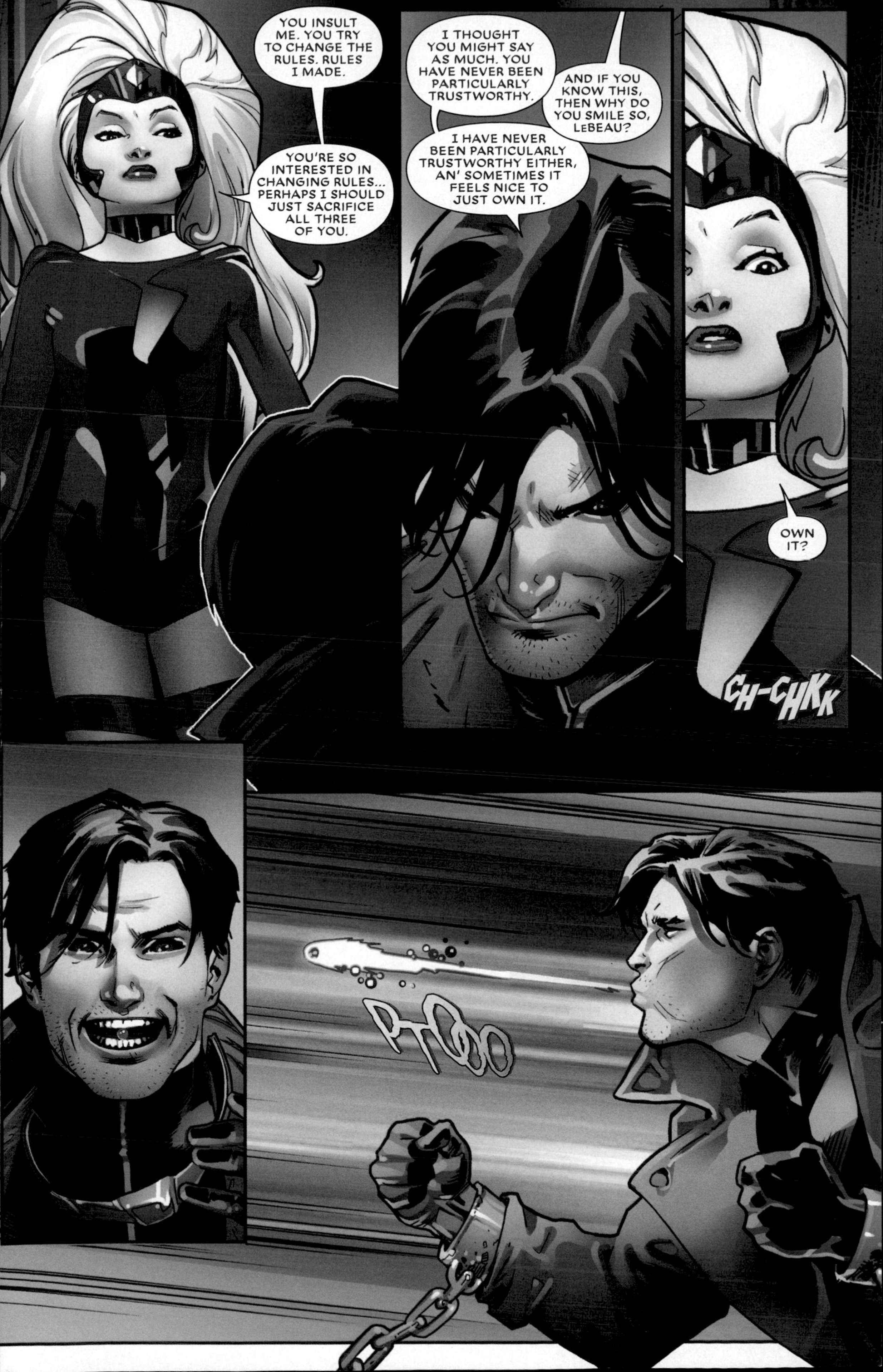
YOU INSULT ME. YOU TRY TO CHANGE THE RULES. RULES I MADE.
YOU'RE SO INTERESTED IN CHANGING RULES... PERHAPS I SHOULD JUST SACRIFICE ALL THREE OF YOU.
I THOUGHT YOU MIGHT SAY AS MUCH. YOU HAVE NEVER BEEN PARTICULARLY TRUSTWORTHY.
I HAVE NEVER BEEN PARTICULARLY TRUSTWORTHY EITHER, AN' SOMETIMES IT FEELS NICE TO JUST OWN IT.
AND IF YOU KNOW THIS, THEN WHY DO YOU SMILE SO, LEBEAU?
OWN IT?
CH-CHKK
PTOO

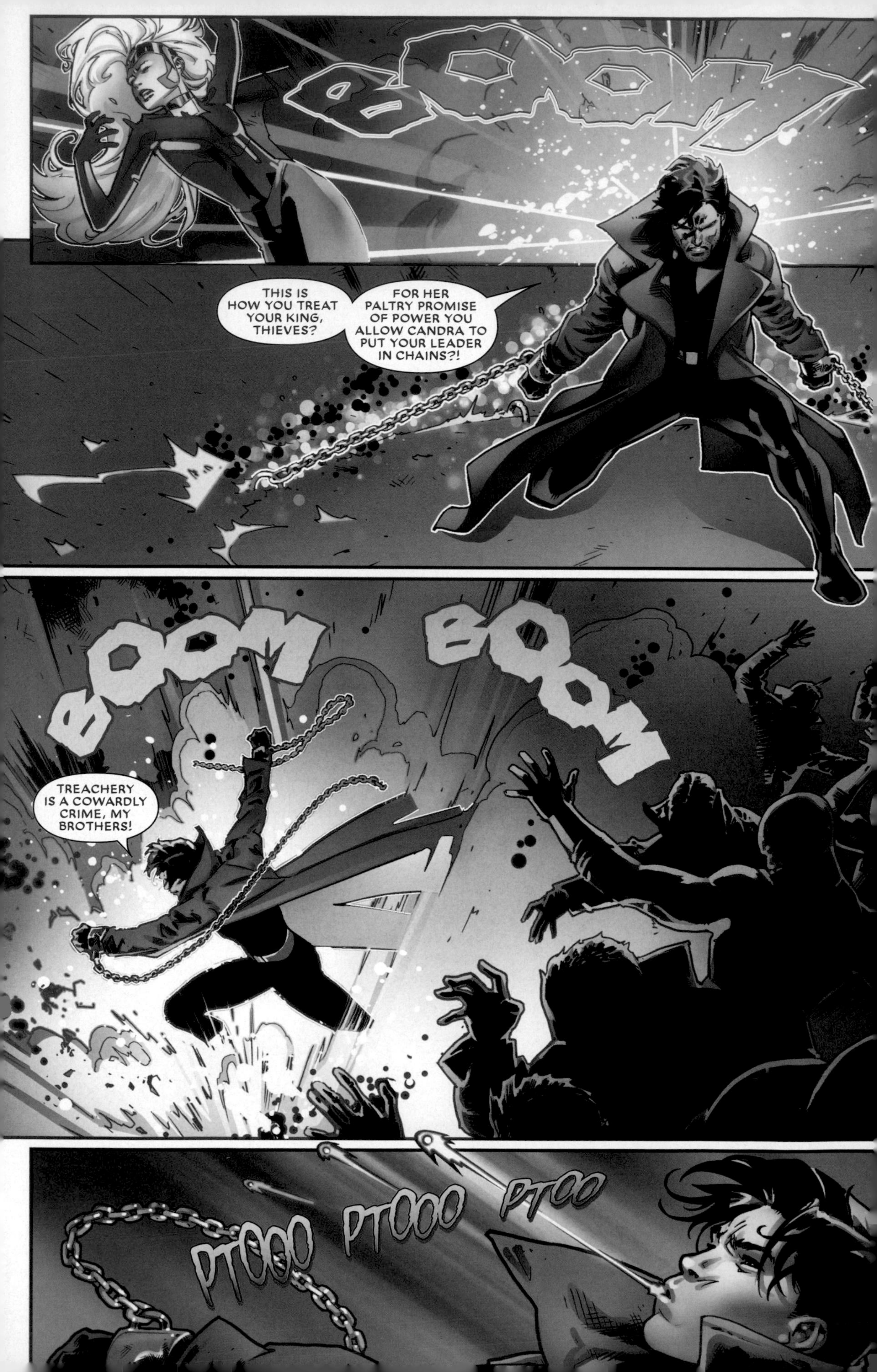
BOOOM
THIS IS HOW YOU TREAT YOUR KING, THIEVES?
FOR HER PALTRY PROMISE OF POWER YOU ALLOW CANDRA TO PUT YOUR LEADER IN CHAINS?!
BOOM
BOOOM
TREACHERY IS A COWARDLY CRIME, MY BROTHERS!
PTOOO
PTOOO
PTOO

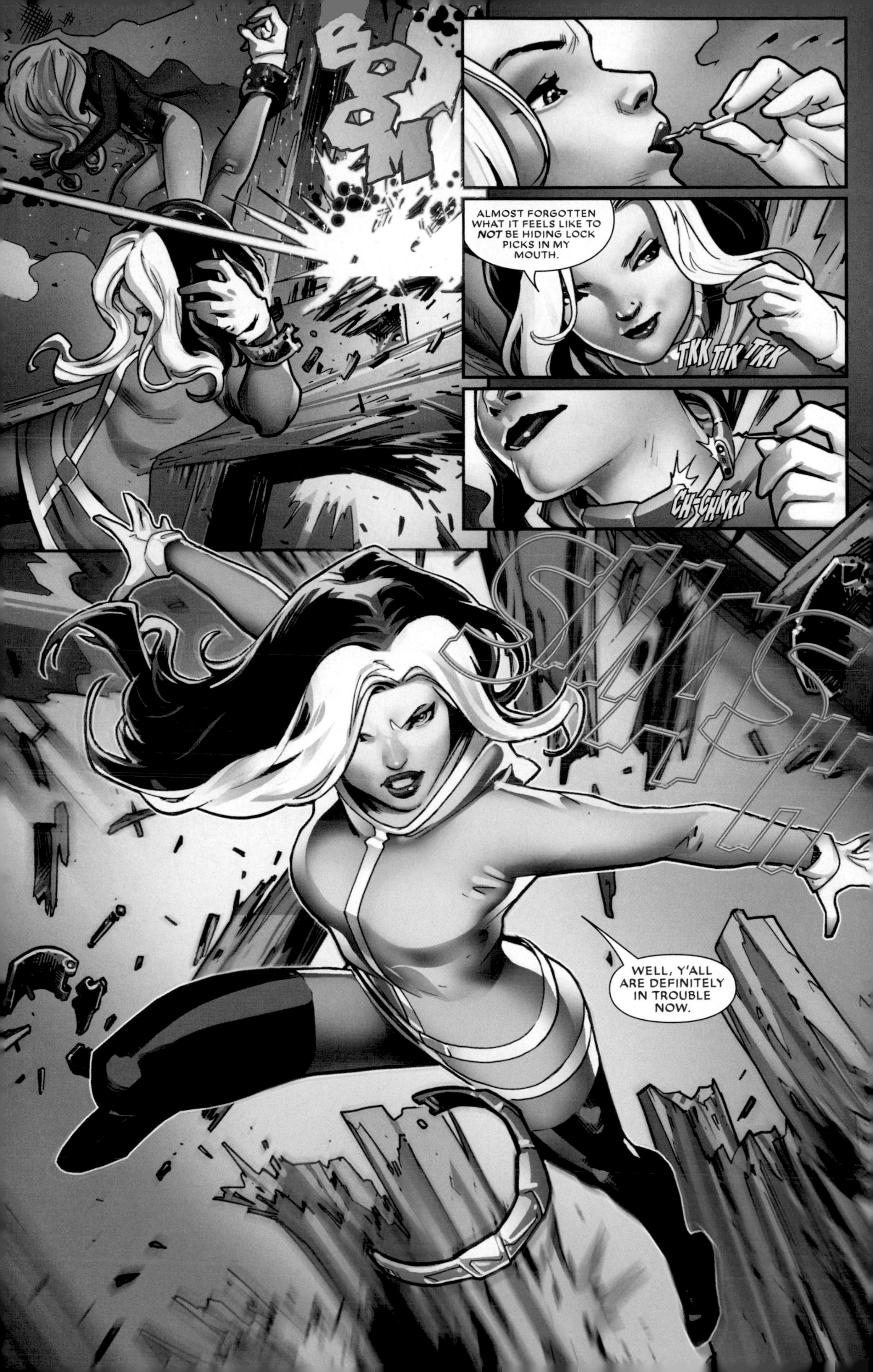
BOOOM
ALMOST FORGOTTEN WHAT IT FEELS LIKE TO NOT BE HIDING LOCK PICKS IN MY MOUTH.
TKK TIK TKK
CH-CHKKK
WELL, Y'ALL ARE DEFINITELY IN TROUBLE NOW.

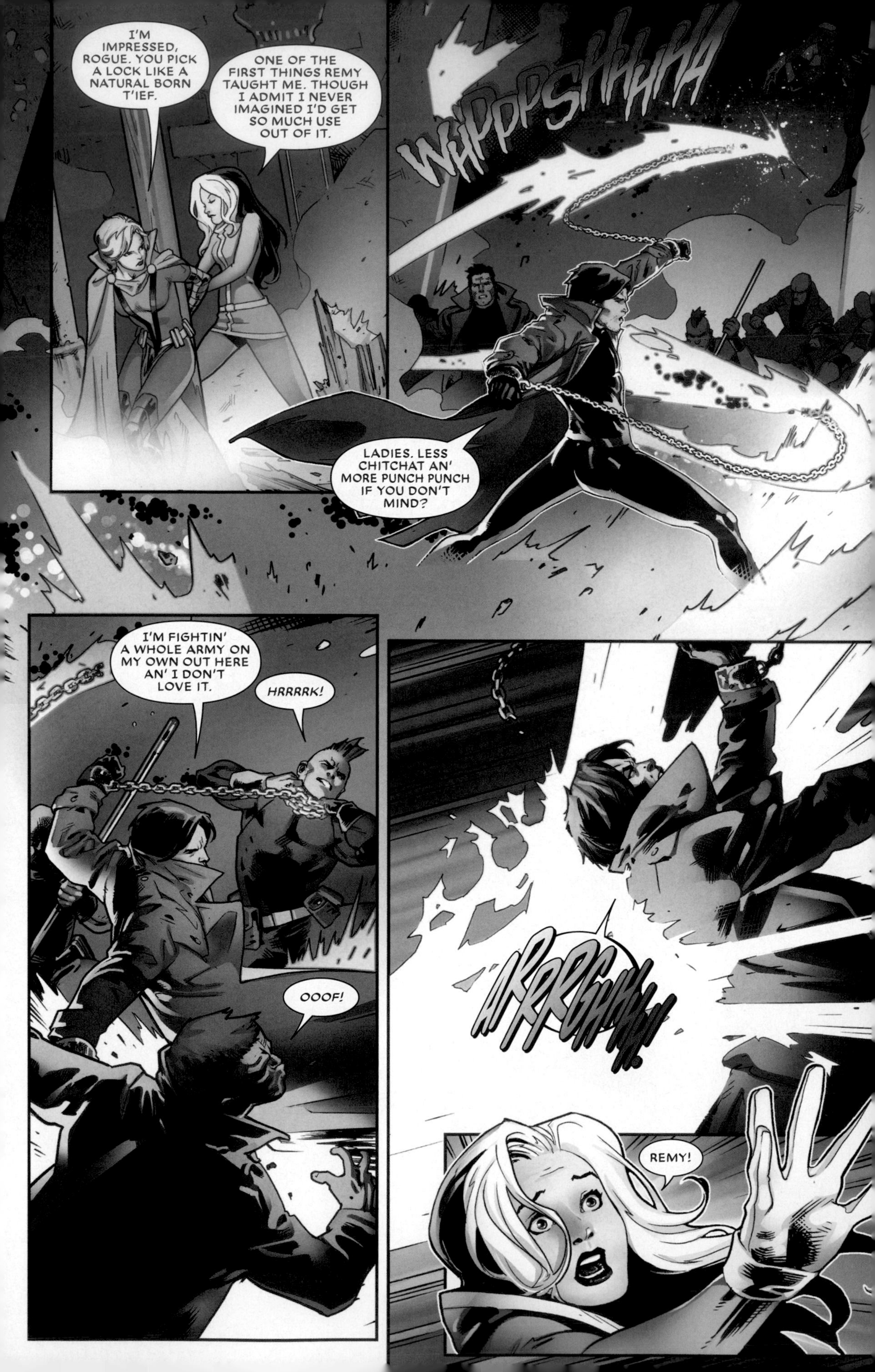

I'M IMPRESSED, ROGUE. YOU PICK A LOCK LIKE A NATURAL BORN T'IEF.
ONE OF THE FIRST THINGS REMY TAUGHT ME. THOUGH I ADMIT I NEVER IMAGINED I'D GET SO MUCH USE OUT OF IT.
WHPPPSHHHHH
LADIES. LESS CHITCHAT AN' MORE PUNCH PUNCH IF YOU DON'T MIND?
I'M FIGHTIN' A WHOLE ARMY ON MY OWN OUT HERE AN' I DON'T LOVE IT.
HRRRRK!
OOOF!
ARRRGHHH!!
REMY!

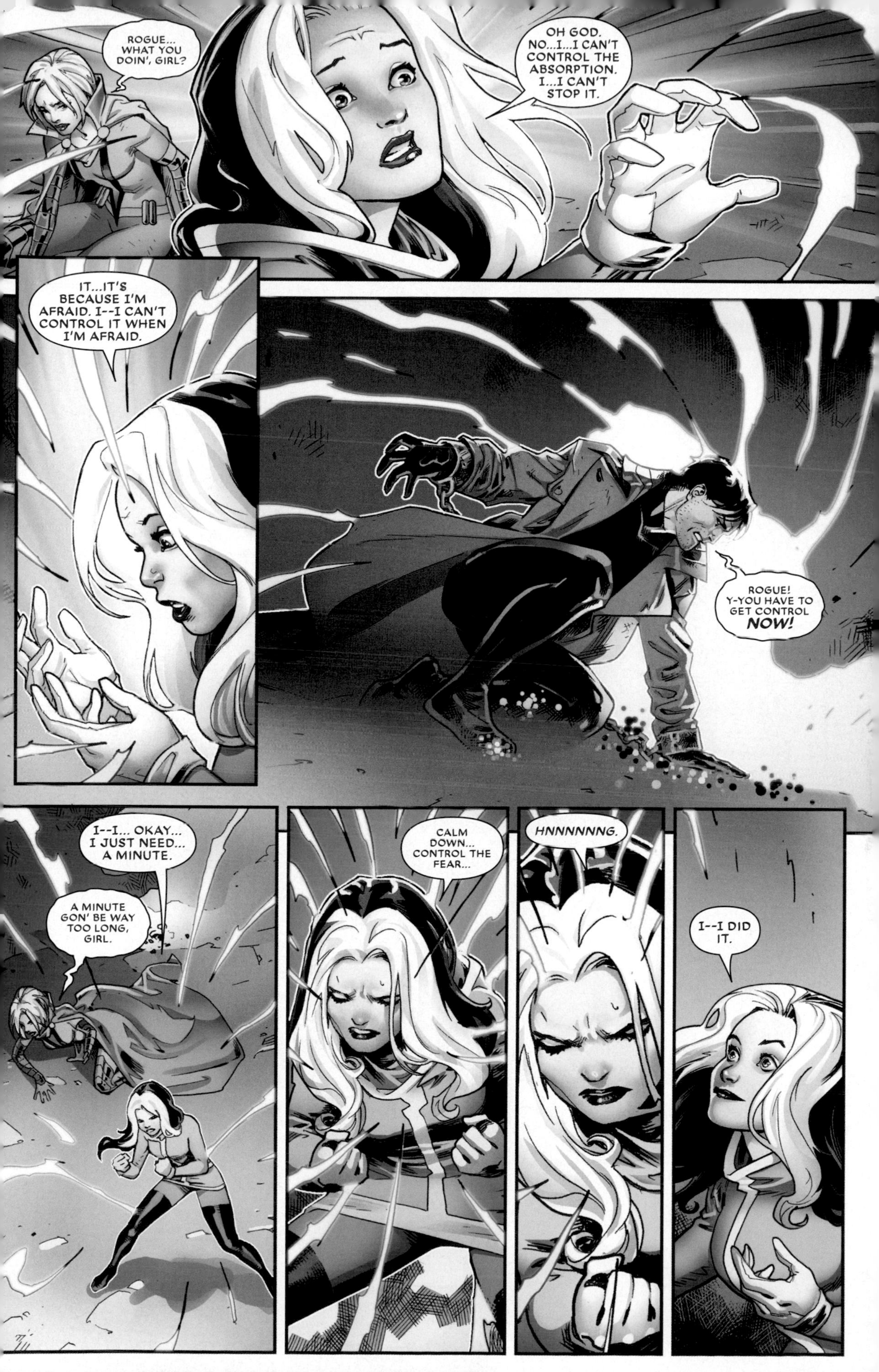
ROGUE... WHAT YOU DOIN', GIRL?
OH GOD. NO...I...I CAN'T CONTROL THE ABSORPTION. I...I CAN'T STOP IT.
IT...IT'S BECAUSE I'M AFRAID. I--I CAN'T CONTROL IT WHEN I'M AFRAID.
ROGUE! Y-YOU HAVE TO GET CONTROL NOW!
I--I... OKAY... I JUST NEED... A MINUTE.
A MINUTE GON' BE WAY TOO LONG, GIRL.
CALM DOWN... CONTROL THE FEAR...
HNNNNNNG.
I--I DID IT.

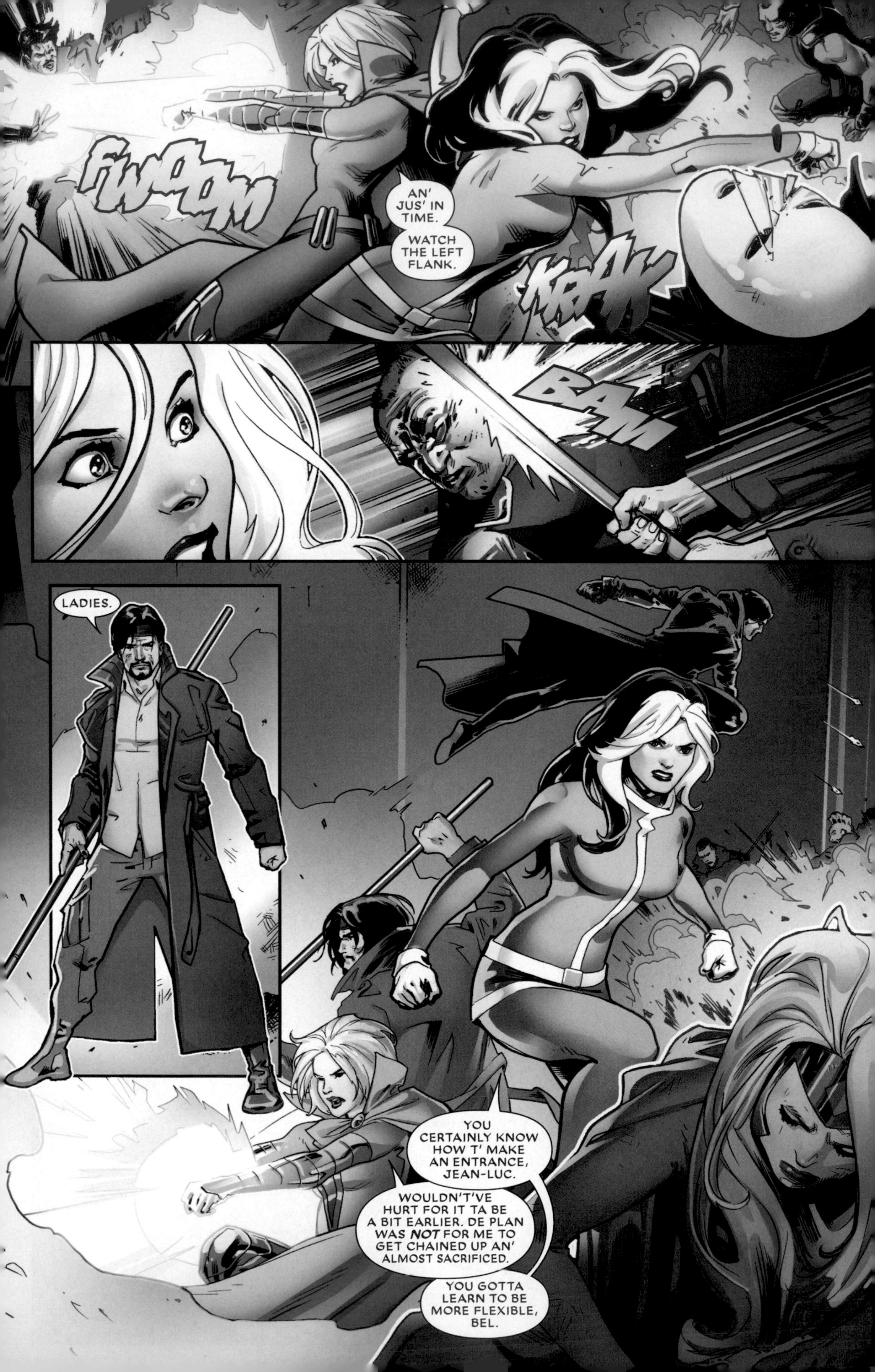
FWOOM
AN' JUS' IN TIME.
WATCH THE LEFT FLANK.
KRAK
BAM
LADIES.
YOU CERTAINLY KNOW HOW T' MAKE AN ENTRANCE, JEAN-LUC.
WOULDN'T'VE HURT FOR IT TA BE A BIT EARLIER. DE PLAN WAS NOT FOR ME TO GET CHAINED UP AN' ALMOST SACRIFICED.
YOU GOTTA LEARN TO BE MORE FLEXIBLE, BEL.

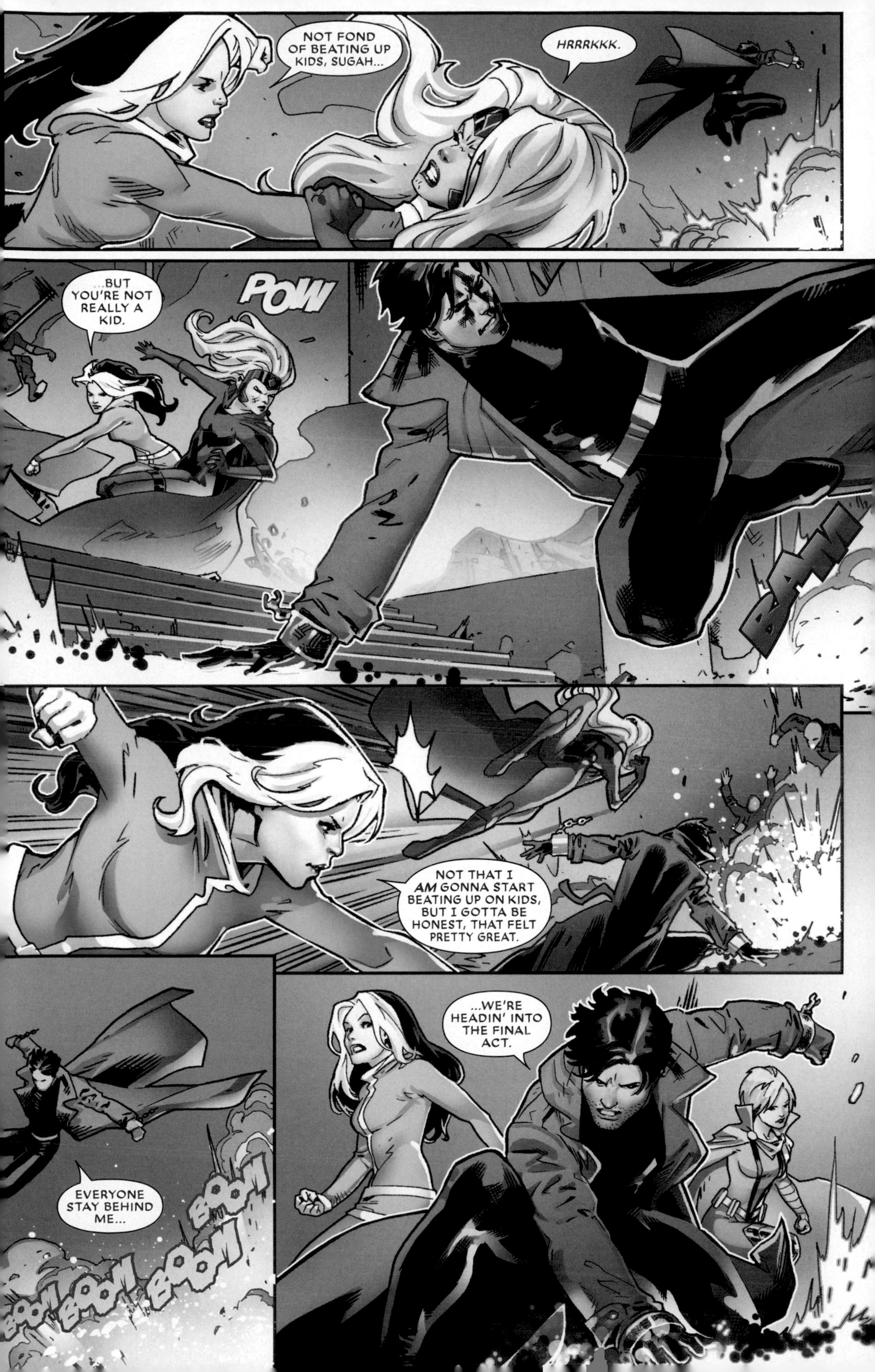
NOT FOND OF BEATING UP KIDS, SUGAH...
HRRRKKK.
...BUT YOU'RE NOT REALLY A KID.
POW
BAM
NOT THAT I *AM* GONNA START BEATING UP ON KIDS, BUT I GOTTA BE HONEST, THAT FELT PRETTY GREAT.
EVERYONE STAY BEHIND ME...
BOOM BOOM BOOM BOOM BOOM
...WE'RE HEADIN' INTO THE FINAL ACT.

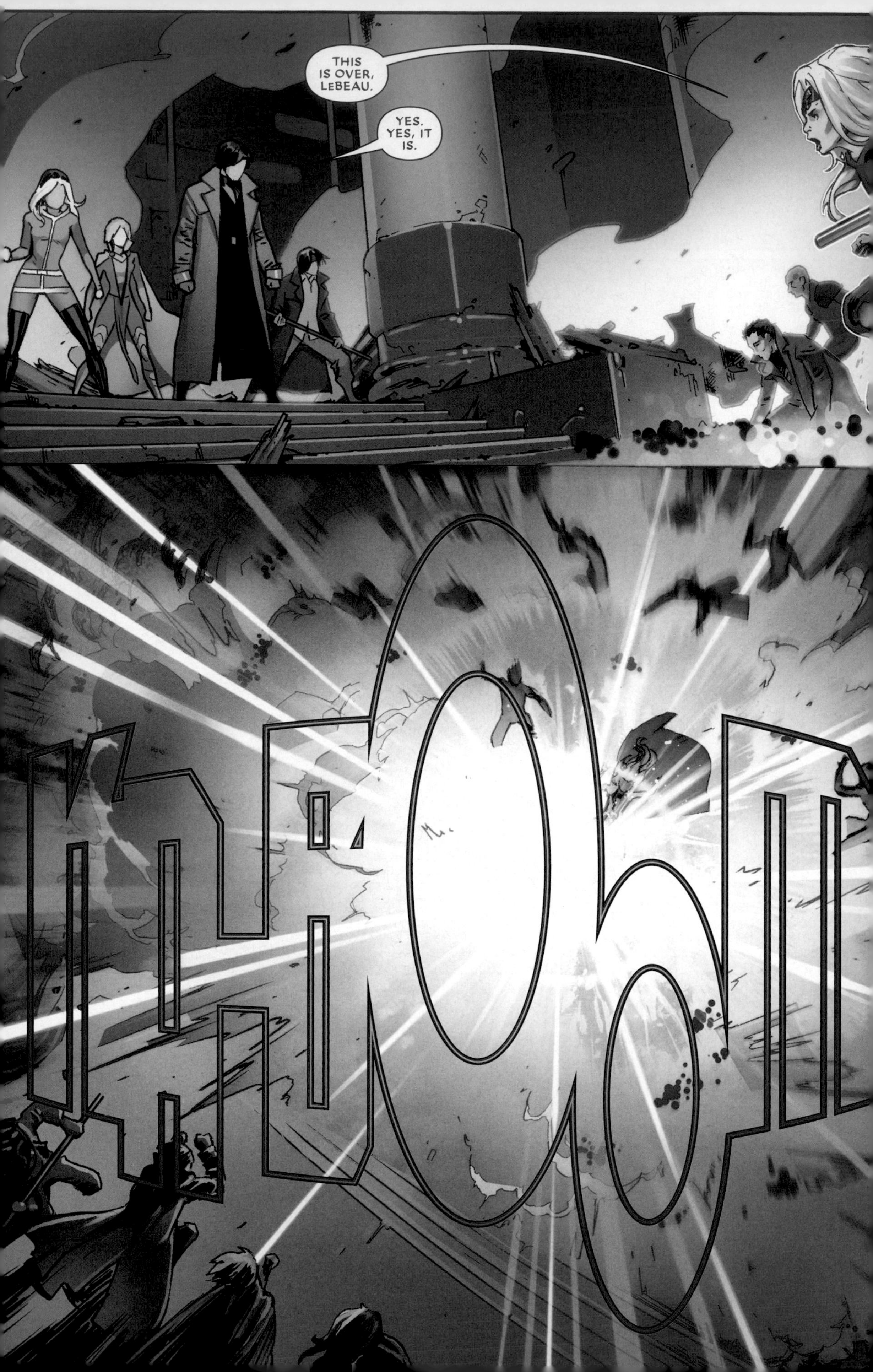
THIS IS OVER, LeBEAU.
YES. YES, IT IS.

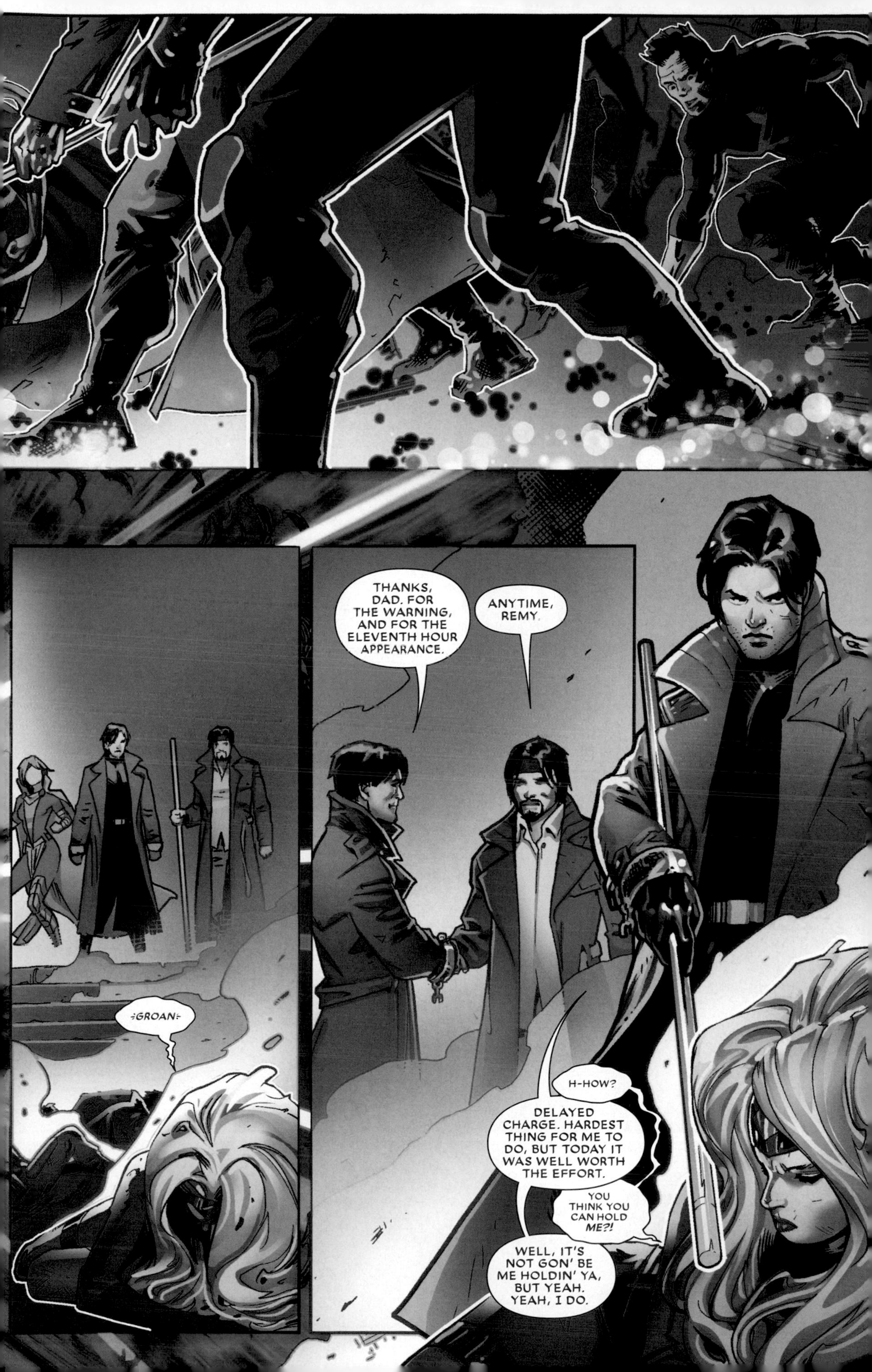

THANKS, DAD. FOR THE WARNING, AND FOR THE ELEVENTH HOUR APPEARANCE.
ANYTIME, REMY.
GROAN
H-HOW?
DELAYED CHARGE. HARDEST THING FOR ME TO DO, BUT TODAY IT WAS WELL WORTH THE EFFORT.
YOU THINK YOU CAN HOLD ME?!
WELL, IT'S NOT GON' BE ME HOLDIN' YA, BUT YEAH. YEAH, I DO.

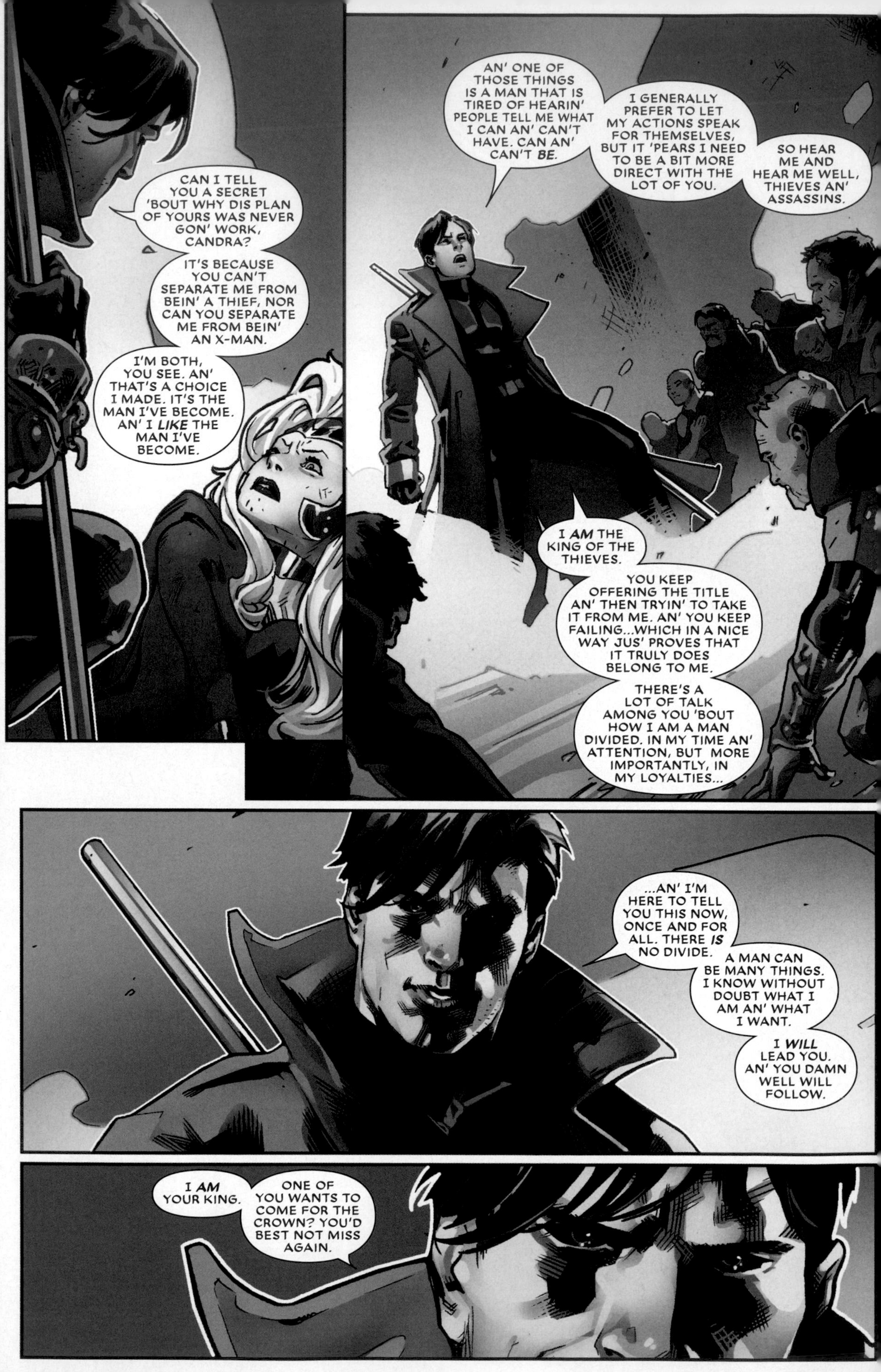
CAN I TELL YOU A SECRET 'BOUT WHY DIS PLAN OF YOURS WAS NEVER GON' WORK, CANDRA?
IT'S BECAUSE YOU CAN'T SEPARATE ME FROM BEIN' A THIEF, NOR CAN YOU SEPARATE ME FROM BEIN' AN X-MAN.
I'M BOTH, YOU SEE. AN' THAT'S A CHOICE I MADE. IT'S THE MAN I'VE BECOME. AN' I *LIKE* THE MAN I'VE BECOME.
AN' ONE OF THOSE THINGS IS A MAN THAT IS TIRED OF HEARIN' PEOPLE TELL ME WHAT I CAN AN' CAN'T HAVE. CAN AN' CAN'T *BE.*
I GENERALLY PREFER TO LET MY ACTIONS SPEAK FOR THEMSELVES, BUT IT 'PEARS I NEED TO BE A BIT MORE DIRECT WITH THE LOT OF YOU.
SO HEAR ME AND HEAR ME WELL, THIEVES AN' ASSASSINS.
I *AM* THE KING OF THE THIEVES.
YOU KEEP OFFERING THE TITLE AN' THEN TRYIN' TO TAKE IT FROM ME. AN' YOU KEEP FAILING...WHICH IN A NICE WAY JUS' PROVES THAT IT TRULY DOES BELONG TO ME.
THERE'S A LOT OF TALK AMONG YOU 'BOUT HOW I AM A MAN DIVIDED. IN MY TIME AN' ATTENTION, BUT MORE IMPORTANTLY, IN MY LOYALTIES...
...AN' I'M HERE TO TELL YOU THIS NOW, ONCE AND FOR ALL. THERE *IS* NO DIVIDE.
A MAN CAN BE MANY THINGS. I KNOW WITHOUT DOUBT WHAT I AM AN' WHAT I WANT.
I *WILL* LEAD YOU. AN' YOU DAMN WELL WILL FOLLOW.
I *AM* YOUR KING.
ONE OF YOU WANTS TO COME FOR THE CROWN? YOU'D BEST NOT MISS AGAIN.

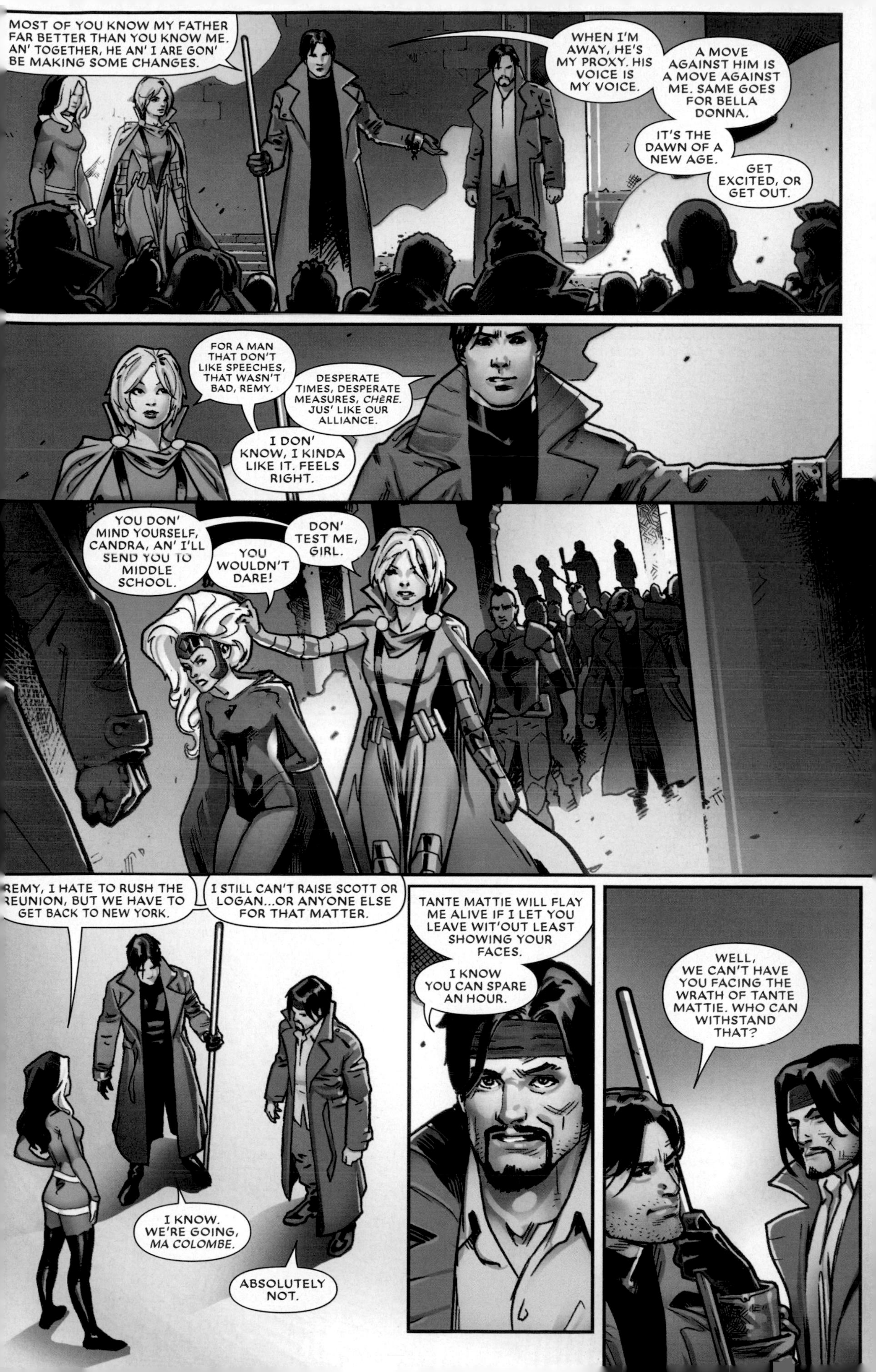
MOST OF YOU KNOW MY FATHER FAR BETTER THAN YOU KNOW ME. AN' TOGETHER, HE AN' I ARE GON' BE MAKING SOME CHANGES.
WHEN I'M AWAY, HE'S MY PROXY. HIS VOICE IS MY VOICE.
A MOVE AGAINST HIM IS A MOVE AGAINST ME. SAME GOES FOR BELLA DONNA.
IT'S THE DAWN OF A NEW AGE.
GET EXCITED, OR GET OUT.
FOR A MAN THAT DON'T LIKE SPEECHES, THAT WASN'T BAD, REMY.
DESPERATE TIMES, DESPERATE MEASURES, *CHÈRE*. JUS' LIKE OUR ALLIANCE.
I DON' KNOW, I KINDA LIKE IT. FEELS RIGHT.
YOU DON' MIND YOURSELF, CANDRA, AN' I'LL SEND YOU TO MIDDLE SCHOOL.
YOU WOULDN'T DARE!
DON' TEST ME, GIRL.
REMY, I HATE TO RUSH THE REUNION, BUT WE HAVE TO GET BACK TO NEW YORK.
I STILL CAN'T RAISE SCOTT OR LOGAN...OR ANYONE ELSE FOR THAT MATTER.
I KNOW. WE'RE GOING, *MA COLOMBE*.
ABSOLUTELY NOT.
TANTE MATTIE WILL FLAY ME ALIVE IF I LET YOU LEAVE WIT'OUT LEAST SHOWING YOUR FACES.
I KNOW YOU CAN SPARE AN HOUR.
WELL, WE CAN'T HAVE YOU FACING THE WRATH OF TANTE MATTIE. WHO CAN WITHSTAND THAT?

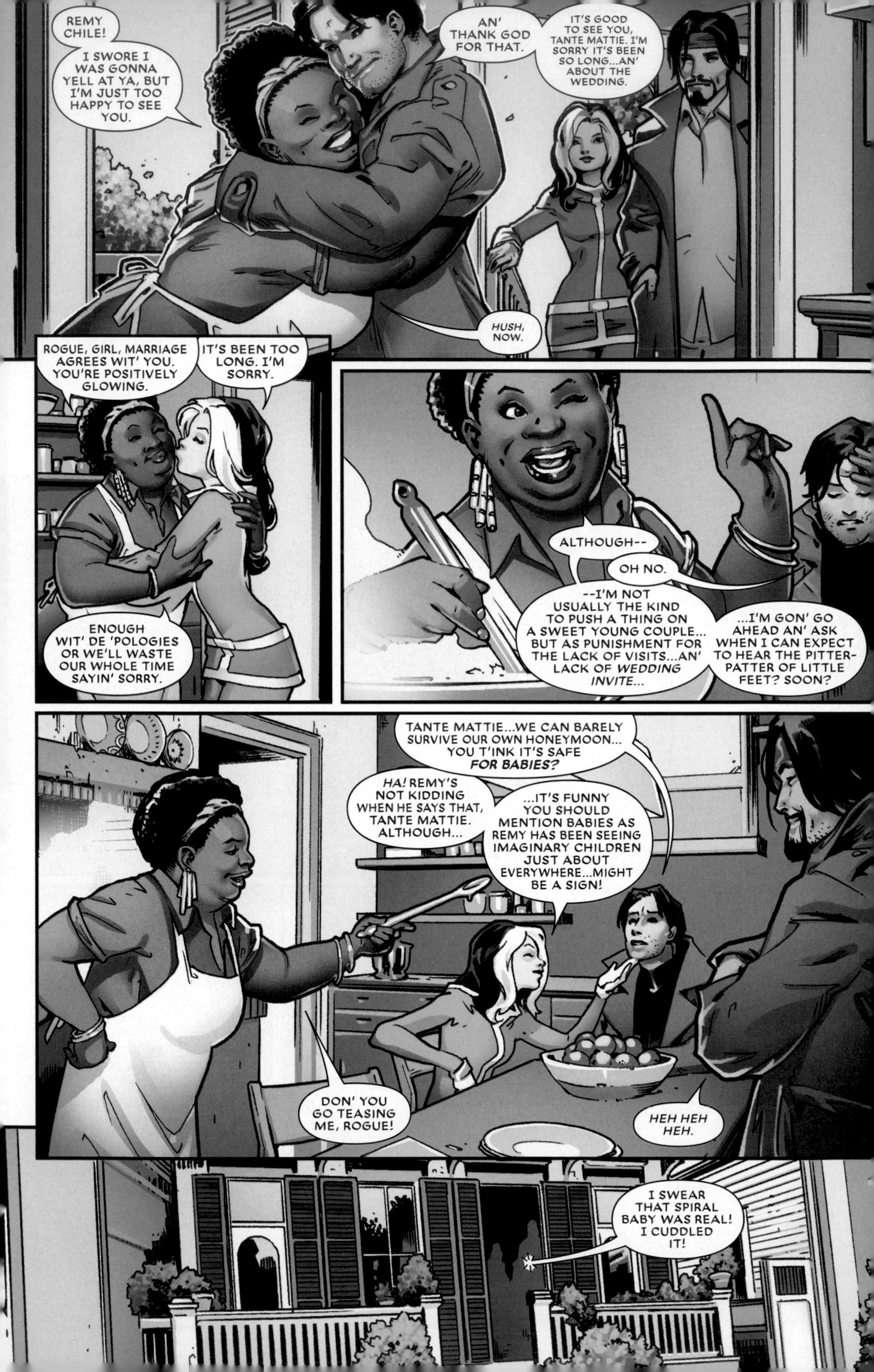
REMY CHILE!
I SWORE I WAS GONNA YELL AT YA, BUT I'M JUST TOO HAPPY TO SEE YOU.
AN' THANK GOD FOR THAT.
IT'S GOOD TO SEE YOU, TANTE MATTIE. I'M SORRY IT'S BEEN SO LONG...AN' ABOUT THE WEDDING.
HUSH, NOW.
ROGUE, GIRL, MARRIAGE AGREES WIT' YOU. YOU'RE POSITIVELY GLOWING.
IT'S BEEN TOO LONG. I'M SORRY.
ENOUGH WIT' DE 'POLOGIES OR WE'LL WASTE OUR WHOLE TIME SAYIN' SORRY.
ALTHOUGH--
OH NO.
--I'M NOT USUALLY THE KIND TO PUSH A THING ON A SWEET YOUNG COUPLE... BUT AS PUNISHMENT FOR THE LACK OF VISITS...AN' LACK OF WEDDING INVITE...
...I'M GON' GO AHEAD AN' ASK WHEN I CAN EXPECT TO HEAR THE PITTER-PATTER OF LITTLE FEET? SOON?
TANTE MATTIE...WE CAN BARELY SURVIVE OUR OWN HONEYMOON... YOU T'INK IT'S SAFE FOR BABIES?
HA! REMY'S NOT KIDDING WHEN HE SAYS THAT, TANTE MATTIE. ALTHOUGH...
...IT'S FUNNY YOU SHOULD MENTION BABIES AS REMY HAS BEEN SEEING IMAGINARY CHILDREN JUST ABOUT EVERYWHERE...MIGHT BE A SIGN!
DON' YOU GO TEASING ME, ROGUE!
HEH HEH HEH.
I SWEAR THAT SPIRAL BABY WAS REAL! I CUDDLED IT!

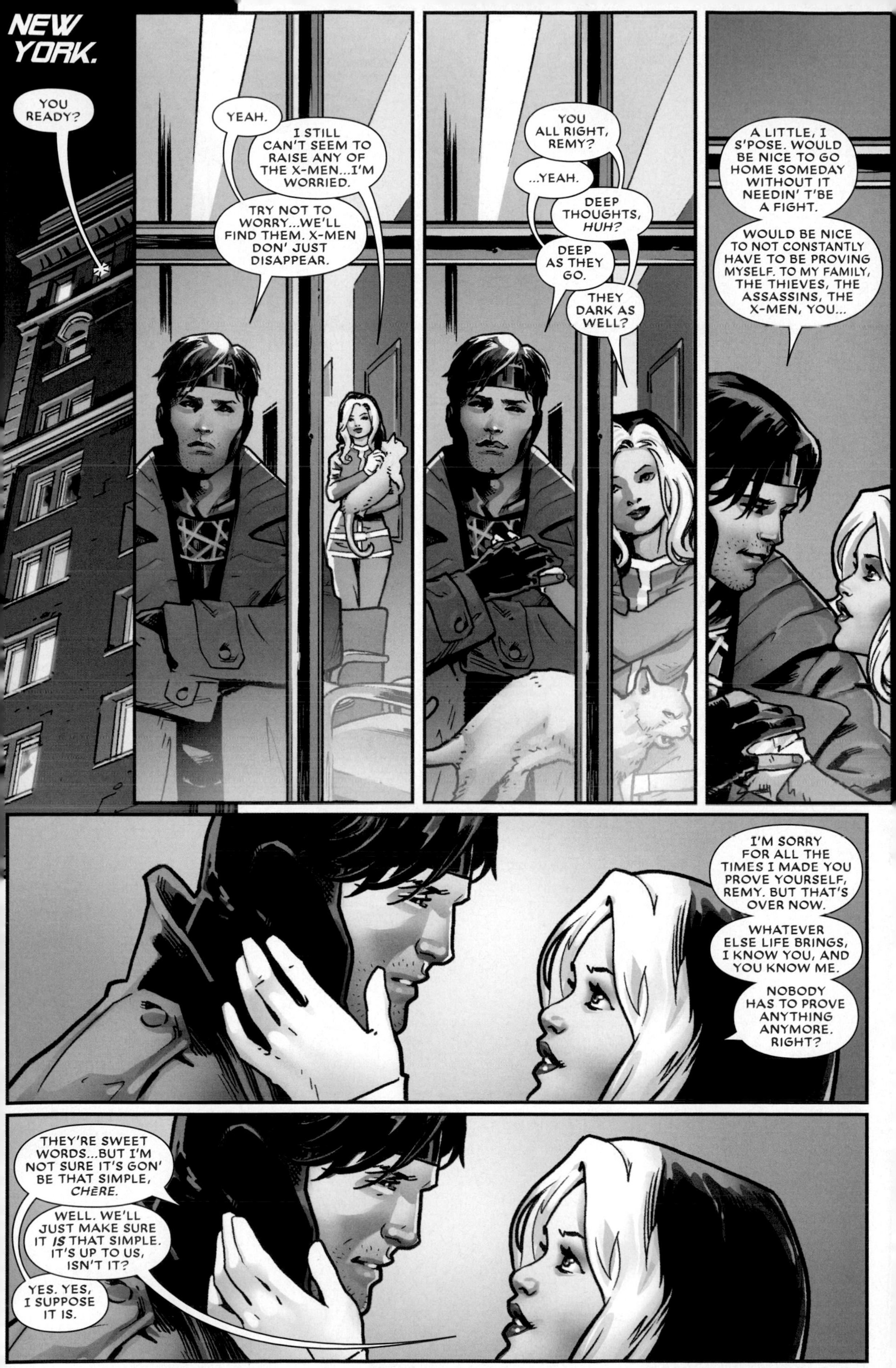
NEW YORK.
YOU READY?
YEAH.
I STILL CAN'T SEEM TO RAISE ANY OF THE X-MEN...I'M WORRIED.
TRY NOT TO WORRY...WE'LL FIND THEM. X-MEN DON' JUST DISAPPEAR.
YOU ALL RIGHT, REMY?
...YEAH.
DEEP THOUGHTS, *HUH?*
DEEP AS THEY GO.
THEY DARK AS WELL?
A LITTLE, I S'POSE. WOULD BE NICE TO GO HOME SOMEDAY WITHOUT IT NEEDIN' T'BE A FIGHT.
WOULD BE NICE TO NOT CONSTANTLY HAVE TO BE PROVING MYSELF. TO MY FAMILY, THE THIEVES, THE ASSASSINS, THE X-MEN, YOU...
I'M SORRY FOR ALL THE TIMES I MADE YOU PROVE YOURSELF, REMY. BUT THAT'S OVER NOW.
WHATEVER ELSE LIFE BRINGS, I KNOW YOU, AND YOU KNOW ME.
NOBODY HAS TO PROVE ANYTHING ANYMORE. RIGHT?
THEY'RE SWEET WORDS...BUT I'M NOT SURE IT'S GON' BE THAT SIMPLE, *CHÈRE.*
WELL. WE'LL JUST MAKE SURE IT *IS* THAT SIMPLE. IT'S UP TO US, ISN'T IT?
YES. YES, I SUPPOSE IT IS.

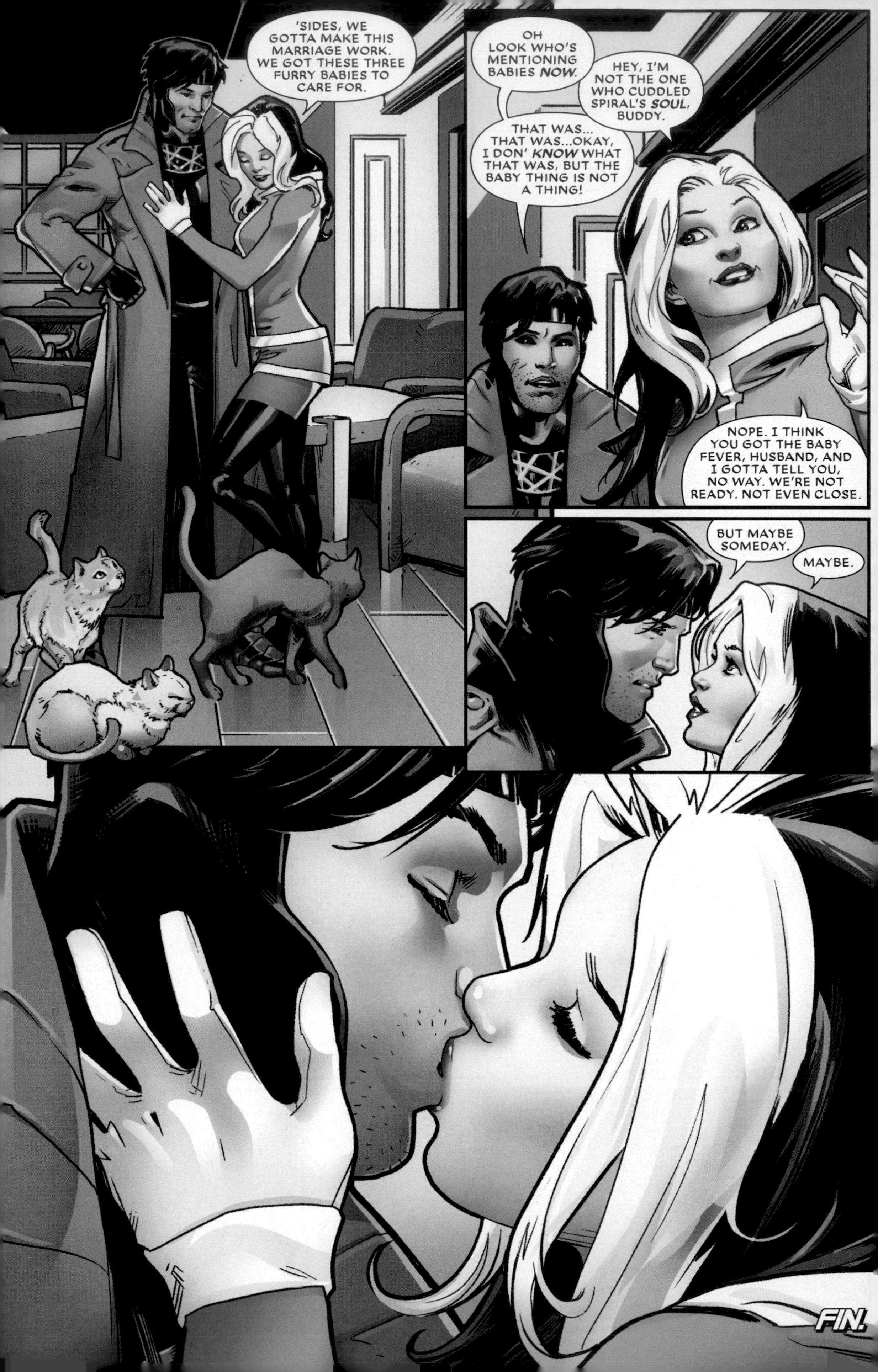
'SIDES, WE GOTTA MAKE THIS MARRIAGE WORK. WE GOT THESE THREE FURRY BABIES TO CARE FOR.
OH LOOK WHO'S MENTIONING BABIES *NOW*.
HEY, I'M NOT THE ONE WHO CUDDLED SPIRAL'S *SOUL*, BUDDY.
THAT WAS... THAT WAS...OKAY, I DON' *KNOW* WHAT THAT WAS, BUT THE BABY THING IS NOT A THING!
NOPE. I THINK YOU GOT THE BABY FEVER, HUSBAND, AND I GOTTA TELL YOU, NO WAY. WE'RE NOT READY. NOT EVEN CLOSE.
BUT MAYBE SOMEDAY.
MAYBE.
FIN.

This ending is bittersweet, no doubt, but that's fitting, I suppose, as I can't think of a word more accurate to describe Gambit and Rogue — so many tumultuous times, but so much sweetness drawing them together over and over again. It's a beautiful thing.

I feel so lucky to have been able to write these two for so many issues — starting back with our ROGUE & GAMBIT miniseries — and getting the chance to get them back together in earnest was an honor and a privilege, not to mention teenage Kelly's childhood dream! I'm so thankful for that opportunity and for all of you who cheered them so passionately.

I think we did something really special here, and that was thanks to a lot of people, including the unbelievable fans. I want to especially thank those of you who championed the book so relentlessly and took the time to let us (and me) know how much you loved it.

But I also need to take a moment to thank all the amazing people who helped make this book possible in the first place — artists Oscar Bazaldua, David Lopez and Javier Pina; colorists Frank D'Armata and Nayoung Kim; letterers Joe Sabino and Travis Lanham; graphic designers Jay Bowen and Anthony Gambino; and of course Terry and Rachel Dodson for bringing us twelve glorious covers. We also had a handful of amazing editors on this book — Annalise Bissa, Danny Khazem and Lauren Amaro — and, of course, our fearless leader Darren Shan and benevolent overlord Jordan White.

Gambit and Rogue deserve a thousand issues and I hope they'll get them, but I'll always be grateful that I was able to contribute even in a small way to their story. I'm excited for the future of these lovebirds, and I hope you guys are too.

Thanks for coming along for the ride. #Rambit4Eva

Kelly Thompson
Portland, Oregon
May 22, 2019